COMPETITION AND TRADE POLICIES

Their Interaction

ORGANISATION FOR ECONOMIC CO-OPERATION AND DEVELOPMENT

Pursuant to article 1 of the Convention signed in Paris on 14th December, 1960, and which came into force on 30th September, 1961, the Organisation for Economic Co-operation and Development (OECD) shall promote policies designed:

- to achieve the highest sustainable economic growth and employment and a rising standard of living in Member countries, while maintaining financial stability, and thus to contribute to the development of the world economy;
- to contribute to sound economic expansion in Member as well as non-member countries in the process of economic development; and
- to contribute to the expansion of world trade on a multilateral, non-discriminatory basis in accordance with international obligations.

The Signatories of the Convention on the OECD are Austria, Belgium, Canada, Denmark, France, the Federal Republic of Germany, Greece, Iceland, Ireland, Italy, Luxembourg, the Netherlands, Norway, Portugal, Spain, Sweden, Switzerland, Turkey, the United Kingdom and the United States. The following countries acceded subsequently to this Convention (the dates are those on which the instruments of accession were deposited): Japan (28th April, 1964), Finland (28th January, 1969), Australia (7th June, 1971) and New Zealand (29th May, 1973).

The Socialist Federal Republic of Yugoslavia takes part in certain work of the OECD (agreement of 28th October, 1961).

Publié en français sous le titre:

POLITIQUES DE LA CONCURRENCE
ET DES ÉCHANGES
Leur interaction

This report has been prepared by the Committee of Experts on Restrictive Business Practices as a first response to a mandate given by the OECD Council meeting at Ministerial level in May 1982 to examine problems arising at the frontier of competition and trade policies. The report was submitted as background material to the 1984 OECD Ministerial Council meeting and subsequently derestricted by the Council on 7th June 1984.

Also available

GUIDE TO LEGISLATION ON RESTRICTIVE BUSINESS PRACTICES
(4th Edition in 4 volumes updated by the first 8 series of supplements) (June 1976)
ISSN 0304-3282

Volume I : Australia, Austria, Belgium, Canada, Switzerland, Germany, Denmark

Volume II : Spain, Ireland, France, United Kingdom

Volume III: Greece, Italy, Japan, Luxembourg, Netherlands, Norway, Portugal, Sweden, Finland

Volume IV: United States, ECSC, EEC

(24 76 01 1) The 4 volumes	£110.00	US$250.00	F1000.00
Subscription to the ninth series of supplements	£6.70	US$15.00	F60.00
Subscription to the tenth series of supplements	£14.60	US$30.00	F120.00
Subscription to the eleventh of supplements	£14.60	US$30.00	F120.00
Subscription to the twelfth series of supplements	£16.70	US$37.50	F150.00

COMPARATIVE SUMMARY OF LEGISLATIONS ON RESTRICTIVE BUSINESS PRACTICES (October 1978)
(24 78 03 1) ISBN 92-64-11831-4   204 pages
£7.60   US$15.50   F62.00

COMPETITION POLICY IN REGULATED SECTORS WITH SPECIAL REFERENCE TO ENERGY, TRANSPORT AND BANKING (September 1979)
(24 79 01 1) ISBN 92-64-11975-2   190 pages
£4.90   US$11.00   F44.00

CONCENTRATION AND COMPETITION POLICY (December 1979)
(24 79 04 1) ISBN 92-64-12014-9   172 pages
£4.20   US$9.50   F38.00

BUYING POWER: THE EXERCISE OF MARKET POWER BY DOMINANT BUYERS (June 1981)
(24 81 03 1) ISBN 92-64-12168-4   178 pages
£4.60   US$11.50   F46.00

ANNUAL REPORTS ON COMPETITION POLICY IN OECD MEMBER COUNTRIES
"Document" series issued twice a year since 1973, countries being divided into two groups. Last issue 1983/No. 2 (June 1984)
(24 84 04 1) ISBN 92-64-12605-8
£6.00   US$12.00   F60.00

COMPETITION LAW ENFORCEMENT: INTERNATIONAL CO-OPERATION IN THE COLLECTION OF INFORMATION (March 1984)
(24 84 01 1) ISBN 92-64-12553-1   126 pages
£6.00   US$12.00   F60.00

MERGER POLICIES AND RECENT TRENDS IN MERGERS (forthcoming)

Prices charged at the OECD Publications Office.

THE OECD CATALOGUE OF PUBLICATIONS and supplements will be sent free of charge on request addressed either to OECD Publications Office,
2, rue André-Pascal, 75775 PARIS CEDEX 16, or to the OECD Sales Agent in your country.

INTRODUCTION, SUMMARY AND CONCLUSIONS

CHAPTER I: TRADE-RELATED COMPETITION ISSUES

A. INTRODUCTION

B. PRACTICES BY ENTERPRISES THAT AFFECT INTERNATIONAL TRADE

1. EXPORT CARTELS AND SIMILAR ARRANGEMENTS

2. IMPORT CARTELS

3. TRADING COMPANIES

4. VOLUNTARY EXPORT RESTRAINTS

5. OTHER BUSINESS PRACTICES AFFECTING
   INTERNATIONAL TRADE

a) Background
b) Vertical restraints
c) Pricing practices
d) Restrictions relating to industrial property
   rights and to the transfer of technology
e) Countertrade

6. MULTINATIONAL ENTERPRISES AND INTRA-FIRM
   AGREEMENTS AFFECTING TRADE: MARKET AND
   PRODUCT ALLOCATION, TRANSFER PRICING AND
   CROSS-SUBSIDISATION.

C. GOVERNMENT INVOLVEMENT IN AND REGULATION OF COMMERCIAL
   ACTIVITIES

1. BACKGROUND

2. GOVERNMENT PROCUREMENT AND STATE TRADING

3. PUBLIC ENTERPRISES

4. REGULATED INDUSTRIES

5. APPLICATION OF COMPETITION POLICY TO REGULATED
   INDUSTRIES AND PUBLIC ENTERPRISES

6. CONCLUSIONS

CHAPTER II - COMPETITION-RELATED TRADE ISSUES

A. INTRODUCTION

B. TRADE POLICY MEASURES (OTHER THAN LAWS RELATING TO UNFAIR TRADE PRACTICES) AFFECTING COMPETITION

    1. ANALYTICAL APPROACHES TO TRADE POLICY FROM A COMPETITION VIEWPOINT

        a) The goals of trade policy and competition policy
        b) Implications of trade policy measures for competition policy

    2. NON-TARIFF MEASURES: THE INSTITUTIONAL SETTING

    3. ANALYSIS OF NON-TARIFF MEASURES OF PARTICULAR RELEVANCE TO COMPETITION

        a) Export promotion policies
        b) Import substitution policies
        c) Export controls
        d) Interchangeability of trade barriers

C. SPECIFIC LAWS ADDRESSING INJURIOUS OR UNFAIR TRADING PRACTICES

    1. INTRODUCTION

        a) Subsidies and countervailing duties
        b) Anti-dumping measures

    2. COVERAGE UNDER THE GATT OF UNFAIR TRADE PRACTICES

    3. NATIONAL LEGISLATION

    4. TRENDS IN ENFORCEMENT OF LAWS RELATING TO UNFAIR TRADE PRACTICES

    5. RELATIONSHIP BETWEEN UNFAIR TRADE LAWS AND COMPETITION POLICY

        a) Use of laws relating to unfair trade practices to restrain competition
        b) Dumping and anti-competitive pricing
        c) Injury
        d) Remedies

D. CONCLUSIONS

CHAPTER III: ISSUES RELATING TO THE FORMULATION AND IMPLEMENTATION OF
TRADE AND COMPETITION LAWS AND POLICIES

A. INTRODUCTION

B. PROBLEMS OF LAW ENFORCEMENT, INCLUDING JURISDICTIONAL ISSUES

1. MAIN FEATURES AND EFFECTS OF JURISDICTIONAL CONFLICTS ARISING
   IN THE AREA OF COMPETITION AND COMPETITION-RELATED TRADE MATTERS

2. APPLICATION OF COMPETITION AND COMPETITION-RELATED TRADE LAWS
   TO FOREIGN CONDUCT AFFECTING DOMESTIC MARKETS AND FOREIGN COMMERCE

   a) Investigating powers
   b) Differences in procedural rules and remedies under competition
      law
   c) Substantive aspects
   d) Parent-subsidiary relationships

3. APPLICATION OF LAWS TO DOMESTIC CONDUCT AFFECTING FOREIGN MARKETS

4. PROBLEMS OF COMPETITION LAW ENFORCEMENT CONCERNING GOVERNMENT
   INVOLVEMENT IN COMMERCIAL ACTIVITIES

   a) "Sovereign immunity" and "Act of State" doctrines
   b) Foreign compulsion

5. NATIONAL AND INTERNATIONAL APPROACHES FOR DEALING WITH PROBLEMS
   OF LAW ENFORCEMENT AND JURISDICTIONAL CONFLICTS

   a) National approaches to resolving disputes
   b) Progress towards co-operation

C. INVOLVEMENT OF COMPETITION AUTHORITIES IN THE DECISION-MAKING PROCESS
ON TRADE POLICY MEASURES

1. PROCEDURES AT NATIONAL LEVEL

   a) Participation of competition officials in the formulation of
      trade policies
   b) Participation of competition authorities in the implementation
      of trade policies and the enforcement of trade laws

2. THE INTERNATIONAL LEVEL

D. CONCLUSIONS

INTRODUCTION, SUMMARY AND CONCLUSIONS

A. INTRODUCTION

Recognising the increasing importance of understanding the links between competition and trade policy and of exploring the gaps and problems that at present exist in the application of these policies, the OECD Council meeting at Ministerial level in May 1982 requested the Committee of Experts on Restrictive Business Practices

"to examine, in particular, possible longer-term approaches to developing an improved international framework for dealing with problems arising at the frontier of competition and trade policies. After consultation with the Trade Committee, the results of the study should be reported to the Council as soon as possible." [C(82)58(Final).

To carry out this mandate, the Committee of Experts on Restrictive Business Practices established a Working Party on Competition and International Trade which has prepared the present report. The advisory bodies to OECD, BIAC and TUAC, have been consulted in the process of preparing the report, and a representative of the GATT Secretariat has participated in the meetings of the Working Party. In the time available it has been possible to take account of the views of the Trade Committee only in the Introduction, Summary and Conclusions and the remainder of the Report has therefore been completed on the authority of the Committee of Experts on Restrictive Business Practices.

The special nature of the mandate given to the Committee with its stress on the problems arising at the frontier of competition and trade policies has led the Committee to focus its report on both trade related competition issues and competition related trade issues. These issues include practices which involve not only enterprises but also governments and which raise concerns for competition policy as well as trade policy. In addition, the report covers issues which are common to the formulation and implementation of both trade and competition policies, in particular jurisdictional issues and the participation of competition authorities in trade policy decisions.

As the report deals with a number of highly complex and politically sensitive issues the Committee took the view that it should aim at a broad coverage and should not seek consensus on all matters. Where divergent views exist, these are recorded as far as possible. The report should be seen as an attempt to alert policy makers and the general public to the concerns raised by certain trends in international trade if improvements are not made in domestic policy formulation and international cooperation. The report suggests an analytical approach for dealing with interrelated competition and trade policy problems. It sets the stage for the consideration of possible action proposals and policy recommendations in the second phase of the Committee's work on these issues.

International trade was a very buoyant feature in the world economy during the 1970s. The share of exports (or imports) of goods and services in OECD GNP rose from about 13 per cent in 1970 to approximately 20 per cent in 1980. Most projections suggest that trade will continue to play a dynamic role in the world economy in the 1980s. However, the volume of world trade was on a declining trend from 1980 to 1982, falling from an average annual percentage increase of 6 per cent in 1979, to 1 1/2 per cent in 1980, 0 per cent in 1981 and an actual decrease of 2 per cent in 1982 (1). However, as the recession in economic activity intensified during 1982 in most countries, substantial progress was recorded in curbing inflation in several industrial countries. Recent estimates and projections by the OECD (2) indicate that a recovery has begun in most OECD countries and is expected to continue in 1984 and 1985, but average figures conceal considerable diversity between OECD countries. It may be expected that international trade has resumed its upward trend which was interrupted at the beginning of the decade.

Despite the recent recovery in trade, there is growing concern that the post-war movement towards freer trade has lost momentum. To deal with domestic problems, governments have resorted to non-tariff trade restrictions, to many forms of domestic subsidisation and to bilateral rather than multilateral approaches to the resolution of international trade problems. Such actions have often had the effect of reducing flexibility in Member countries'economies by sheltering them from market forces and by acting as a brake on the shift of resources to industries or enterprises with greater potential for growth and employment creation. Short term relief thus gained has sometimes taken precedence in policy formulation over longer term considerations. It has become apparent how closely trade problems are linked with macro-economic policies and with domestic industrial, regional, social and other policies with which competition policy is also concerned. The Organisation is presently engaged in a multi-faceted approach to examine these interrelated problems in a longer term perspective with a view to strengthening international cooperation on trade and trade-related issues in the 1980s. The interface between trade and competition policies is an important part of this approach.

The report is organised in three chapters. Chapter I is concerned with trade-related competition issues, i.e. those practices by enterprises or, as appropriate, by governments in their commercial activities which fall within the scope of competition policy and which have implications for international trade. Chapter II of the report examines a range of trade policy measures, in particular non-tariff barriers, from the perspective of competition policy, with a view to presenting a framework governments could use to assess the economic effects of such policies, including their impact on market structures. In addition, this chapter deals with specific laws addressing unfair or injurious trade practices examining the extent to which competition policy considerations can be brought to bear in the application of such laws. Chapter III discusses problems of law enforcement, including jurisdictional issues, relating to the problem areas identified in the previous two chapters and analyses the scope for improved participation of competition authorities in the decision-making process on trade and trade-related matters.

The analysis of the subjects covered in the report is based on the experience acquired by the Committee in its past activities, on theme papers as well as information provided by Delegations in response to a questionnaire and additional research. Due to the time constraints in preparing the report, it was not possible to undertake in depth studies on the wide range of issues raised nor does the report attempt to give an exhaustive description of the position of each Member country. References to Member countries' law and experience therefore do not pretend to be all-inclusive; their purpose is rather to provide illustrative examples of the issues identified and of the possible approaches for dealing with such issues.

B. SUMMARY OF THE MAIN ISSUES DEALT WITH IN THE REPORT

The enactment of national competition laws and policies is largely a development of the post war period. In general terms, competition policy seeks to ensure the efficient allocation of resources by means of open and competitive markets. Toward that end, competition laws prohibit or grant authorities the right to prohibit or monitor anticompetitive practices or practices which are contrary to the public interest such as collusive activity among firms to jointly fix prices or output, as well as other conduct that substantially restrains competition, e.g. by raising entry barriers or creating excessive market concentration. Since its inception, the Committee has issued a series of reports analysing the national competition laws pertaining to business practices and commercial behaviour, including their effects on international trade (see Annex I). In addition, the Committee has attached high priority to international competition issues in order to enhance cooperation between Member countries and in 1967 and 1973 established mechanisms for international cooperation in the field of restrictive business practices which were consolidated in a 1979 Council Recommendation concerning cooperation between Member countries on restrictive business practices affecting international trade [C(79)154(Final)].

In the final analysis, trade liberalisation measures and competition policy share a common economic objective. Competition policy is aimed at ensuring the efficient functioning of markets by the removal or control of restrictive business practices. Trade liberalisation policies focus upon the removal of barriers to international trade both through action to reduce tariff levels and through agreements to limit the effects of non-tariff measures.

In this context, it should be noted that in certain circumstances trade-limiting actions are permitted under the GATT. Moreover, divergences have arisen in some circumstances between the goals and implementation of both competition and trade policy at least within the short run. In particular, when trade policy measures are designed to protect or promote domestic industries, they may limit the role of foreign enterprises in national markets and weaken competition in those markets. In recent years such policies have most commonly been implemented by means of non-tariff barriers such as Orderly Marketing Agreements (OMAs), Voluntary Export Restraints (VERs), quotas and in certain instances the abuse of administrative procedures and product standards. To the extent trade policy measures disregard longer term effects on the economy they may conflict with competition policy principles.

At the international level, problems can arise due to conflicts between the trade promotion policies of one country and the competition laws and policies in effect in the markets to which that country exports its goods and services. For instance, in order to promote their export trade, countries often encourage the creation of export trade arrangements, such as export associations and joint ventures. Although these arrangements may provide scale efficiencies and thus expand trade opportunities, to the extent that they restrain competition on foreign markets, e.g. through collusive setting of prices or output, they can violate the competition laws of other countries depending on the scope of these laws and the nature of the arrangements involved. Thus, trade policies adopted in one Member country may give rise to problems of competition law enforcement in others, which may be magnified by jurisdictional conflicts. Enterprises in importing countries, with or without the support of their governments, may resort to import cartels or other joint practices to countervail foreign export cartels. If this led to a general trend of cartelisation of export and import trade, this would affect competition in the markets of all countries concerned and impair the functioning of international trading relations.

A major issue dealt with in the report is the involvement of governments in restrictive business practices affecting international trade, through the granting of exemptions from competition laws, de facto acceptance, advice, encouragement or even compulsion. In some instances restrictive business practices by enterprises are in close correlation with restrictive trade policies. Government sponsored business practices that are at variance with principles of competition law and policy may be immune from challenge under such doctrines as "act of state" or "sovereign compulsion" suggesting the need for diplomatic or multilateral approaches to resolve such problems. The use of VERs in trade illustrates many of these issues, as these are measures which lie squarely at the interface of trade and competition policy. Although they are generally conceived as an instrument of trade policy, and accordingly imply a substantial degree of government involvement in their operation, VERs can resemble restrictive business practices such as cartels and are potentially subject to competition laws in a number of Member countries, while their status under the GATT is unclear.

The increasing resort in recent years to selective trade restrictions such as OMAs and VERs presents inherent problems for the functioning of the international trading system. In the first place, such arrangements result in discrimination between exporters, normally at the expense of the most competitive. Secondly they distort the adjustment process in the importing country. Thirdly, the cartellisation of exports which OMAs and VERs tend to encourage has the effect of reducing competition in both the exporting and importing country. A fourth factor is the possible transfer of resources from the importing to the exporting country when minimum price provisions form part of the arrangement. Finally, in most cases, consumers or users in the importing country bear the costs of such arrangements. Although there is a general reservation on the part of Member countries with respect to the use of VERs, some countries that have subjected their exports to VERs view them as a means of avoiding the adoption of more formal protectionist measures in import markets and thus enter into VERs to avoid more serious dislocations to the free trade market. One of the main features of the present report consists in the further development of an analytical framework aimed at improving, inter alia, from a competition point of view, the economic assessment of the OMAs, VERs and other forms of trade restrictions to provide policy-makers with a better basis for their decisions.

Another source of potential conflict revolves around the commercial activities of governments. The government role in commercial sectors, either through subsidies, public enterprises or the regulation of industries, appears to be growing in some OECD countries and is a significant factor in the economies of most OECD countries. While this activity is generally aimed at strengthening domestic economies, it can have repercussions on trade and on competition in foreign markets. For example, government subsidies to domestic firms may provide them with competitive advantages in export markets. This may also arise where public enterprises are used as instruments of government policies and benefit from competitive advantages resulting from various forms of government support. As to regulated sectors, distortions in international competition can occur where a monopolistic regulated sector trades with competitive sectors in other countries.

Competition policy has substantial reasons for being concerned with a nation's trade policy. A principal one is that international trade serves to sharpen competition in the domestic market place in terms of price, quality, variety and incentives to innovate new products and production processes, while trade barriers which shelter particular domestic industries have, in certain circumstances, anti-competitive effects on domestic markets. In this context, non-tariff barriers are of particular relevance to competition policy as these measures often act as serious impediments to trade flows and thus their impact on market structures can be both direct and substantial. In addition, the way certain types of non-tariff measures such as quotas, VERs and OMAs are implemented can induce collusive behaviour by exporting and/or importing enterprises and lead to cartelisation of world markets. Although designed to redress competitive disequilibria, laws relating to unfair trade practices, if improperly used, can act as barriers to trade and restrain competition on domestic markets.

Problems of competition law enforcement arise where restrictive practices by enterprises and government trade policies are closely interlinked and such problems can be magnified by jurisdictional conflicts. In the long run, managed international trade and inward oriented trade policies can frustrate the effective implementation of competition policy by favouring market structures unresponsive to competitive pressures. It is, therefore, important to explore practical possibilities for giving greater weight to competition policy considerations in the decision-making process on trade and trade-related issues having a significant impact on competition.

Although steps have been taken to improve cooperation within the spheres of competition and trade policy, it appears that little attention has been focused to date on developing a framework to address the types of problems that arise at the interface between these two policies and that are identified in the report. The earlier Recommendations and work of the Committee of Experts on Restrictive Business Practices have served, on both a procedural and substantive level, to improve cooperation among competition authorities on issues relating to international business conduct. However, as stated by the Council in 1982, there is a need for longer term approaches to improve cooperation concerning problem areas where trade policies by governments and restrictive practices by enterprises are closely inter-linked. The Committee believes that the present report identifies some major issues, provides a basis for analysis and sets the stage for developing further international cooperation on these problems.

C. <u>CONCLUSIONS</u>

1. TRADE-RELATED COMPETITION ISSUES

a) <u>Practices by enterprises that affect international trade</u>

The focus of this part of the report is on the treatment under competition policy of the various ways in which enterprises conduct or structure transactions in international trade. Accordingly, a wide variety of practices, including export cartels, import cartels, trading companies, voluntary export restraints, territorial restrictions linked to exclusive dealing or licensing agreements, countertrade and intra-group arrangements by multinational enterprises, are considered. The interrelationships which often exist between such practices and government policies are highlighted throughout the discussion and reflected in the following conclusions.

i) <u>Export cartels</u>

Export cartels are generally considered to be arrangements between firms which have substituted an agreement on prices, output or related matters for independent decision-making in relation to goods or services to be exported to foreign markets. As this definition implies, not all co-operative arrangements among export firms are considered to be export cartels, but only those which seek to restrain competition through cartel-like behaviour. Existing data do not permit an adequate assessment of the number and significance of national and international export cartels in world trade. Only four countries - Germany, Japan, UK, the US - require or provide for notification of export cartels and in all except Japan, the available information is inconclusive. The notification system in some of these countries also covers other export arrangements and the information notified is confidential in Germany and in the United Kingdom.

On the basis of such incomplete information, it is difficult to draw conclusions as to the trend in these cartels over the last ten years. However, the small number of new registrations or notifications each year in the four countries and the estimated small percentage of total exports accounted for by export cartels in a few countries have been noted and the trend in these countries would appear stable or declining. No conclusions can be drawn about the majority of OECD countries which do not keep records of export cartels and which do not require their notification. One suggestion, however, made by the Committee of Experts on Restrictive Business Practices in its earlier report on export cartels would seem equally appropriate at the present time, namely that Member countries should consider notification of export cartels or similar procedures and vigilant enforcement of such a provision to obtain more information about the nature and extent of export cartels, subject to relevant confidentiality requirements.

It should be noted that export cartels, whether national or international, have given rise to investigations and prosecutions in some countries at which they are aimed on the grounds that they have harmful effects on the domestic markets of the investigating countries. This suggests that there is concern in those countries, particularly in the case of international export cartels, about the trade-distorting and competition-restricting effects of such arrangements. It might therefore act as a deterrent to firms which are participants in exempted national export cartels if they are made aware that their conduct may still infringe the competition laws of other countries. Governments should not encourage the creation of export cartels but should ensure that their policies are at least neutral in respect of the formation of such cartels. The governments of the countries where export cartels are located should also be ready to cooperate, as far as their laws permit, with the competition authorities of other countries in any investigation into possible anti-competitive effects of arrangements located in their countries, recognising the jurisdictional difficulties that sometimes arise when information is sought from abroad or where the parties to a restrictive agreement are located abroad. The OECD 1979 Council Recommendation concerning cooperation on Restrictive Business Practices affecting international trade, the 1976 OECD Guidelines for Multinational Enterprises as well as the United Nations Set of Multilaterally Agreed Equitable Principles and Rules remain appropriate instruments for such cooperation.

ii) Import cartels

On the basis of available information it would seem that import cartels do not present serious problems as regards manufactured products. However, there is some evidence that such cartels have occurred in the raw materials sector. The increasing cross-penetration of developed countries' markets suggest that the conditions for an import cartel to be established and sustained will not be very commonly realised; and where they are, the cartel is likely to come to the attention of the competition authorities in the importing country because of the likely adverse effects on competition in that country.

Nevertheless, it is possible that importers could arrange the coordination of imports without restricting competition in the domestic market. This is perhaps most likely where the imported product is a raw material. Moreover, if the import arrangement is of an informal or tacit kind, it may escape the attention of the competition authorities, even if it does restrict competition in the domestic market. In these circumstances the adverse effects on the trade of the exporting country, a lower quantity of exports and a lower price for those exports, will not be corrected by action by the competition authorities in the importing country. Among Member countries Australia has drawn attention to this situation and the potential adverse effects on its trade. Countries adhering to a strict application of the territoriality principle of jurisdiction cannot take action against import cartels located in other countries which damage their export trade.

Where exporting countries inform the competition authorities in the importing country of the existence of an import cartel, or their suspicion of a cartel, those authorities should take appropriate steps to ensure that the cartel members are not in breach of the importing country's own laws. Where applicable under their national laws, they should cooperate to the fullest extent possible with the authorities of the exporting country in the provision of information and take what steps are open to them under their national laws to minimise the adverse effects of actions by their own importers on international trade.

iii) Trading companies

Trading companies vary considerably in size, structure, functions and frequency of use from one country to another. They are tending however to become increasingly significant in the export and import trade of a number of Member countries, accounting for a considerable share of total foreign trade or of trade in particular product groups. Whilst action against them under competition law has so far been relatively rare, their growing influence in certain sectors, in particular primary products, has led some authorities to consider the possible anti-competitive effects which may arise from the power certain trading companies possess in particular geographical and product markets. Governments should closely follow the growth of trading companies and, where appropriate, apply their competition laws to any anti-competitive practices in which such companies engage.

iv) Voluntary export restraints

In recent years, there has been a growing resort to VERs as a means for controlling or limiting imports. Designed to protect domestic industries from import competition, VERs have been relatively frequently used in such sectors as steel, automobiles, footwear, and consumer electronics. They may be arranged between governments or between individual firms with or without government sponsorship. VERs generally arise as a result of pressure or requests from an importing country for the exporting country to limit its exports of specific products; they may be regarded by the exporting country as preferable to other, more restrictive, trade barriers.

An important distorting feature of VERs is the fact that they may limit or restrict competition by their selective nature. Moreover, in some instances, these agreements have been resorted to where injury resulting from imports cannot be determined under the provisions of the GATT. Although they can produce cartel-like effects, VERs are often not subject to challenge under RBP laws, either because they fall outside the jurisdictional limit of these laws or due to government involvement in their creation or implementation. Further, since there are at present, with the exception of a few countries, no requirements to notify VERs to the government, private agreements may simply go unidentified. Thus, the introduction or extension of notification requirements to private VERs, which can be considered as cartels, would facilitate enforcement of competition law with respect to these arrangements.

VERs may conflict with the fundamental objectives of competition policy, as they lessen competitive pressures on domestic producers which may give rise to special problems in already concentrated markets. While they can produce short-term benefits, it appears from various studies that their costs for consumers and the economy of the importing country can be substantial.

They may also have detrimental effects on countries not party to the agreement. It would seem that greater steps are needed to increase the transparency of VERs, to monitor their effects and to consider their treatment under trade and competition laws. Competition authorities have an important role to prevent harmful effects on domestic market structure. Bringing VERs under international surveillance and control would be an important first step in regulating their use in a manner consistent with an effectively functioning international trading system. The Committee intends to cooperate with the Trade Committee to continue the analysis of VERs and their effects on trade and competition.

v) Other business practices affecting international trade

There are a number of other practices that are common features in commercial transactions on the domestic and international level. From the standpoint of competition policy, one principal concern is that the terms and conditions in the vertical distribution of goods and services or in the transfer of technology are not abused to allocate and divide world markets. Analysis of these practices, and of business arrangements such as joint ventures, rests on a determination as to whether they excessively restrict competition. With regard to joint ventures, this issue is already being addressed in the work programme of the Committee. The Committee is also planning to review experience under the 1973 Council Recommendation on Restrictive Business Practices relating to the use of Patents and Licences.

Although recognising the various reasons why countertrade agreements are used, in light of their potentially harmful effects on trade and competition, their uncertain status under competition laws, and their growing role in world trade, such agreements should be kept under review and, in particular, consideration should be given to steps that can be taken to increase the transparency of these agreements.

vi) Intra-group arrangements by multinational enterprises

Practices like intra-group allocations, transfer pricing, and cross-subsidisation and their effects on trade and competition are of interest to policy makers, given the large proportion of international trade attributable to intra-group transactions. Competition laws in most OECD Member countries provide that intra-group practices are not considered harmful in and of themselves unless they amount to an abuse of a dominant position adversely affecting competition outside the affiliated enterprises. In dealing with such practices, cooperation between governments in the exchange of information according to the Committee's recent report on competition law enforcement is an essential element. In addition, Member countries should continue to use the consultation process provided in the 1979 Recommendation where problems of obtaining information arise. Similarly, use should be made of the provisions of the OECD Guidelines relevant to intra-group practices.

b) Government involvement in and regulation of commercial activities

The commercial activity of governments, be it through procurement policies, public enterprises or regulation of industries, is of considerable importance in the domestic economies of OECD Member countries. As a result, such activity can exert a significant impact on competition in domestic markets and on international trade. Of particular concern is the extent to which the government's role, through, for example, specific procurement regulations or product standards, or through subsidies or financial support to enterprises at better than market terms, affects competition in domestic and foreign markets. Further, it may be more difficult for competition officials to apply their laws against the commercial activities of foreign governments that restrict competition in their markets than would be the case with private competition restraints. Greater transparency as to the Government's role in commercial activity is a necessary basis for assessment of effects of such action on trade and competition.

In the experience of several countries, efforts to apply competition laws to regulated sectors through deregulatory reforms have proved beneficial. Countries that have taken steps to deregulate certain sectors may however experience problems in trading with countries where regulation remains the rule and in applying their competition laws to such transactions. To improve this situation, cooperation between government authorities, including those responsible for competition policy, is necessary. The 1979 Council Recommendation on Exempted or Regulated Sectors is particularly relevant in this regard, since it calls upon Member countries to reconsider the continuing validity of present regulatory frameworks and whether the same objectives could be achieved by the operation of competition or through measures which restrict competition to a lesser degree. The Committee intends to examine in its future work programme the way this Recommendation has been applied.

II. COMPETITION-RELATED TRADE ISSUES

a) Trade policy measures (other than laws relating to unfair trade practices) affecting competition

Trade policy measures can have a significant impact on the competitive processes in both national and international markets. Where such measures restrict the pro-competitive effects of international trade in markets in terms of price, quality and incentives to innovate new products and production processes, they are of direct concern to competition policy authorities. In some cases restrictive trade measures can be conducive to increased collusion between market participants. In the long run, measures designed to shelter sectors from the incentives resulting from effective competition can reduce the ability of these sectors to innovate and grow in the domestic economy and to compete internationally, even though the stated purpose of the measures may be to give the sector time to adjust and become more competitive.

The Committee therefore is of the view that policy-makers should, when considering a prospective trade measure, undertake as systematic and comprehensive an evaluation as possible of the likely effects of the measure, including, inter alia, the impact of the measure on the structure and functioning of the relevant markets and the long-term effects on the structural adaptation of the affected sector. A checklist of the important effects of trade measures has been developed to provide a framework for such analysis (see paragraph 242 and Annex II). It is understood that it would have to be adapted to the particular situation in question and that governmental policy considerations will determine the weight given to each item. Competition policy authorities could make an important contribution to such analyses, particularly with respect to the evaluation of the likely impact of the measure on the structure of the relevant markets and the competitive process within those markets.

While a number of interesting national case studies of the economic effects of various trade measures have been identified, the Committee believes that considerable further analysis is needed to increase understanding of these often complex effects, particularly with respect to the newer forms of trade protection such as VERs and OMAs. Within the OECD, it would be desirable to have further discussions, including, <u>inter alia</u>, exchanges of views and comparisons of national experiences with such measures from the perspective of both competition policy and trade policy authorities using the indicative checklist as a framework for the discussion. The Committee has noted in this regard a need for exploring possible ways and means for increasing the transparency of these measures so that their effects can be better identified and monitored.

b) <u>Competition policy and the application of laws relating to unfair trade practices</u>

With respect to laws addressing injurious or unfair trade practices, the Committee noted that these laws and competition policy share the common objective of seeking to remove artificial distortions in the marketplace. While competition policy is designed to preserve competitive domestic market structures and the efficient allocation of resources, laws dealing with unfair trade practices aim to protect domestic industry from unfair import pressures causing injury to domestic competitors. Accordingly, in the enforcement of anti-dumping and countervail laws, different standards are applied to import pricing practices than if such practices were examined under competition statutes. As a result, some actions brought under the unfair trade laws can reduce competition in domestic markets, particularly where high levels of concentration already exist, through the foreclosure of foreign firms.

The Committee therefore considers that consensus should be sought on the extent to which policy-makers and enforcement authorities should give consideration to the impact on competition in domestic markets of actions taken under laws dealing with unfair trade practices. First, care should be exercised to avoid a misuse of unfair trade proceedings by enterprises seeking to restrain foreign competition. Second, further consideration should be given to the extent to which in administering laws dealing with unfair trade practices, it would be appropriate to take into account the structure and the functioning of markets and the competitive situation within these markets and the pro-competitive impact of foreign firms in domestic markets. Injury and its causal relationship to unfair trade practices should continue to be assessed on the basis of objective criteria, in accordance with international rules, and following procedures where all interested parties are given an opportunity to express their views.

III. ISSUES RELATING TO THE FORMULATION AND IMPLEMENTATION OF TRADE AND COMPETITION LAWS AND POLICIES

a) Problems of law enforcement including jurisdictional issues

In light of the increasing internationalisation of business conduct, the rising importance of trade as a component of national economies and the development of competition law in most OECD Members, there is a strong interest in controlling restrictive practices on the part of either foreign or domestic firms which create anti-competitive effects on domestic markets. On the other hand, policies designed to promote export trade or to regulate imports, through the creation of such structures as export cartels, import cartels, trading companies or joint ventures, can be of limited effect depending on the jurisdictional reach of the competition laws existing in target markets. In this context, jurisdictional rules and international arrangements need to reflect the growth and development of the world trading system to ensure that all relevant interests are considered and disputes avoided as far as possible when questions of jurisdiction over international conduct arise and to provide businesses with reasonable certainty as to the laws applicable to their transactions. Although there seems to be growing observance of moderation and self-restraint, in the absence of multilaterally agreed upon criteria, unilateral approaches are not likely to be successful in resolving all conflicts which may arise. With due regard to the situs of conduct, jurisdictional rules should be based on reasonable standards that allow for the consistent and effective implementation of the laws and policies of the countries affected. In this connection, while significant differences remain among Member countries, the Committee recognises the desirability of achieving international agreed criteria for avoiding or resolving jurisdictional differences of this nature.

There is a strong common interest among OECD Member countries in overcoming difficulties arising from competing claims of jurisdiction over international business activities and there have been encouraging signs in the development of cooperation between governments, in particular in the competition area. On whatever basis jurisdiction is applied, competition authorities may need to obtain information located outside the national territory in order to adequately evaluate the nature of practices under review and the impact of such practices on competition in the domestic market. The notification and consultation procedures provided for under international instruments and bilateral agreements have provided a useful first step in creating channels to resolve conflicts between the competition policies and trading interests of countries.

b) The Involvement of Competition Authorities in the Decision-making Process on Trade Policy Measures

Given their expertise with the functioning of markets and the short and longer-term effects of restrictive business practices on market structures, competition officials can make an important contribution to the formulation and implementation of trade policies. In most countries, arrangements of a formal or more frequently informal nature exist to obtain the advice of competition authorities on trade policy measures likely to affect competition. Nevertheless, experience shows that procedures do not always suffice to bring to bear on trade policy any real influence based on the criteria of competition. This situation could be significantly improved if policy makers undertook, where appropriate with the assistance of competition authorities, an analysis of the likely effects of prospective trade measures, guided by a checklist of quantitative and qualitative criteria as described in Annex II of this paper.

Given the diversity of government structures in Member countries, it is neither possible nor desirable to propose a single institutional framework in which coordination between trade and competition policies could be organised. Stress should be laid not on rigid procedural arrangements, but rather on creating the necessary conditions under which competition policy considerations can effectively be brought to the attention of policy-makers in the formulation and implementation of trade policies. For this purpose, competition authorities should be provided, subject to legal constraints, in a timely manner with relevant information on the nature and motivation of proposed trade policy decisions and be invited to express their views on all such decisions likely to have a significant impact on competition. Corresponding to different organisational patterns of government and public administration, there are various options for organising such participation, such as informal but regular contacts, establishment of standing interdepartmental committees or formal public hearings. On their part, competition authorities should be sensitive to the realities and developments in international trade including in particular trade rules and the growing internationalisation of markets. Thus, there is a need for a two-way co-operation between trade and competition authorities so as to better promote the efficient functioning of markets within an open international trading system.

IV. ACTION TO IMPROVE COOPERATION IN COMPETITION AND COMPETITION-RELATED TRADE MATTERS

The Committee's report has identified key issues arising at the frontier between competition and trade policies where further action is needed to improve international cooperation and has provided an analytical framework for such efforts. Such issues include: export cartels, trading companies and other export promotion arrangements between enterprises, the use of import cartels or other forms of collective purchasing practices in particular in the raw materials area, voluntary export restraints, government involvement in commercial activities, subsidies, safeguard restrictions and other non-tariff barriers, counter-trade, the relationship between competition policy and the enforcement of laws dealing with unfair trade practices, and jurisdictional issues arising in these areas. In addition the Committee's current and future activities on joint ventures, international mergers, patents and licences and the intended review of the implementation of the 1979 Recommendation on Competition Policy in Exempted or Regulated Sectors will highlight the important international trade aspects related to these issues. Continuing attention will also be given to intra-group practices of multinational enterprises to the extent that they affect competition and trade. On the basis of the conclusions set out in the report, the Committee in the next stage of its work intends, in accordance with the mandate given to it by the 1982 Ministerial Council, and taking into account the views to be expressed at the 1984 Ministerial Council, to explore the possibility for developing policy approaches and recommendations, in particular in those areas where it has been shown in the Committee's work to date that conflicts may arise between the trade and competition policies and practices of Member countries.

The Committee also intends to review existing mechanisms for considering related competition and trade issues and resolving disputes involving OECD Member countries. In this context, it will study the means by which the instruments that have proved beneficial in promoting cooperation in the competition area could be strengthened and whether they could be applied to trade matters having a substantial effect on competition. The review of the 1979 Recommendation concerning cooperation on restrictive business practices affecting international trade which is presently underway will be an important part of that exercise. Within the Organisation, the Committee intends to continue to closely cooperate with the Trade Committee and other bodies dealing with trade or trade-related matters within their areas of competence. It will provide, where appropriate, its advice to these bodies on issues likely to have a bearing on competition.

NOTES AND REFERENCES

1.   See GATT report on international trade 1982/1983, Geneva, 1983, p. 1, Table 1.

2.   OECD Economic Outlook, No. 34, December 1983, p. 7.

LIST OF REPORTS BY THE COMMITTEE AND OF COUNCIL RECOMMENDATIONS ON COMPETITION ISSUES OF RELEVANCE TO INTERNATIONAL TRADE

a) Reports

Restrictive business practices relating to patents and licences (1972)

Export cartels (1974)

Restrictive business practices of multinational enterprises (1977)

Restrictive business practices relating to trademarks (1978)

Competition policy in regulated sectors, with special reference to energy, transport and banking (1979)

The role of competition policy in a period of economic recession (1981)

Competition law enforcement: international cooperation in the collection of information (1984)

b) Council Recommendations

Recommendation concerning action against restrictive business practices relating to the use of patents and licences [C(73)238(Final)]

Recommendation concerning action against restrictive business practices relating to the use of trademarks and trademark licences [C(78)40(Final)]

Recommendation concerning action against restrictive business practices affecting international trade including those involving multinational enterprises [C(78)133(Final)]

Recommendation concerning cooperation between Member countries on restrictive business practices affecting international trade [C(79)154(Final)]

Recommendation on competition policy and exempted or regulated sectors [C(79)155(Final)]

INDICATIVE CHECK-LIST FOR THE ASSESSMENT OF TRADE POLICY MEASURES

a) What are the expected direct economic gains to the domestic sector, industry or firm in question (technically, the increase in producers' surplus) and also what jobs are expected to be created or protected by the measure?

b) What are the expected direct gains to government revenues (e.g. from tariffs, import licences, tax receipts) and/or increased government costs (e.g. export promotion, government subsidies, lost tax revenues)?

c) What are the direct costs to consumers due to the resulting higher prices they must pay for the product in question and the reduction in the level of consumption of the product (technically, the reduction in consumers' surplus)?

d) What is the likely impact of the measure on the structure of the relevant markets and the competitive process within those markets?

e) In the medium and longer term perspective, will the measure, on balance, encourage or permit structural adaptation of domestic industry leading over time to increased productivity and international competitiveness or will it further weaken and delay pressures for such adaptation? What will be the expected effect on investment, by domestic firms in the affected sector, by potential new entrants, by foreign investors?

f) What would be the expected economic effects on other sectors of the economy, in particular, on firms purchasing products from, and selling products to, the industry in question?

g) How are other governments and foreign firms likely to react to the measure and what would be the expected effect on the economy of such actions? Is the measure a response to unfair practices in other countries?

h) What are the likely effects of the measure on other countries? How can prejudice to trading partners be minimized?

CHAPTER I

TRADE-RELATED COMPETITION ISSUES

A. INTRODUCTION

1.   Chapter I of this study is concerned with trade-related competition issues. By this is meant those practices of enterprises or, as appropriate, of governments in their commercial activities, which fall within the scope of competition policy and which have implications for international trade and therefore for the interests of a country's trading partners. In view of the increasing interdependence through trade of national economies, and the importance of imports and exports as proportions of GNP in many of them, the subject matter of the chapter is very wide. However, it can be narrowed down to a number of major topics which are dealt with separately in subsequent sections of the chapter.

2.   First, the chapter deals with cartels, that is restrictive arrangements involving agreements or concerted actions by two or more enterprises. It is in relation to these that competition policies are most developed. A number of cartel arrangements affect international trade, most obviously export cartels and import cartels. These are discussed in Sections 2 and 3. In addition to formal agreements between enterprises there may be tacit understandings between enterprises in different countries not to compete in each others' domestic markets.

3.   Recently, there has been the development of trading companies which play a major part in exporting and importing many products. These are discussed in Section 4. It would seem that such activities have so far been of little concern to competition policy but at the very least such enterprises and agencies may deploy considerable buying power and by reciprocal and other dealing arrangements can have a significant impact not only on trade but also on competition.

4.   A major recent development which is also discussed is voluntary export restraints (VER's). Although these could equally be classified as trade issues they involve business practices by enterprises and often include the involvement of governments. Section 5 deals with these practices from a competition policy perspective while the broad economic implications of the trade policies giving rise to VERs are discussed in Chapter II of this report.

5.	Enterprises which have a dominant position in their domestic markets may also engage in practices which restrict competition, including competition from imports, and which therefore have incidental effects on trade. But the main concern in Section 6 of this chapter is with a variety of business practices in international trade which may impact directly on competition in foreign markets and on trade flows. These include vertical restraints, restrictions relating to the transfer of technology, pricing practices and countertrade.

6.	Given the significant share of intra-group trade in total world trade, the operations of multinational enterprise have a significant impact on trade flows between Member countries and competition in national and international markets. Section 7 is focussed on intra-group practices where trade and competition aspects are most closely linked, i.e. intra-group allocations of production and markets, transfer pricing and cross-subsidisation.

7.	The final part of this chapter deals with the effects on trade and competition of three types of government intervention in commercial activities namely, public procurement policies, public enterprises and government regulated industries.

8.	The basic questions to which each of the separate sections of the chapter may be considered to be addressed are:

a) To what extent do practices by enterprises act as substitutes for trade barriers? What is the relationship of such practices to trade policies pursued by governments? Are they reactions to imposed trade restrictions by governments? Are they condoned, encouraged or even compelled by government action? Do competition laws apply to those practices? Are there any specific problems of enforcement of competition laws in these areas?

b) What is the influence of government involvement in commercial activities (i.e. government procurement and public enterprises) and of government regulation of industries on competition and international trade? To what extent are such activities subject to competition laws and competition policy considerations?

c) Is the position adopted by competition policy on these various practices and arrangements contrary to, consistent with or neutral towards the stance taken on trade policy grounds?

d) To counter increasing pressures towards protectionism are there possibilities for competition policy to play a greater role in the control of business practices affecting trade, involving a more harmonised approach for instance to export cartels and VERs?

B. PRACTICES BY ENTERPRISES THAT AFFECT INTERNATIONAL TRADE

1. EXPORT CARTELS AND SIMILAR ARRANGEMENTS

a) Background

9.   To sell their goods and services abroad, and, in particular, to enter new markets or to increase their share where they already do business, firms may enter into cooperative arrangements with their competitors. These arrangements include but are not limited to export cartels. An individual firm's decision as to how best to enter into export trade will depend, inter alia, on the size of the firm, the type of product or service involved, the capital requirements of export trade, the nature of the entry barriers likely to be encountered and the existing regulations to be found in foreign markets. In turn, joint export arrangements can offer exporters distributional and other scale efficiencies, expertise, familiarity with foreign markets, and promotional assistance that individual firms could find difficult and expensive to acquire on their own. From the standpoint of trade policy, these export arrangements are generally encouraged, since they are perceived as a means to promote and expand trading opportunities of domestic firms particularly in the face of import-restricting measures adopted in other countries. In addition, certain export cartels have been approved by governments in response to requests by importing countries to limit their exports and in these cases the export cartels resemble voluntary restraint or orderly marketing arrangements, which are discussed in subsequent sections of this report. During periods of recession and decline in world trade, as in the most recent period, several countries have taken legislative action to facilitate the creation of export cartels and similar arrangements and one of the means pursued to achieve this objective has been to provide clearer guidance as to the application of competition policy to different export trade arrangements.

10.   The application of competition policy to export trade arrangements reflects two basic policies. First, most countries do not apply their competition laws to their national export agreements, unless these agreements produce effects on the domestic market. Nonetheless, due to the enactment of competition laws in many OECD countries during the past two decades, export arrangements may be challenged under the competition laws of Member countries in which they trade. Thus there is a potential for conflicts between the trade policies of one country and the competition laws of its trading partners. Second, business arrangements that achieve or facilitate inter-firm collusion are viewed with scepticism under competition policy. National competition laws widely prohibit collusion among firms to restrain competition through such practices as joint horizontal price fixing. Consequently, attempts by firms, whether at national or international level, to control output and prices in markets or to divide world markets (these being the classic "cartel-like" effects) are usually in direct violation of competition laws in the markets affected, subject to the territorial scope of a particular country's competition law.

11.   In light of these policies, cartel-like behaviour in export trade, the effect that export cartels can produce on trade, and their effect in domestic markets has been a subject of concern to competition authorities. In 1974, the Committee issued a report on export cartels, focusing on their

significance in world trade and their status under competition law. Other business arrangements used to effectuate trade have not received the same degree of examination, in part due to their relative newness, and the fact that certain other practices are common only in a few countries. Regardless of the particular form adopted for purposes of export trade, the principal issue remains to reconcile the interests of national trade policies in expanding trade opportunities through joint export arrangements with the competition policy of trading partners, which generally forbid inter-firm collusion and attempts to exercise market power to control prices and output in markets. It is this question which serves as the focus of this section on export cartels and similar arrangements.

b) Definition

12.   Export cartels are generally considered to be arrangements between firms which have substituted an agreement on prices, output or related matters for independent decision-making in relation to goods or services to be exported to foreign markets. They may also have anti-competitive effects on national markets. As this definition implies, not all co-operative arrangements among export firms are considered to be export cartels, but only those which seek to restrain competition through cartel-like behaviour. Consequently, determination that an arrangement is an export cartel involves consideration of the structure, purpose and effects of the arrangement. An export cartel generally involves direct cooperation among industry members. In contrast, foreign trade can also be conducted through joint ventures, where an independent firm or unit is created by industry members or others to handle exports, and through companies that specialise in trade and exist independently of producers and manufacturers, such as export agents. While these latter arrangements may serve to facilitate collusion among industry members, they do not amount to horizontal arrangements among competitors.

13.   Export cartels are usually classified by the nationality of their members and by their objectives. National cartels consist only of firms within a single country, while international cartels include firms from two or more nations. Cartels can also be classified by their intended sphere of influence. In its 1974 Report, the Committee defined "pure" export cartels as those cartels which cover exclusively competition on foreign markets, while "mixed" export cartels are those which affect competition both on foreign and domestic markets (1). Of course, it needs to be recognized that pure export cartels may, even if unintended, have effects on the domestic market. For that reason, a few countries do not distinguish between pure and mixed cartels in their competition laws. And indeed the very real possibility that "pure" cartels can give rise to collusion concerning domestic markets is one of the reasons for the great interest that competition authorities take in the activities of export cartels.

c) Present trends in export cartels

14.   In the period between the two world wars, export cartels were one of the major vehicles for conducting international trade. One study of export cartels estimated that immediately prior to World War II, international cartels controlled from 30 to 50 per cent of world trade (2). Another study by the U.S. Department of Justice noted the existence of 179 international cartels in 1940 (3). Of course, this was a period when most OECD countries did not possess competition laws or policies. Between 1940 and 1949, the U.S.

Justice Department filed approximately 60 cases involving international cartels, involving a wide range of products (4). As U.S. firms were forced out of these cartels, and as other OECD countries adopted and enforced competition laws, many of the large cartels disbanded. The climate of international business changed and the 1950's ushered in a period of expansion and dynamic change in world trade.

15. The break-up of international cartels during the postwar period not only contributed to an expansion of world trade but also the creation and extension of new forms of trade structures. Multinational enterprises establishing production and distribution facilities in many countries, have increased their share in world trade. Trade arrangements other than export cartels, e.g. joint ventures and trading companies, have also become more prominent. These developments have probably resulted in the relative stability or decline in the importance of export cartels in the last decade.

16. At present, knowledge about the extent of export cartels in trade is limited in OECD countries. The main reason for this is that "pure" export cartels, whether national or international, are in many countries considered to be outside the jurisdiction of competition authorities. As a result, few countries monitor, let alone control pure export cartels, thus making it difficult to quantify the significance of such cartels in international trade. The situation is however more transparent with mixed export cartels.

17. On the basis of available data, it would appear that the level of export cartels has remained relatively stable since 1972, when the Committee last examined this subject in those few countries which keep a record of numbers of export agreements (Germany, Japan, UK and US). Only in the United States has there been a slight increase in the number of registered Webb-Pomerene associations over the last five years. The German figures from 1972 to 1982 show a slight decline while the Japanese data show a considerable decline. The United Kingdom figures were the same in 1972 and 1982.

18. These figures are subject to several qualifications. For example, in the United States, there is no compulsory notification when export agreements are abandoned so that the actual numbers do not reflect whether registered export agreements or associations are still active. In the United States, export associations are not required to register with the government, so the available data is limited in this respect. As regards the trend in recent years, figures do exist on new export agreements registered each year. These show for Germany that only two export cartels have been notified in the period 1980-1982; for the United Kingdom, over the period 1972 to 1982, 13 new export agreements were notified (one of which was subsequently abandoned): there were no new cartels at all registered in 1975-1976 and 1981-1982. In Japan, between 1973 and 1983, 29 new cartel agreements were registered, while 135 existing cartel agreements were abolished. In the United States, as of December 29, 1977, there were 30 registered Webb-Pomerene associations. The number of associations created, each year, during the period 1973 - 1977 was as follows: 1973-1, 1974-0, 1975-4, 1976-5 and 1977-4. Of those registered, one had been inactive for several years, another had been incorrectly registered in 1977, and subsequently dropped from the rolls and a third terminated its registration effective December 31, 1977. Three of the remaining associations reported that they were also inactive. As of November 1, 1978, there were 32 registered Webb-Pomerene associations, 29 of which were believed to be active. As of the end of 1982, there were

42 registered Webb-Pomerene associations in existence and believed to be active. From 1979 through 1982, the following number of new associations were registered each year: 1979-5, 1980-4, 1981-3 and 1982-8. During the same time period, 12 associations dissolved or became inactive.

19. For other OECD countries, information about export cartels is very limited. Denmark reported the existence of 17 registered agreements which contained export restrictions, 5 of which have since been terminated. 12 of these concerned national enterprises and the remaining 5 were international export cartels.

20. As regards the share of export cartels in total exports, again little data was available except for Germany, the United Kingdom and the United States. In Germany, the share of national and international export cartels in total German exports was approximately 2 per cent in 1982, showing little change over the last decade. In the United Kingdom, the recent figure is unlikely to be higher than 5 per cent and likely to be significantly lower. In the United States, a Federal Trade Commission staff report of 1967 (6) found that Webb-Pomerene associations accounted for only 2.4 per cent of total US merchandise exports between 1958 and 1962. The 1976 FTC report (7) confirmed these findings and found that Webb-Pomerene assisted exports in 1976 were only 1.5 per cent of total US merchandise exports. In 1981, in the House of Representatives hearings on the Foreign Trade Antitrust Improvements Act, there was testimony that Webb-Pomerene associations had declined from a peak of 19 per cent of total US exports in 1930-1935 to less than a 2 per cent share in 1981 (8).

21. Data on the product or industry coverage of export cartels was available for five countries -- Denmark, Germany, Japan, the UK and the United States (9). For Denmark, most of the registered agreements containing export restrictions concerned the agricultural and dairy products sectors. However other sectors included air transport, linoleum, film rights and paint. In Germany, whilst no detailed breakdown is possible, export cartels are currently found for example in the electrical industry, including electronics, chemical, engineering, food and the iron and steel industries. In Japan, in 1983 there was a total of 53 export cartels in existence, with textiles accounting for 27, machinery and equipment for 9, chemical products for 6, miscellaneous products for 5, followed by metal products (4) and agricultural and fishery products (2). In the United Kingdom, the broad sectors covered by export agreements (1973-1980) were engineering goods (6), consumer goods (2), producer services (1) and consumer services (1). For the United States, Webb-Pomerene associations in existence prior to 1973 covered the following products: wood pulp, chips, and fibre, still and motion films, picture negatives, phonograph records, textile machinery, liquid sulphur, clay, anthracite coal, bit coal, phosphate rock, and agricultural products (general; fruit and vegetables, dried fruit and tree nuts, frozen poultry, milled rice, beef tallow, raw cotton). The product coverage of new Webb-Pomerene associations registered since 1973 has concerned predominantly agricultural products and raw materials.

22. As regards the functions performed by export cartels, again due to lack of reporting or registration requirements, little data was available on the actual activities. Only in the United States, in the two reports on the operation of Webb-Pomerene associations mentioned earlier was some information provided on functions. Of the 27 Webb associations active in 1978, the

predominant functions were: exporting in the name of the association, freight consolidation/rate negotiation/ship chartering and market research. Next came statistical services, price setting, credit information and collection facilities. Allocating business was relatively infrequent. Only three associations indicated that they engaged in this practice (10).

23.   The 1978 FTC staff report also analysed other characteristics of the associations for a more recent period as had the 1967 report for the earlier period (11). As regards membership of the associations, the 1978 analysis showed that only 4 associations (of 30 registered associations in 1978) had more than 20 members and more than two-thirds had less than 10 members. No data was collected concerning size and characteristics, but such data tended to confirm the 1967 report's findings that large firms predominated in the average association and that small firms appeared to have received little assistance from the Act, although the Act was primarily directed towards helping them.

d) The trade rationale and effects of export cartels

24.   The assessment of the trade rationale for and effects of export cartels needs to consider both the interests of industry and governments and should provide a means for distinguishing cartel-like agreements from co-operative trade arrangements that do not restrain competition.

25.   In the classical and historic sense, international cartels provided a means for producers and manufacturers of different nationalities to divide and allocate world markets. By joining together, they acquired collective market power enabling them to foreclose competitors from their individual markets and to control price, output and sales. As a result, competition was diminished in all the affected markets, trade flows were restricted and non-cartel members could be forced out of markets. It is for these reasons that competition policy played an active and decisive role in prosecuting international cartels.

26.   On the other hand, countries seek to strengthen and expand their export trade by allowing domestic firms to enter into cooperative agreements, which may include national export cartels. The rationale for this policy is that inter-firm co-operation to achieve scale efficiencies by pooling personnel, equipment or other resources, or to spread high risks, capital outlays or demands on capacity imposed by export activities may be needed to enable medium and small firms to engage effectively in trade. Further, such arrangements may serve as a mechanism to collectively acquire and share the special skills and knowledge needed to successfully export to foreign markets such as where restrictions on imports distort export trade. In some cases export cartels may also be used to countervail joint buying practices in the importing country. To the extent that these policies enable firms to export that would not otherwise be able to do so, national export cartels may increase competition in foreign markets. This may be particularly the case where a co-operative arrangement provides the types of efficiencies that allows national firms to enter new export markets, but does not endow them with, or where they otherwise lack, sufficient market power to distort competition in those markets through control of output or prices.

27.   To the extent that these policies include the promotion of national export cartels, their success will depend in part on whether a national export

cartel prompts either defensive measures or prosecution in foreign markets. This will depend on a number of factors, including the size of the cartel, the number of industry members it represents and the types of activities it engages in. When a cartel accounts for only a small share of output, its ability to raise export prices will be diminished since it will be subjected to competitive pressures from non-cartel members. On the other hand, where a national cartel includes a significant percentage of domestic producers and production, it may be difficult to maintain. This is because more efficient members of the cartel will be tempted to lower their prices below the cartel price to gain a competitive advantage.

28.   The limited available evidence (mostly from the United States) suggests that policies to facilitate the creation of national export cartels often do not achieve their objectives. In fact, such evidence indicates that export cartels are not typically composed of small firms, but rather require a relatively small number of (large) members producing a homogeneous product to succeed (12). In its 1974 Report, the Committee concluded, on the basis of experience in some Member countries, that the expectations underlying policies to encourage national export cartels and exempt them from competition laws in their home countries have not been fulfilled and that small firms, who would be expected to benefit from reductions in overhead costs of exporting, have received little assistance (13). The Report further noted that "legal authorization of export cartels by one country may be an incentive for other countries to grant similar exemptions", raising the threat of an increase in cartelised trade (14).

29.   Of particular concern to competition authorities are the likely spillover effects from a national export cartel in the domestic market. From a structural standpoint alone, the ability of domestic firms to co-operate in their foreign trade through participation in a cartel facilitates collusion in the domestic market. This can occur, for example, where firms exchange information on prices and production costs. Moreover, in many instances the factors leading to a successful cartel will heighten the possibility of spillover effects. If an export cartel comprises a large share of domestic industry output, thus increasing the possibility it will be able to exercise market power in foreign markets, it is likely that the cartel will be able to divert output to the higher priced export market as well as engaging in collusive pricing in the domestic market. Thus, successful export cartels are likely to produce effects on the domestic market (15).

30.   National export cartels may also be approved pursuant to government trade policies other than export promotion or expansion. In some instances, export cartels may be used by governments to regulate trade in response to trade restrictive measures or requests from trading partners. Thus, in Japan, some export cartels have been approved by the government to limit exports to other countries and in this case they resemble VERs or OMAs.

31.   In other cases, governments, particularly those that export national resources, may encourage the formation of national export cartels to overcome import cartels, restrictive government purchasing policies or other monopsonistic practices in foreign markets. In some situations, import cartels have been established as a counter measure to foreign export cartels, rather than the other way round. Thus, in response to the U.S. cartel of sulphur exporters (SULEXCO) which grouped 75 per cent of world sulphur supplies, import cartels were established in Australia, New Zealand and the

United Kingdom to negotiate lower price increases than those desired by the members of the export cartel. However, there have also been instances where the formation of export cartels has been explained by joint buying practices or monopsonistic power in the importing country. The 1978 FTC report (16) found that only three U.S. Webb-Pomerene associations listed a private import cartel as a customer. However, there is evidence that these associations deal with government agencies and State trading firms. The same report mentioned that 16 associations had such customers in the Eastern bloc countries or in developing countries (17).

e) Legal status of export cartels

32.   As already noted, most OECD countries have an explicit or implied exemption from their competition laws for export agreements which do not affect the domestic market. In general, these exemptions do not distinguish between joint export arrangements which serve only to facilitate trade and those arrangements which produce cartel-like effects in foreign markets. There are, however, significant differences between countries as to the nature of the exemption. In four countries (Australia, Germany, Japan and the United States) a specific statutory exemption applies to export cartels only if certain requirements are met. Otherwise, the permissibility of export cartels is evaluated under generally applicable competition law standards. These requirements concern i) formal notification or registration of the export agreement to the national competition authorities before the agreement is put into effect;   ii) the satisfaction of varying substantive criteria.

33.   In other countries whose legislation is based on control of abuses, there is usually a special provision in the competition law which exempts export agreements from the provisions applicable to other kinds of restrictive agreements. In Australia, Canada, Germany, Norway, Sweden and the US, spillover domestic restraints of competition contained in export agreements are not exempt from control. In the UK, export cartels governing the export of goods from the UK may be referred to the Monopolies and Mergers Commission under the legislation concerning monopolies for consideration as to whether or not they are in the public interest. They are however exempted from the legislation concerning restrictive agreements, except for the obligation to notify the competition authorities of their existence. The information notified however remains confidential. In Italy, there is no competition legislation as such, and therefore no controls are placed on export cartels.

34.   In Germany, export cartels providing for domestic restraints may be allowed if such restraints are necessary to ensure the desired regulation of competition in markets outside Germany and if the following five other criteria are satisfied: a) the export cartel must cover trade in goods or services within Germany;   b) the restraint on the domestic market must be necessary to ensure the desired regulation of competition in foreign markets; c) the export cartel must not violate principles accepted by the Federal Republic in international treaties with other nations;   d) the effects on the domestic market must not lead to substantial restraints of competition and the interest in preserving competition must prevail;   and e) the agreement must not be abusive within the meaning of Section 12 of the Act. In practice very few "mixed" cartels have been authorised. During the period 1972-1982 only 1 such mixed cartel was authorised. At the end of 1982, only 3 such cartels were in existence. It should be noted that the 4th Amendment to the Act against Restraints of Competition (1980) also clarified the provisions

relating to "pure" export cartels. In a judgment of 1973 (1), the Federal Supreme Court ruled that a "pure" export cartel with anticompetitive effects outside Germany alone was outside the jurisdictional reach of the Act against Restraints of Competition. As a result parties to "pure" export cartels having no domestic effects were no longer obliged to notify these to the Federal Cartel Office. The 1980 Amendment, however, introduced a mandatory prior notification requirement for all export cartels in which enterprises located in the Federal Republic of Germany, including West Berlin, participate. This provision requires German parties to submit the full texts of agreements and decisions, including any subsequent modifications and amendments, to the Federal Cartel Office before the export agreement has been put into effect. On the other hand, "pure" export cartels are not placed on a public register so that they are kept confidential by the cartel authority. In addition, the 1980 Amendment strengthened the abuse control system on "pure" export cartels to permit action even against "pure" export cartels the effects of which "substantially impair predominant foreign trade interests of Germany". Enforcement of this provision has been entrusted to the Federal Minister of Economics because of the close relationship between the control of export cartels and the foreign trade interests of Germany.

35.   In addition to Germany, three other countries -- Greece, Norway and Sweden -- have introduced a qualification to the exemption for export agreements, in their competition laws specifying that such cartels must be compatible with the provisions of international conventions or agreements entered into. Other countries have not felt the need for a specific provision of this kind in their competition law since their international obligations are deemed self-executing according to the terms of the conventions and treaties to which they are party.

36.   In Japan, export cartels are in principle subject to the Anti-Monopoly Act. However, under the Export and Import Trading Act and the Act concerning the promotion of export fisheries, export cartels may be exempted from the Anti-Monopoly Act subject to authorisation by the competent ministers or to a report being filed by the parties. In granting exemptions, the competent ministers must consult with or notify the Fair Trade Commission. The Commission, if it finds that the agreements are compatible with certain criteria (e.g. that they do not lead to undue harm to consumers' interests), may request the competent minister to take the necessary dispositions. The same situation also applies to export associations.

37.   In the United States, there are three principal provisions that govern joint export activities. First, a joint exporting arrangement may be organised without benefit of any special antitrust exemption and its legality tested under normal antitrust standards (18). Since the 1982 Amendments to the Sherman Act, the law does not reach agreements unless they produce a "direct, substantial and reasonably foreseeable effect on domestic commerce on import commerce or on export commerce of a US person insofar as the activity injures that person's export business". The impetus for this legislation was the need felt by Congress to respond to complaints by US exporters that uncertainty about the reach of the antitrust laws to export trade had deterred some legitimate export cartels. Thus a price-fixing conspiracy directed solely at exported products or services would not have the required effects on domestic or import trade, in the absence of spillover effects on the domestic market. It should be noted, as was expressed in Congress, that the 1982 Act

in no way prevents a foreign government from taking action against a US export cartel which has unlawful effects on its territory.

38.   Secondly, the Webb-Pomerene Act provides a limited, non-discretionary exemption from the Sherman Act for export trade associations formed for the sole purpose of engaging in export trade under two primary conditions. First, the export trade association, or acts or agreements in connection with its activities, must not restrain trade within the United States or restrain the export trade of any domestic competitor of the association. Second, the export trade association may not enter into any agreement, understanding or conspiracy, or do any act, which artificially or intentionally enhances or depresses prices within the United States of the commodities of the class exported by the association, or which in any other way restrains trade in the United States. In addition, the Webb-Pomerene Act extends the prohibition against "unfair methods of competition" in the Federal Trade Commission Act to unfair methods of competition used in export trade, even though done outside the territorial jurisdiction of the United States.

39.   Both the Federal Trade Commission and the Department of Justice have investigated the activities of Webb-Pomerene associations and have taken action against associations whose anti-competitive activities exceeded the scope of the exemptions granted (19).

40.   In the first judicial interpretation of the Webb-Pomerene Act, United States v. Alkali Export Association (20), the district court held that a Webb Association violated the Sherman Act by: (1) participating in foreign cartels; (2) engaging in practices which result in "the use of monopoly power to extinguish the competition of independent domestic competitors engaged in the export trade"; and (3) carrying out practices which stabilize domestic prices by removing surplus products from the domestic market. In the second major decision, United States v. Minnesota Mining & Manufacturing Co. (21) the court held that an export association could not establish or operate jointly-owned production facilities abroad. Significantly, the court affirmed the legality of a Webb Association, representing certain members of a highly oligopolistic industry, in refusing to handle the products of the remaining competing American firms.

41.   The Minnesota Mining decision stands on its own for providing illustrative examples of conduct that Webb Associations may lawfully carry out. Thus, business firms can

    1) Create an association by a majority of American manufacturers;

    2) Use the association as the members' exclusive foreign outlet;

    3) Agree that goods will be purchased only from member producers;

    4) Fix resale prices for the association's foreign distributors; and

    5) Fix export prices and establish quotas for members.

42.   Finally, the Export Trading Company Act of 1982 is also relevant to export activities (see Section 3 below for a discussion of its provisions).

f) Competition cases involving national and international export cartels

43.   The exemption, general or limited, for national export cartels from national competition laws has inevitably meant that there have been few cases of enforcement of competition laws against "pure" export cartels by the authorities in the cartels' home country. Unless the cartels were thought to have exceeded the terms of the authorisation or exemption granted them, there would indeed be no basis for such action.

44.   The situation is not the same for the country or countries at which the national export cartel is directed, or where an international cartel whether or not it involved a domestic firm, is thought to be adversely affecting a particular country's interests. Six countries reported investigations since 1973 involving national export cartels or domestic firms participating in international export cartels -- Canada, Denmark, Norway, Sweden, United States, as well as the EEC. Thus, while a national export cartel may be exempted from its domestic competition laws, it nevertheless remains subject to the applicable competition law in its export markets, and as these cases suggest, in applying their competition laws, countries are increasingly less likely to defer to the policies of their trading partners of granting exemption to export cartels. In Australia, there have been two investigations of export agreements by the Trade Practices Commission. One concerned the export of liquefied gas and the other concerned the construction of an alumina smelter in Queensland involving various US and Japanese companies, which was geared to the export market. Following investigation, neither project was challenged, since they were viewed as bringing substantial public benefits to Australia.

45.   In Denmark, in 1981, the Monopolies Control Authority took action against an agreement between a sales organisation engaged in exporting bacon, principally to Britain, and Danish bacon producers on the main grounds that the price-fixing method used caused unreasonable effects on the domestic market, in particular, higher prices to certain domestic purchasers. Following intervention by the MCA, the agreement was abandoned by the parties.

46.   In Germany, there has been only one recent case in which the Federal Cartel Office ("FCO") challenged a foreign export cartel. In the course of abuse control, the German FCO required a foreign export cartel consisting of steel foundries to modify their information agreement covering export transactions. The informations system was used by member firms, inter alia, for costing purposes. The information about price elements also included direct-to-customer sales which members had made or intended to make with domestic independent export dealers on enquiry from the latter. By including such transactions in the reporting system, it was alleged that the manufacturers unlawfully restrained competition. At the instigation of the FCO, the necessary changes were made in the information agreement so as to avoid harmful effects on competition.

47.   In Japan, the Fair Trade Commission took a decision in 1972 (Decision of 27th December 1972) designed to secure the withdrawal of 14 Japanese textile manufacturers from international export cartels concluded with European man-made fibre manufacturers concerning rayon yarn, staple fibre, nylon filament, polyester filament and acrylic yarn. With regard to acrylic yarn, the Japanese firms had concluded an international cartel at the request

of the German Worsted Yarn Association in order to limit exports to West Germany. The FTC held these agreements to be a substantial restraint of competition in the export trading field for each of the commodities and therefore a violation of Section 6(1) of the Antimonopoly Act. In a similar 1973 case (Decision of 12th January 1973) the Fair Trade Commission ordered four Japanese manufacturers of felt and canvas who accounted for the bulk of exports from Japan to withdraw from an international price agreement operated by the European Felt Industry. The FTC found that this agreement caused a substantial restraint of competition in the export of felt and canvas. In Norway, the Price Council took action against an state-owned Israeli export cooperative of citrus fruits which had refused importer status to a Norwegian wholesaler. As a result of the intervention which was based on jurisdiction according to the effects doctrine, the cooperative granted the wholesaler status as an importer.

48.   In Sweden, the Competition Ombudsman has intervened in several cases involving international export agreements relating to electrical equipment, carbon brushes, doors, particle boards, insulating material, paper, cast-iron rolls, mink pelts and fertilizers. Most of the cases concerned price, output and market-sharing agreements affecting the Swedish market.

49.   In the United States, there have been many cases against international export cartels, some of which have involved national export cartels. There have also been various private actions in the United States against international cartels. Most of the public actions have involved international market-sharing, production quota and price-fixing agreements in sectors as diverse as lithium, dyes, mink pelts, books, diamond grit, persulfates, wigs, bank security equipment, wheelchairs, potash, air fares, uranium, ocean shipping, industrial nitro-cellulose and motor freight transport.

50.   In one international cartel case [U.S. v. National Board of Fur Farm Organisations, Inc., Giv. No. 74-546 and Crim No. 17-211 (E.D. Wis. 1974)] the government alleged that several American companies, in conjunction with foreign mink rancher corporations named as unindicted co-conspirators, namely the Scandinavian Fur Farm Organisations, and Canada Mink Breeders Association, had conspired by fixing prices and establishing quotas for the sale of mink pelts. Pleas of nolo contendere were entered and fines imposed in the criminal action; a consent decree was entered in the civil suit.

51.   Finally, in 1981 the European Commission began an investigation into allegations of price fixing in the sale to the Common Market among an international group of wood pulp producers, including a U.S. registered Webb-Pomerene association of wood pulp exporters, and issued a statement of objections. The investigation was specifically aimed at an alleged pattern of price announcements and other price communications for wood pulp involving North American and European producers. Although the case is still pending, the Commission did note that export association activities that have substantial anti-competitive effects in the Common Market may violate EC competition law, even if those activities are authorised in the association's home country.

g) Conclusions

52.   Export cartels are generally considered to be arrangements between firms which have substituted an agreement on prices, output or related matters

for independent decision-making in relation to goods or services to be exported to foreign markets. As this definition implies, not all co-operative arrangements among export firms are considered to be export cartels, but only those which seek to restrain competition through cartel-like behaviour. Existing data do not permit an adequate assessment of the number and significance of national and international export cartels in world trade. Only four countries -- Germany, Japan, UK, the US -- require or provide for notification of export cartels and in all except Japan, the available information is inconclusive. The notification system in some of these countries also covers other export arrangements and the information notified is confidential in Germany and in the United Kingdom.

53.   On the basis of such incomplete information, it is difficult to draw conclusions as to the trend in these cartels over the last ten years. However, the small number of new registrations or notifications each year in the four countries and the estimated small percentage of total exports accounted for by export cartels in a few countries have been noted and the trend in these countries would appear stable or declining. No conclusions can be drawn about the majority of OECD countries which do not keep records of export cartels and which do not require their notification. One suggestion, however, made by the Committee of Experts on Restrictive Business Practices in its earlier report on export cartels would seem equally appropriate at the present time, namely that Member countries should consider notification of export cartels or similar procedures and vigilant enforcement of such a provision to obtain more information about the nature and extent of export cartels, subject to relevant confidentiality requirements.

54.   It should be noted that export cartels, whether national or international, have given rise to investigations and prosecutions in some countries at which they are aimed on the grounds that they have harmful effects on the domestic markets of the investigating countries. This suggests that there is concern in those countries, particularly in the case of international export cartels, about the trade-distorting and competition-restricting effects of such arrangements. It might therefore act as a deterrent to firms which are participants in exempted national export cartels if they are made aware that their conduct may still infringe the competition laws of other countries. Governments should not encourage the creation of export cartels but should ensure that their policies are at least neutral in respect of the formation of such cartels. The governments of the countries where export cartels are located should also be ready to cooperate, as far as their laws permit, with the competition authorities of other countries in any investigation into possible anti-competitive effects of their arrangements, recognising the jurisdictional difficulties that sometimes arise when information is sought from abroad or where the parties to a restrictive agreement are located abroad (22). The OECD 1979 Council Recommendation concerning cooperation on Restrictive Business Practices affecting international trade, the 1976 OECD Guidelines for Multinational Enterprises as well as the United Nations Set of Multilaterally Agreed Equitable Principles and Rules remain appropriate instruments for such cooperation.

a) Introduction

55.   Import cartels are agreements between firms in a particular country made for the purpose of coordinating the importation into that country of a good or service. The agreement therefore relates to purchases of a good or service. Cooperation between buyers occurs in many markets. Many arrangements to coordinate buying will be innocuous in competition terms in that they enable small firms to share transaction costs, insurance or storage costs, or managerial costs and to obtain pecuniary economies of scale from discounts and rebates for which their bulked purchases may be eligible. In so far as such coordination improves the efficiency of the participants, involves firms which together account for a small proportion of the market and does not extend to cartelisation of the market(s) in which the participants sell, then the agreement will have no adverse effects on competition, or, where the purchases are of imports, on international trade. Such agreements -- which perhaps hardly merit the term "cartel" -- are therefore of little significance for the purposes of this report.

56.   Import cartels which are of interest are those which limit competition with respect to imports by coordination of the price, quantity or other terms of purchase of imports with a view to the acquisition and exercise of market power. Market power may be exercised in the domestic market for the sale of the product or in the relevant market for the purchase of the product, or both.

b) Market power in the domestic market for sale of the product

57.   An import cartel which controls the importation of a product into a country so that non-members of the cartel are unable to obtain supplies, or able to obtain them only on disadvantageous terms, will enable the members of the cartel to restrict supplies in the domestic market and hence to raise prices on the domestic market. Where the importers do not have monopsony power, and are therefore not able through their coordinated purchases to drive down the price of the imported products, the effects of the control they exercise over imports are analogous to the detrimental effects in the domestic market of any agreement among domestic producers to restrict supplies and raise price. Consumers will pay higher prices than if the market was competitive and the efficiency of the domestic industry may be reduced by the blunting of the competitive pressures to which the members of the cartel are exposed.

58.   This type of cartel will only be possible or sustainable where non-members can be excluded from the market in which the cartel buys and where foreign suppliers are denied access to the domestic market other than through the cartel. Cartel members may have exclusive purchasing arrangements with foreign sources of supply or otherwise control the distribution of the product into the domestic market. There may be government restrictions preventing the emergence of competition with the cartel. For internationally traded goods and services, the exclusion of competition will not be easy to organise. But if the cartel is successful in this respect there will be detriments not only to domestic consumers but also to foreign suppliers denied access to that market otherwise than through the cartel. The cartel will therefore restrict trade as well as competition in the domestic market.

c) Market power in the relevant market for purchase of the product

59.   Import cartels will be of particular significance from the trade point of view where the members have the power to influence the price at which they import the product. The cartel members may have sufficient monopsony power to drive down the price of the imported product below what it would be in a competitive market. This is the precise analogue of the market power exercised by a cartel of sellers. The exporting nation will suffer in that the cartel will both restrict purchases of the item compared with where the buyers purchase independently and secure a lower price. The benefits of the buyers'power will accrue to them and not, or not necessarily, to consumers in the importing country. For an import cartel to have monopsony power, the cartel members must possess substantial market power in the relevant overseas market, conceivably the world market, for the imported product. There are likely to be few products for which the industry of one country is the dominant purchaser. Some countries may however be a sufficiently important customer for the products of another country so that an import cartel could exert a degree of monopsony power in that market, at least in the short run. This may be more likely with primary products than with manufactured products. Some member countries, notably Australia, have drawn attention to the potentially adverse trade implications for raw material producing countries of coordinated buying arrangements between importers (23).

60.   An import cartel with monopsony power is likely to cause the usual detriments of any cartel in the domestic market, i.e. higher prices than those that would occur under competitive conditions and, probably, a lower level of efficiency in the industry with detriments to consumers and a general loss of economic welfare in the importing country. Where the import cartel is concerned with the importation of a raw material which is an input for a domestic manufacturing industry, the agreement among the importers may extend beyond the coordination of purchases of the raw material to an agreement on prices of the finished output on the domestic market, again with detrimental effects to consumers and to efficiency and welfare.

61.   An import cartel may serve to countervail the market power of foreign suppliers. This may be the market power of a dominant foreign supplier or the market power of an export cartel (whether of all domestic suppliers in an exporting country or an international export cartel). The effects of such a situation are not easy to predict since they depend upon the relative bargaining strength and market power of the parties on the two sides of the market. If both sides are fully monopolised, the price of the imported product is likely to be less and the quantity imported more than if the export side alone was monopolised. The effect of an import cartel on the pattern of trade will then be beneficial compared with where the exporters' market power is not countervailed. Domestic consumers will also benefit compared with the alternative situation, although the outcome will be less beneficial to consumers than if competition prevailed on both sides of the market. If an import cartel is to be an effective purchaser of an imported item it must have market power in the domestic market. But this market power may be less than that of a complete monopoly when competition with non-cartel members may mean that more of the benefits of the cartel are shared with consumers.

d) Treatment under competition law

62.   An agreement between firms to coordinate imports into the domestic

market with the objective or effect of raising prices in that market will be subject to a country's competition law in the same way as any other agreement to restrict supplies and fix prices. Member countries' laws therefore do not recognise this type of import cartel as distinctive from other domestic cartels.

63.   In the United States, however, Section 1 of the Sherman Act, which is the basic statute on cartels and which applies to any agreement which restricts U.S. trade or commerce among states or with foreign nations, is supplemented as far as import cartels are concerned by the Wilson Tariff Act. Under Section 23 of that Act, "every combination, conspiracy, trust, agreement or contract made by or between two or more persons either of whom .... is engaged in importing any article from any foreign country into the United States .... is illegal and void if intended to operate in restraint of trade or to increase the market price of any imported article in any part of the United States or of any manufacture into which such article enters or is intended to enter". A number of cases have been brought under the provisions of the Sherman Act and the Wilson Tariff Act.

64.   In the late 1920's an injunction was sought against a group of American corporations and one Mexican corporation which had effected a plan to monopolise the supply abroad, and the domestic supply and price, of sisal, a fibre used to make twine (24). The Court noted that the "fundamental object [of the plan] was control of both importation and sale of sisal". The Sisal decision was expressly approved by the Supreme Court in a 1962 case (25).

65.   There have also been cases in other countries involving import cartels. In the United Kingdom, the members of the various constituent associations of the British Jute Trade Federal Council were parties to various agreements which in effect required imported goods to be priced substantially the same as goods produced in the UK. The Restrictive Practices Court ruled against the agreements (26). The Japanese Fair Trade Commission required the only four Japanese soda ash manufacturers, which were also the only firms that imported soda ash from the United States, to terminate a cartel agreement which set the overall quantity to be imported, established the share that each of the four would import, and imposed other restrictions on storage terminal facilities to discourage new entrants from circumventing the cartel (27).

66.   The laws of some Member countries expressly provide for the exemption or approval of cartels which are considered necessary to countervail sellers' market power, including sellers of imported products. These countries are the United Kingdom, Germany and Spain.

67.   In the United Kingdom, under the Restrictive Trade Practices Act, 1976, the parties to an agreement which has restrictive provisions which are registrable under that Act and which the Act presumes operate against the public interest may argue before the Restrictive Practices Court that the restrictions are justified in that they are necessary to obtain "fair and reasonable terms" from a preponderant supplier of the product (or service) and that the benefits thereof are not outweighed by any other detriments that may result from the restrictions. The National Sulphuric Acid Association, a trade association of the manufacturers of sulphuric acid, formed a sulphur pool by means of which it operated as the sole importer of sulphur for making acid in the UK. The several restrictions in the agreement, namely common prices, terms and conditions on which members bought imported sulphur from the

pool, sulphur acquired from the pool not to be sold to anyone not a member of the pool, were considered by the Restrictive Practices Court to be justified as necessary to obtain fair and reasonable terms from Sulexco, a United States Webb-Pomerene export trade association which controlled a preponderant part of the supply of sulphur to the UK market. As the court also found that the advantages of the pool outweighed any detriments they declared that the agreement did not operate against the public interest and should be allowed to stand (28).

68.   In Germany, Section 7 of the Act Against Restraints on Competition exempts buyer cartels from the general prohibition of cartels in Section 1 of the Act insofar as the agreement regulates only to imports into the Federal Republic and the German buyers face no competition, or insignificant competition, among their suppliers. The exemption of such a buyers' cartel requires the authorisation of the Federal Cartel Office. This provision of the Act is regarded by the German authorities as justified where the exercise of countervailing power enables price advantages to be obtained by the buyers which will benefit the German market. However, the authorities report that the provision has been of no practical significance. Since the Act came into force in 1958, only six applications for authorisation of an import cartel have been filed and only two were granted by the FCO. Both cartels, however, are no longer in operation.

69.   In Spain, the Act Against Restraints of Competition prohibits agreements "whose object or effect is to prevent, to distort or to limit competition in the national market", but Section 5 provides that the Court for the Protection of Competition may authorise such an agreement provided that both of two conditions are fulfilled; i) a general condition that the agreement contributes to improving production or distribution or promoting technical change or economic progress while reserving to consumers or users an adequate share of the benefits and so long as the restrictions on competition are essential for the attainment of those benefits, and ii) a specific condition that the agreement relates to imports from foreign markets in which there is no free competition and provided that the restriction of competition by the agreement is not detrimental to the market. So far no use has been made of this provision of the Spanish law.

70.   There are interesting similarities in the rationale of these three countries' provisions for permitting import cartels where necessary to countervail power on the suppliers' side of the market, although it is notable that very few cartels have sought to take advantage of these provisions.

71.   In the United States, the Department of Justice indicated in the early 1970's in a series of Business Review Letters (by which companies are advised of the likely reaction of the authorities to any of their practices) that action would not be taken against US oil companies which dealt collectively with the OPEC oil producing cartel. By 1974, however, the Department had indicated that because of changed conditions in the oil market and its own concern about the competitive behaviour of the US oil industry, the US companies should no longer assume that collective arrangements in relation to importing of oil products would be immune from antitrust action. This illustrates that competition authorities may adopt a flexible attitude to import cartels notwithstanding the absence of express provisions in their law.

72.   Most Member countries' laws do not extend to other countries' import cartels even if those cartels have effects upon their own trade.   In the United States, however, there have been instances where antitrust action has been taken in such circumstances.   One such case involved a Department of Justice civil complaint in 1982 against eight Japanese fishing and trading companies that formed an import cartel in Japan to fix the price they would pay to Alaskan processors of tanner crab (29).

e) Conclusions

73.   On the basis of available information it would seem that import cartels do not present serious problems as regards manufactured products.   However, there is some evidence that such cartels have occurred in the raw materials sector.   The increasing cross-penetration of developed countries' markets suggest that the conditions for an import cartel to be established and sustained will not be very commonly realised;   and where they are, the cartel is likely to come to the attention of the competition authorities in the importing country because of the likely adverse effects on competition in that country.

74.   Nevertheless, it is possible that importers could arrange the coordination of imports without restricting competition in the domestic market.   This is perhaps most likely where the imported product is a raw material.   Moreover, if the import arrangement is of an informal or tacit kind, it may escape the attention of the competition authorities, even if it does restrict competition in the domestic market.   In these circumstances the adverse effects on the trade of the exporting country, a lower quantity of exports and a lower price for those exports, will not be corrected by action by the competition authorities in the importing country.   Among Member countries Australia has drawn attention to this situation and the potential adverse effects on its trade.   Countries adhering to a strict application of the territoriality principle of jurisdiction cannot take action against import cartels located in other countries which damage their export trade.

75.   Where exporting countries inform the competition authorities in the importing country of the existence of an import cartel, or their suspicion of a cartel, those authorities should take appropriate steps to ensure that the cartel members are not in breach of the importing country's own laws.   Where applicable under their national laws, they should cooperate to the fullest extent possible with the authorities of the exporting country in the provision of information and take what steps are open to them under their national laws to minimise the adverse effects of actions by their own importers on international trade.

3. TRADING COMPANIES

a) Definition and effects

76.   There is no precise definition of trading companies.   They are generally considered to be firms of variable size established to conduct trade in goods and services, on both the export and import side.   Their prime functions are those of buying and selling products rather than production or manufacture.   While they are often private enterprises, in some countries

there is considerable government involvement in their operations. In many countries, trading companies have been set up in particular sectors to channel exports and imports on behalf of small and medium-sized enterprises. In Japan, however, there exist a few general trading companies engaged in many sectors of activity not limited to buying and selling.

77.   In Japan, the trade industry is classified by the government into trading companies, department stores, manufacturers and others. Although there are many small trading companies, the most widely known trading companies are the 9 "sogoshosha", that employ over 50,000 persons and operate worldwide. They are involved in all aspects of trade and their principal function is to act as intermediaries in trade. They provide access to distribution networks, arrange international joint ventures, organise supplies of raw materials and provide research, transportation and financial services. They also often have a financial interest by means of interlocking directorships or partial ownership in a wide variety of manufacturing enterprises.

78.   As with other business practices in international trade, competition authorities have an interest in assessing the role of trading companies and their effect on competition. Since they can operate on both the export and import side, analysis of a particular trading company and its effect on competition and trade will depend very much on its particular function and method of operation. In general, trading companies can exercise a positive effect on both competition and trade. On the export side, they can offer specialised skills and services, financing, etc. to enable export firms, and in particular small enterprises, to enter foreign markets and thereby stimulate competition. On the import side, trade companies can serve to provide distributional efficiencies, increase access to markets and thus strengthen the competitiveness of foreign firms in export markets. Further, the growing role of countertrade in international transactions (see, discussion infra at section 6) creates an additional need for specialised trading companies, as a means of selling and distributing goods to and from particular (usually centrally-planned) countries. Consequently, some countries are presently encouraging the formation of trading companies, especially on the export side (e.g. new legislation in the United States), as a means to promote trade.

79.   Trading companies can, on the other hand, impact negatively on competition and trade. This is not due to the mere presence of trading companies in and of themselves, but rather where trading companies are of such a size as to achieve a dominant position in a product or service sector, and are therefore able to exercise market power in their spheres of operation. In this regard, a particular concern arises that, on the import side, one or more trading companies can effectively control distributional networks and, to the extent they abuse their power by discriminating against foreign producers, lessen competition and restrain trade. Other competitive concerns may arise on account of the diversification of some trading companies activities whether in the form of interlocking directorates or partial acquisitions of interest, which might lead to excessive concentration of particular markets. Therefore, should trading companies continue to be a significant mechanism for conducting trade, their status under competition laws should receive increased attention, particularly with regard to their import activities.

b) Significance

80.   While little quantitative data is available on the extent of trading companies in OECD countries' trade, they would appear to be important in a number of countries' exports and imports, in particular in Australia, Austria, Canada, Ireland, Japan and the United States, and especially significant in certain product areas such as agricultural and dairy products and raw materials. State trading enterprises have frequently been established also in these sectors, although no country was able to supply a precise breakdown by public or private type.

81.   Since there is no commonly-accepted definition of trading companies, data on their activities is not strictly comparable among countries. Quantitative data was available for 5 countries. For example in Japan, the total sales of the six largest general trading companies (Sogo Shosha) amounted in the fiscal year 1981 to 27.7 per cent of GNP, to more than 40 per cent of total exports and to more than 50 per cent of imports. In 1982, the 13 largest companies exported $13 billion of goods to the United States, representing approximately 36 per cent of total Japanese exports to the United States.   In the United States, the National Association of Export Companies estimated that in 1980 US export trading companies accounted for $12 billion in manufactured goods, $25 billion in agricultural commodities and $7 billion in mixed ore exports. This approached 19 per cent of total US exports.   In addition, Japanese trading companies, operating through their subsidiaries, were estimated to handle another 10 per cent of all US exports ($21.7 billion). In Canada, trading company activities accounted for 15 per cent of Canadian exports in 1980.   Their activities concerned the agricultural and fisheries sectors in particular. Two state trading enterprises exist in the agricultural sector -- the Canadian Wheat Board and the Canadian Dairy Commission -- and a third has recently been approved for other agricultural and food products -- Canagrex. In addition, there are three non-agricultural state trading companies for freshwater fish, saltfish and liquor. There are also several private trading companies.' In the Netherlands, while there are no offical data available, rough estimates indicate that one-quarter of exports and one-half of imports are channelled through trading companies.   In Spain, it is estimated that trading companies account for approximately three to four percent of exports and five to six per cent of imports.

82.   As regards qualitative data, Australia, Finland, Greece and Sweden provided some analysis of the activities of export trading companies.   In Australia, Japanese trading companies are particularly active in exports of commodities such as coal, iron ore, manganese, mixed sands, steel, dairy products, wool and grains. For example, with regard to iron ore exports to Japan, they provide technical services in relation to scheduling of vessels and delivery times, weighing and sampling of ore and arrangements for payments. In Finland, trading companies are active in the processed wood, agricultural, steel, machinery and apparatus sectors. On the import side, the major product group handled by the trading companies are fuels and minerals, steel, machinery and technical apparatus, construction materials and chemicals.   In Greece, the major product groups handled by trading companies are consumer goods on the import side and agricultural products, to a lesser extent, with regard to exports. In Sweden, trading companies account for a limited share of total Swedish foreign trade and their major importance lies in certain markets outside Europe.

45

83.   The type and structure of trading companies vary considerably from one country to another. In Japan, trading companies comprise a few very large firms engaged in exporting and importing a whole range of goods and services, as well as in other activities. In most other countries they are typically associations of small and medium-sized enterprises established for exporting particular products.

84.   In Japan, a recent survey by the Fair Trade Commission revealed a number of further distinctive features of the six largest Japanese trading companies. In addition to their buying and selling activities, Japanese trading companies are active in financing transactions and, in acquiring financial interests in other enterprises (although since the 1977 Amendment to the Anti-monopoly Act, ceilings have been placed on such holdings). The number of interlocking directorships remains high although there was no significant difference in the number of such directorships involving the six companies between 1974 and 1982. The survey also showed that only 12 per cent of purchases and 5 per cent of sales were intra-group transactions.

c) Treatment under competition law

85.   For the most part, trading companies are generally subject to national competition laws in OECD countries, but are not specifically mentioned in such statutes. Thus, as with other forms of enterprise, trading companies will be subject to competition law enforcement if their practices excessively restrain competition, and in particular, where they abuse any dominant position they may hold in particular markets. However, there are relatively few cases under competition law involving trading companies.

i) Export activities

86.   The status of trading companies under competition law and assessment of their effect on competition varies depending on whether one is looking at the export or import side of their activity. In the export market, the activities of a trading company, as is the case with other exporting mechanisms, will in most countries not be subject to competition law unless that activity produces a spillover effect in the domestic market. However, where a trading company controls a significant share of export trade in a particular product or sector, concern could arise if it exercises undue power to prevent entry to a particular export market.

87.   Recognizing that trading companies can expand trade opportunities by providing export networks for manufacturers, most countries generally accept or encourage their use in export trade, so long as possible anticompetitive effects in the home market are controlled. For example, the United States has recently implemented legislation which provides a certification process to grant export trading companies immunity from U.S. competition laws and to expand the financing bases for trading companies. The Export Trading Company Act of 1982 specifically extended the existing limited exemptions from the antitrust laws for export trading companies in order to promote their formation. One of the purposes of the Act is to encourage small and medium-sized US enterprises which produce exportable goods or services (the Webb-Pomerene Act applies only to goods) to form export trading companies to reduce the costs of exporting. Secondly, the Act permits bank holding companies and similar companies to invest in export trading companies and reduces restrictions on trade financing provided by financial institutions.

The Act also provides for the issuance of export trade certificates of review to give exporters greater certainty concerning the antitrust implications of export activities. These certificates cover specified export conduct and protect the holder from private treble damage actions and government suits under federal or state antitrust laws with respect to the conduct specified. There are several exceptions. The Attorney General may sue to enjoin certified conduct "threatening clear and irreparable harm to the national interest". Further, persons injured by the certified conduct may sue for injunctive relief and for actual damages if the conduct is inconsistent with the statutory standards for exemption.

88. To qualify for a certificate under the Act, the applicant's export-related conduct must satisfy four specified standards. It must (1) not substantially lessen competition or restrain trade in the United States or restrain the export trade of a US competitor; (2) not unreasonably enhance, stabilise or depress prices in the United States; (3) not be an unfair method of competition against export competitors; or (4) not reasonably be expected to result in a sale or resale in the United States of the exported goods or services.

89. Given the fact that in most Member countries competition laws do not apply to export trade which does not affect the domestic market of the exporting country, competition authorities in these countries to date have not taken any action against the export activities of their trading companies. However, as is the case with export cartels, the immunity from competition law in the home market will not protect a trading company against competition laws applicable in foreign markets. If trading companies expand the opportunities for trade, particularly for small and medium-sized producers, they can be seen as lowering entry barriers and increasing the forces of competition in foreign markets. On the other hand, if the activities of trading companies acting in concert with other trading companies or exporters, cause such cartel-like effects as price-fixing or output control in their export markets, they may be prosecuted under the competition laws of the countries affected.

90. In the United States, there have been some, mostly private, actions brought against the export activities of foreign trading companies. One case involved several Japanese trading companies and other corporations (and in some instances, their American subsidiaries) who were engaged in the manufacture, importation, and sale of steel products (30). However, the Court found Japanese steel mills which sold steel to Japanese trading companies for distribution in the United States were not subject to U.S. jurisdiction. In a case filed in 1975, Industrial Investment Development Corp. sued Mitsui & Co., a Japanese company, its US subsidiary, and an Indonesian corporation alleging an antitrust conspiracy to keep plaintiff out of the business of harvesting trees in Indonesia and exporting logs and lumber from Indonesia to the United States and other countries (31).

ii) Import activities

91. Somewhat different considerations may attach with respect to the import activities of trading companies. Here, both competition authorities in the importing country as well as their colleagues in exporting countries will be concerned with the competitive and trade effects of trading companies. To the extent that they act as import cartels (see discussion in the preceding section), concern may arise on the part of exporting authorities (always

provided that the behaviour is considered within jurisdictional reach), if trading companies acquire and exercise market power in the purchase of goods for export. Authorities in the importing country will also be concerned if this market power is abused in the distribution of goods in the importing countries. Whether this is the case will depend on an analysis of the facts in each instance, and in particular the size of a trading company, its share of the market and the presence of alternative trade mechanisms. To date, there have not been many cases of this kind.

92.   In one recent case, the United States Department of Justice filed a civil complaint against eight Japanese fishing and trading companies (32), alleging that they conspired to fix the price they would pay to Alaskan processors for tanner crab. A consent decree was entered in October, 1982 (33). It enjoins the defendants from engaging in any conduct or exchange of information that would have the effect of fixing or depressing prices for processed Alaskan seafood. Each defendant is also required to establish an antitrust compliance programme which must include annual distribution of a copy of the final judgment to all employees involved in pricing decisions.

93.   Another concern on the part of both domestic and foreign competition authorities is the role trading companies play in distributing imported products. In view of their familiarity with conditions in their home markets, trading companies can usefully enable foreign firms to penetrate new markets and strengthen their competitiveness relative to domestic suppliers. On the other hand, where trading companies exercise monopolistic or abusive control over distribution networks, their activities can amount to barriers to trade.

94.   In Japan, the Fair Trade Commission recently concluded a study on the competitiveness of national distribution networks for imported goods and the role of trading companies in distribution. Among its findings, the Report concluded that imported goods are not treated unfairly as compared to domestically-produced goods. The Fair Trade Commission will continue to monitor the activities of trading companies to ensure that they do not infringe the provisions of the Anti-monopoly Act.

d) Conclusions

95.   Trading companies vary considerably in size, structure, functions and frequency of use from one country to another. They are tending however to become increasingly significant in the export and import trade of a number of Member countries, accounting for a considerable share of total foreign trade or of trade in particular product groups. Whilst action against them under competition law has so far been relatively rare, their growing influence in certain sectors, in particular primary products, has led some authorities to consider the possible anti-competitive effects which may arise from the power certain trading companies possess in particular geographical and product markets. Governments should closely follow the growth of trading companies and, where appropriate, apply their competition laws to any anti-competitive practices in which such companies engage.

4. VOLUNTARY EXPORT RESTRAINTS

a) Background

96.   In recent years voluntary export restraints (VERs) have emerged as one of the more frequently used devices to control and limit imports. Although they are generally conceived of as an instrument of trade policy, and accordingly imply a substantial degree of government involvement in their operation, VERs can resemble restrictive business practices such as cartels. The degree to which VERs are subject to competition laws depends on the methods used for their implementation.

97.   One of the most striking features of VERs is the flexibility of this instrument which eludes precise definition. Broadly speaking, three types of actions to limit exports can be distinguished:

-- The first is based on an agreement or understanding between governments. To the extent that formal intergovernmental agreement are involved these are generally classified as Orderly Marketing Agreements.

-- Another type of VERs are government sponsored arrangements among exporting firms to limit their exports to a level which is predetermined by understandings reached between the governments concerned.

-- Third, there are VERs which do not imply any direct form of government involvement. These are agreements or arrangements between exporting firms to limit their exports and, in some instances, raise prices in anticipation of protectionist pressures in the importing countries. Such arrangements most closely resemble national export cartels or international cartels as the case may be and are sometimes condoned by the governments of the countries concerned.

98.   VERs prompt a number of concerns on the part of competition policy, since they ultimately involve actions by exporting firms to limit their volume of exports, and in some instances, to raise prices. This, in turn, can promote collusive behaviour among firms and weaken competitive forces in both markets. While the effect of VERs on competition and trade flows resembles other quantitative barriers in some aspects, there are significant differences as well. Perhaps most significantly, the uncertain status of VERs under both trade laws (e.g. the GATT) and competition legislation has facilitated their increased use and has raised difficult issues for trade and competition authorities.

99.   Although there is a general lack of enthusiasm on the part of Member countries with respect to the use of VERs, there are noticeable differences in approach. Some countries generally consider VERs as an impediment to trade and contrary to the basic principles of an open multilateral trading system. Nevertheless some of these countries have used VERs as a device to avoid serious adjustment difficulties in certain sectors or to provide "breathing space" for the development of new industries or for structural adjustment in established sectors.

100. There is another group of countries which view VERs although undesirable in principle, as viable and flexible instruments, to provide relief in specific sectors without resort to more formal or stringent measures such as the imposition of tariffs or quotas. Countries that have subjected their exports to VERs view them as a means to avoid the adoption of more formal protectionist measures in import markets and thus enter into VERs to avoid more serious dislocations to the free trade system. Further, they believe that VERs should be limited in scope and duration and should be accompanied by industrial restructuring in the country seeking the VER. Despite these differences in approach to VERs, all Member countries agree that such instruments wherever used should only serve as a temporary expedient and that they should be flanked by suitable adjustment policies.

101. The following section, after describing the various types of VERs and their actual use, discusses their possible effects on competition as well as the regulatory framework applicable to them under competition laws. It should be emphasised that the focus of this discussion is on competition policy considerations and issues of competition law enforcement, whereas criteria for economic analysis of the trade policy aspects of these measures are considered within the analytical framework developed in Chapter II of this report.

b) Description and trends

102. Although there are no specific definitions of VERs in competition or trade law, they bear a number of distinguishing features and thus can be differentiated from private restrictive practices such as export cartels and formal trade policy measures, such as orderly marketing arrangements ("OMA's"). For the most part, these differences are of form and motivation, rather than effect. While VERs resemble in effect other practices that impose or result in quantitative restrictions, differences emerge in the motivation underlying VERs and in the methods used to implement them, and these differences have important implications for the status and legality of VERs under competition law.

103. VERs generally arise as a result of pressure or requests from an importing country for the exporting country to limit its exports of specific product(s). Although discussions often take place between the two trading partners, the final action as to the number of exports and means of limitation is often taken unilaterally by the exporting country. These arrangements may relate to prices or quantities, or both. And while VER's at the inter-governmental level have attracted considerable attention, in other instances, VERs are privately arranged between companies in the exporting and importing market. Among the OECD countries, while some governments will seek to directly arrange VERs to relieve import pressures, other countries leave such actions to the private sector.

104. Two other factors are important in delimiting the nature of VERs. First, they are temporary in nature. Of course, such arrangements can be extended by the parties involved. In addition, if a VER between two countries leads to an upsurge in exports to other markets, other countries may seek a VER or import relief from the exporting country. Second, VERs are limited in scope, applying to specific products and to particular trading partners. Thus, a VER may be arranged with one country that exports a product, while other countries and firms that export the product into the market are not

affected.   Therefore, VERs are generally applied on a selective and
discriminatory basis.

105.   The above description suggests some of the differences between VERs,
OMAs and other measures to limit imports.   Although they may produce similar
effects, the motivations and methods underlying VERs and export cartels are
different.   Unlike VERs, export cartels are not formed in response to requests
from an importing country, but rather are designed to increase export revenues
in overseas markets.   Nevertheless, export cartels approved by governments
have in certain instances been used as a device for implementing VERs.   OMAs
are distinguished from VERs by their more formal nature and greater degree of
government involvement.   OMAs are typically the direct result of bilateral and
multilateral discussions and formal negotiations among trading partners, a
prominent example being the multi-fibre agreement.   In addition, in some
countries, legislation specifically authorizes governments to negotiate OMAs
to relieve pressures in the domestic market caused by increases in
imports (34).   While each of these practices and policies can result in import
limitations, these differences in form and motivation can affect the extent to
which they are subject to enforcement under competition law.

106.   It is difficult at present to quantify either the number and extent of
VERs, or their effect on trade flows (35).   This is due to a number of
factors.   Private arrangements are often not publicly disclosed, and most
countries do not require that these practices be notified to the trade or
competition authorities (see discussion, infra).   Thus, several countries
reported that they had no data on VERs.   Even where VERs are the result of
inter-governmental discussions, in the absence of precise definitions,
governments may choose not to characterize such arrangements as VERs or to
disagree as to the nature of the understanding reached.   Finally, it may be
difficult to isolate the effect of VERs on trade flows, especially where an
arrangement applies to some, but not all of the exporters to a market.   In
addition, governments do not seem to systematically monitor or report on the
effects of VERs after they have become operational.

107.   It would appear, however, that there has been a growing trend in the
use of VERs and other quantitative restraints in the past decade and in
particular sectors.   VERs appear to be particularly common in such sectors as
steel, automobiles, food, clothing and textiles, machine tools, footwear and
consumer electronics (36).   VERs have been used to protect both new high
technology industries and established industries.   Among the exporting
countries, firms in Japan and the developing industrial countries of Asia have
most frequently been subject to VERs, and, recently, firms in the European
Communities have also been subject to such restraints.

108.   A brief sampling of arrangements reached between trading partners
exemplifies the nature of VERs and recent trends in their use.   In 1981, the
U.S. and Japan entered into a VER by which the latter decided to limit their
automobile exports to the U.S. to 1.68 million units annually, for a period of
three years.   This action followed a decision by the U.S. International Trade
Commission that Japanese imports were not a substantial cause of serious
injury to the U.S. automobile industry, which is the required test for
obtaining relief under legal provisions applicable to the proceeding.   No
formal negotiations took place between the two countries, and Japan ultimately
acted unilaterally to limit its exports (37).   The Japanese Government decided
as a temporary measure to continue the VER in 1984.   In early 1983, Japan for

the first time decided to exercise export moderation for particular products to the entire EEC, this arrangement taking the form of a series of official forecasts of Japanese exports to the EEC countries. The number of videotape recorders ("VTR") it sells in the EEC, establishment of a floor price for VTR sales and a market for 1.2 million units produced by European manufacturers are provided for in the arrangement. An ostensible reason for such arrangement was to protect the development of European firms in this growing segment of the consumer electronics industry. Other products covered by this arrangement included colour television tubes, light commercial vehicles, forklift trucks, small motorcycles, quartz watches, stereo equipment and machine tools.

109.   A number of other VERs were mentioned in country submissions. In 1982, the United States requested that its major suppliers of beef and veal, Canada, Australia and New Zealand, agree to limit their shipments to the U.S. The U.S. offered its major suppliers the options of avoiding quotas by agreeing to limit exports to ensure that trigger levels leading to quotas under the U.S. meat import law would not be reached. Accordingly, the three exporting countried concluded a VER with respect to exports of sheep, beef and veal to the U.S. in 1982 and 1983. Other VERs and OMAs mentioned by the United States involved colour television receivers, non-rubber footwear (Korea, Taiwan), carbon steel products (EC), cotton (Egypt) and machine tools (Japan). Lastly, the United Kingdom noted that although it has not negotiated any VERs, it benefits from a number of arrangements, particularly in textiles and clothing, negotiated by the EEC. Further, British firms have reached understandings relating to orderly marketing practices with firms in supplying countries in such sectors as vehicles, footwear, cutlery, consumer electronics and pottery.

c) Legal Status

110.   One of the reasons for the growing use of VERs appears to lie in their uncertain status under national and multilateral trade laws and agreements and under competition legislation. As will be discussed in Chapter II, it remains an unresolved issue within GATT as to the extent to which (if any) VERs are subject to the safeguard provisions in Article XIX. With respect to competition law, VERs may be subject to provisions prohibiting cartels and other forms of collusive behaviour by firms. However, the actual application of such laws to VERs is sharply limited by the extent to which specific VERs meet statutory definitions of collusive behaviour, the jurisdictional reach of competition laws and whether VERs are authorized or admistered by governments or are privately arranged. Thus, the flexible nature of VERs and the specific ways in which they are established and implemented will determine whether they are subject to trade or competition laws.

111.   As will be discussed in Chapter II, VERs have a significant impact on both trade and competition. In the importing market, a VER reduces competitive pressures on domestic firms and by limiting the volume of exports, can produce effects similar to a cartel and thus lead to higher prices. Concern may also arise where domestic firms initiate actions under domestic laws as a means to compel foreign firms to curtail or cease exports through VERs or voluntary undertakings. These effects can be particularly strong when the market is already concentrated and a VER applies to a significant share of exports. A VER can also reduce competition among firms in the exporting country. Where VERs are implemented through fixed export quotas for individual firms, these companies may lack incentives to innovate or achieve

efficiencies to increase their share of the import market. Further, firms not subject to a VER may be excluded from the import market under the terms of the arrangement. Therefore, VERs may result in the kinds of anticompetitive effects that competition policy seeks to eliminate if arising from private restrictive business practices.

112. The application of competition laws to VERs and other quantitative restraints will vary depending upon the terms, structure of the agreement, the degree of government involvement and the existence of provisions in national law, if any, which authorise the negotiation or implementation of the restraints. Thus, from an enforcement perspective, distinctions can be drawn between OMAs, which are the result of formal, bilateral, government negotiations and which in some countries may be authorised in certain situations under national law, VERs unilaterally decided upon by governments in exporting countries, and VERs which are largely or purely private in nature. Therefore, even though they may produce similar effects on trade and competition, these distinctions will determine whether an agreement is potentially subject to enforcement under competition law in either the importing or exporting country. OMAs are less likely to be subject to competition law, since they are formal, bilateral agreements between governments, whose negotiation and implementation may be authorised under specific provisions of national law.

113. The issue is more complex with respect to VERs which may be governmental or private in nature. Where a VER has been negotiated or decided at governmental level, there is a general policy in many countries that since the VER is motivated by mutual trading interests, actions taken by private firms to implement the VER in response to government decisions will not be subject to challenge under the competition laws of either country. In the EEC, this policy is generally explained by the fact that quantitative restrictions arranged between the EEC and third countries are trade policy matters not subject to competition law. Measures which fall into the framework of trade agreements between the Community and a third country as well as agreements imposed on firms of third countries by the authorities of those countries, are regarded as measures of external trade policy which are not covered by Article 85 of the Treaty of Rome. In the case of the measures adopted in January 1981 by the Japanese Government in the machine tools sector, the Commission therefore felt that they were not covered by Article 85. In Switzerland, a VER entered into or instigated by the Federal Council would not be within the scope of the Cartels Act. In Sweden, if a VER has been approved by the government, it will not be deemed to have harmful effects contrary to the public interest.

114. In the United States, however, the government lacks general statutory authority to enter into VERs (except in certain specific sectors) and private firms are able to initiate litigation under the competition laws. Thus, an important issue is whether the actions of the government in the exporting country in implementing its decision to limit exports of its firms to the U.S. are such as to provide these firms with immunity from antitrust prosecution. To resolve this dilemma, a VER can be structured so that its implementation requires the government in the exporting country to compel its producers to limit their exports, thereby providing a defence under the "sovereign compulsion" doctrine in the event that any litigation should ensue. For instance, in the VER by Japan on passenger car exports to the U.S., the Japanese Authorities expressed concern that the arrangement could result in

liability for their car producers under U.S. competition laws. (38) It was felt that implementation of the VER through the issuance by Japan of "administrative guidance" to its automobile companies might not be sufficient to invoke the sovereign compulsion doctrine, since these were not mandatory controls. To resolve this problem, the Japanese government indicated that to enforce the VER, it would issue directives establishing export quotas, and would require export licenses (accompanied by sanctions for violations) if it appeared that exports might exceed the limits set by the VER. The Department of Justice provided its view that since the VER was based on compulsory measures by the Japanese government, it did not appear to give rise to antitrust liability (39).

115.   Where VERs are essentially private, i.e. arranged between firms in the importing and exporting countries, they closely resemble international cartels and will generally be subject to provisions in competition laws prohibiting cartels or other forms of collusive anticompetitive behaviour among competitors. Application of the laws to these types of VERs may be limited, however, by jurisdictional principles and, where provided for in the laws, by the extent to which a VER is perceived to be in the trading interests of the countries.

116.   In Australia, there is no specific mention of VERs in the RBP laws, and to be actionable, an agreement must usually produce an impact on a market in Australia and not be exempted under provisions pertaining to export activity. In Canada, arrangements to restrict imports which are not made pursuant to a valid statute would be subject to provisions of Section 32 of the competition laws, to the extent that they involved Canadian entities. In Finland, the competition laws would not be applicable unless an agreement directly affects the Finnish market. In Norway, there are no special laws covering VERs. In Sweden, competition laws apply in principle to VERs if they have effects in the domestic market. There is no specific mention of VERs in Spanish law. In Switzerland, a VER is subject to the cartel law unless authorized by the government. In the United States, VERs are generally subject to the competition laws, in the absence of offsetting defenses, e.g. sovereign compulsion.

117.   In the EEC, the application of Article 85 cannot be excluded in principle in the case of private agreements which have been adopted unilaterally by firms of third countries, or after consultation with the corresponding European firms. Nevertheless, any implementation of Article 85 with regard to private agreements involving certain sectors and certain community countries would need, in order to be realistic, to be viewed in the overall framework of the measures implemented in the various Member States, and in the relevant sectors, to eliminate or narrow the trade gap between the country in question and the Community.

118.   Whether or not a particular VER is subject to these laws depends largely upon whether the behaviour of the exporting firms meets the statutory requirements. This determination can rest upon the structure of the VER and the manner in which the limitations are allocated among firms. Where the government of the exporting country allocates export quotas among its firms, there may be no collusion between firms sufficient to give rise to a violation. Thus, in the U.S.-Japan auto VER, the Japanese government individually assigned export allotments to its firms, obviating the need for inter-firm cooperation. In contrast, privately-agreed VERs may be more

suspect under competition laws, although collusion can be difficult to detect. Moreover, where a VER results from pressures placed on foreign firms by companies in the domestic market, the private arrangement resembles an international cartel.

119. Another problem in applying competition law to private VERs is that these arrangements can be difficult to detect. In assessing the number of VERs and their impact, it has been noted that transparency with regard to the disclosure of these arrangements is a problem. In many Member countries, the competition laws require that firms notify restrictive agreements to the authorities. Nonetheless, with the exception of Finland, and in certain circumstances the United Kingdom, no countries require under their competition laws that VERs be notifed to the competition authorities.

120. This lack of transparency with respect to private VERs may also make it more difficult to modify or "roll-back" these arrangements in the event of changes in trade policies.

121. The involvement of competition authorities with respect to VERs is not limited to enforcement of RBP laws. In countries which provide general procedures for competition officials to advise or comment on proposed or ongoing trade policies, competition authorities can exercise their powers to comment on VERs as well. (See Chapter III of this report). Competition authorities have used these procedures to comment both on the effect of VERs on competition and the extent to which individual VERs and other restraints could be subject to challenge under the competition laws.

122. In some instances, competition officials have taken action against VERs. In Australia, the Trade Practices Commission considered a VER between a domestic paper manufacturer and New Zealand softwood pulp suppliers which involved restrictions on imports from New Zealand. Australian Paper Manufacturers Ltd. ("APM") had sought authorization for an agreement with three New Zealand companies which limited the sale of packaging materials and converted products in Australia as well as limiting the quantity and conditions of supply to APM's competitor in Australia. The agreements were claimed to have been made in furtherance of the aims of the New Zealand - Australia Free Trade Agreement. The Commission indicated that some of the provisions were anticompetitive and in 1978, APM amended the agreements to reduce the possible anticompetitive effects. Consequently the Commission found the VER generally acceptable under the circumstances.

d) Conclusions

123. In recent years, there has been a growing resort to VERs as a means for controlling or limiting imports. Designed to protect domestic industries from import competition, VERs have been relatively frequently used in such sectors as steel, automobiles, footwear, and consumer electronics. They may be arranged between governments or between individual firms with or without government sponsorship. VERs generally arise as a result of pressure or requests from an importing country for the exporting country to limit its exports of specific products; they may be regarded by the exporting country as preferable to other, more restrictive, trade barriers.

124. An important distorting feature of VERs is the fact that they may limit or restrict competition by their selective nature. Moreover, in some

instances, these agreements have been resorted to where injury resulting from imports cannot be determined under the provisions of the GATT. Although they can produce cartel-like effects, VERs are often not subject to challenge under RBP laws, either because they fall outside the jurisdictional limit of these laws or due to government involvement in their creation or implementation. Further, since there are at present, with the exception of a few countries, no requirements to notify VERs to the government, private agreements may simply go unidentified. Thus, the introduction or extension of notification requirements to private VERs, which can be considered as cartels, would facilitate enforcement of competition law with respect to these arrangements.

125. VERs may conflict with the fundamental objectives of competition policy, as they lessen competitive pressures on domestic producers which may give rise to special problems in already concentrated markets. While they can produce short-term benefits, it appears from various studies that their costs for consumers and the economy of the importing country can be substantial. They may also have detrimental effects on countries not party to the agreement. It would seem that greater steps are needed to increase the transparency of VERs, to monitor their effects and to consider their treatment under trade and competition laws. Competition authorities have an important role to prevent harmful effects on domestic market structure. Bringing VERs under international surveillance and control would be an important first step in regulating their use in a manner consistent with an effectively functioning international trading system. The Committee intends to cooperate with the Trade Committee to continue the analysis of VERs and their effects on trade and competition.

5. OTHER BUSINESS PRACTICES AFFECTING INTERNATIONAL TRADE

a) Background

126. There are a number of other business practices that can significantly affect trade and competition, and which are generally dealt with under competition laws. In the sale and distribution of their goods, manufacturers may attempt to restrict their wholesalers and retailers by, inter alia, requiring them to enter into exclusive dealing arrangements or to agree not to resell in other territories or re-export the goods. To increase market share or as a market penetration strategy, manufacturers or dealers may reduce prices of goods below cost levels in order to gain sales and eliminate competition. In the sale or transfer of technology, licensors may attempt to exploit their industrial property rights (patents, trademarks or copyrights) by limiting the use which the licensor can make of the technology, e.g. by preventing the resale or export of goods produced under the grant. While these practices can facilitate efforts by businesses to enter new markets and can thereby increase trade opportunities, they may be subject to challenge where their effect is to excessively restrain competition. For this study, a principal question is the extent to which these business practices can be used to restrict competition and allocate markets either through contractual terms and conditions that are used in the distribution of goods and services, including pricing provisions, or through the sale and licensing of industrial property rights. This question has taken on particular significance in the European Community, which applies its competition policy so as to promote the

creation of a unified market and to check business practices which enforce
territorial restraints along the lines of national boundaries.

127.   Although commonly-considered as a trade practice, countertrade or
reciprocal-dealing agreements between firms or trading partners can resemble
more traditional vertical restraints if they lead to market foreclosure on the
sale or supply side.   Thus, this chapter briefly considers these practices,
their qualitative effect on trade and their status under competition law and
policy.

b) Vertical restraints

128.   Vertical restraints generally refer to the terms and conditions that
attach to the transfer of goods along the distribution chain from manufacturer
to ultimate user and are commonly classified as either a price or non-price
restraint.   For the most part, the practices examined under the heading of
vertical restraints do not have any particular role or effect on international
trade nor are distinctions drawn between domestic and foreign firms.
Nonetheless, business practices such as exclusive dealing arrangements between
manufacturers and dealers can facilitate entry into markets by ensuring
adequate distribution networks for new products or by creating distributional
efficiencies.   The application of competition law to non-price vertical
restraints varies in OECD countries, reflecting in part differences in the
size and structure of domestic and regional markets.   A principal concern is
that vertical restraints are not used to excessively restrict competition,
particularly in already concentrated markets, through market or territorial
restrictions.   This can come about, for instance, through exclusive dealing
agreements where the supplier controls a high market share of both the product
market and of distribution outlets, and, in addition, new entry into
distribution must be difficult.   Likewise, territorial restrictions, which
limit the purchaser as to where he can resell, and absolute territorial
restrictions or modified restrictions like dealer location clauses, may also
have anticompetitive effects in similar circumstances.   However, where
inter-brand competition is strong, restrictions on intra-brand competition of
the type noted here may have little effect on market outcomes.

129.   In the EC, the approach taken toward vertical restraints under
competition policy has been largely determined by the basic objective of the
EEC Treaty -- the unification of the various national markets and the creation
of a single market resembling an internal market.   This has led the Community
to develop a rather different view of territorial restrictions than might have
been the case if only traditional competition policy objectives had been
pursued.   Thus, while on the one hand seeking to encourage agreements and
practices which promote the interpenetration of national markets, the
Communities seek to prevent the resurrection by undertakings of the barriers
to trade between Member states which the founding of the EEC and the efforts
of the Community institutions have removed.   Territorial restrictions of all
kinds (which range from outright export or import prohibitions to obligations
to concentrate activity in a given territory or the obligation not to deal
with or license any other person in a territory) are of course apt to be used
for the creation or maintenance of divisions between the national markets of
the EEC and must be seen in this light.

130.   The Community has always considered that territorial restrictions are,
except in exceptional circumstances, by their very nature restrictions of

competition falling within the scope of Article 85 and therefore require exemption under Article 85(3) if they are to be permissible. This is clearly the case when the territorial restrictions operate within the Common Market (40). Restrictions on imports into the Common Market as a whole are also considered as falling under Article 85. Restrictions on exports from the Common Market, on the other hand, do not fall within Article 85 if the possibility of subsequent reimports can be excluded (41).

131. Territorial restrictions arising from exclusive dealing arrangements are also subject to challenge under EEC law, especially where the clauses allocate dealers along national boundaries. In 1966, the Court in the Grundig-Consten case prohibited an agreement between a German manufacturer and its exclusive distributor for sales in France. Under the agreement, the French distributor attempted to block parallel imports of Grundig radios from Germany into France on the basis that the imports violated the trademark rights in France held by the exclusive distributor (42). Subsequently, the Commission issued Regulation 67/67 which granted a block exemption to certain types of bilateral exclusive distribution agreements complying with specified conditions, primarily the absence of any restrictions on parallel imports or re-exports across Member state boundaries (43). As from 1st July, 1983 this Regulation has been replaced by Regulation No. 1983/83 for exclusive distribution agreements and by Regulation No. 1984/83 for exclusive purchasing agreements (44).

132. The policy followed by the EEC attempts to balance the goals of market integration with the reasonable needs of businesses seeking to enter new markets or expand in their present areas. Territorially restricted (i.e. usually exclusive) distribution agreements are a valuable means of promoting the interpenetration of national markets and of facilitating and improving distribution within the Community. They are often the best or even the only means for a manufacturer in one Member State to sell his products in another Member state. This is especially true of small and medium-sized undertakings which are not established in, and do not have the organisation or financial resources required to expand their activities into, another Member state. Even for established products, exclusive dealing continues to have economic advantages in rationalising and simplifying distribution.

133. Recognising the economic benefits flowing from exclusive distribution, the Commission grants exemption for these arrangements under certain conditions. In considering whether exclusive dealing agreements can benefit from an exemption under Art. 85(3) the Commission seeks to ensure that territorial restrictions in such agreements do not in fact lead to absolute territorial protection or the isolation of a part of the Common Market. Exemptions are granted by category to exclusive distribution agreements so long as intermediaries and users have an alternative source of supply. Alternative sources of supply through parallel imports must also not be impeded or rendered difficult in practice. There is, therefore, an additional provision which provides that the exemption will cease to apply if measures, for example in the exercise of industrial property rights, are taken to impede or render more difficult such parallel imports.

134. The relationship of competition laws to exclusive dealing and territorial restrictions has evolved in a different manner in countries where market integration is not a goal or has already been achieved. In the United States, restrictive practices may be characterised as "per se" violations of

the law, or they may be analysed under a "rule of reason" standard, by which their procompetitive effect can be weighed against the extent to which they restrain competition. At one stage, the courts held that territorial resale restrictions were "per se" unlawful as an allocation of markets (45). More recently, the courts reversed themselves and have held that the rule of reason should apply to vertical territorial and customer restrictions (46). This reversal was based in part on the view that the reduction that vertical restraints can have on intrabrand competition can be more than offset by increases to interbrand competition that may arise by allowing a manufacturer to achieve certain efficiences in the distribution of its products. Thus, the courts have placed emphasis in assessing these practices on their effect on horizontal competition.

135.   Although there are differences in policy and enforcement strategy among countries, it can be seen that competition policy generally does not bar exclusive dealing arrangements or territorial restrictions, insofar as these agreements promote horizontal competition. However, it is recognised that vertical restraints should not be allowed as a de facto means of preserving national trade boundaries as trade barriers. Accordingly, exporters are permitted considerable leeway under the competition laws to enter new markets through agreements with dealers that ensure, for example, that goods will be promoted and properly serviced. This can enable exporters to overcome the initial reluctance of buyers in new markets to purchase their products and contribute to trade flows. Nonetheless, considerable practical questions remain as to the appropriate level and circumstances under which exclusive dealing agreements and territorial restrictions are consistent with competition policy and the method by which their competitive effects can best be measured.

   c) Pricing practices

136.   Competition policy applies both directly and indirectly to the prices of products and services. In most OECD countries, emphasis is placed on ensuring that markets remain free and open, and that prices are set in response to competitive pressures. Practices which distort such competition, e.g. collusive price-fixing or price cartels, are strictly controlled or prohibited. As part of their analysis of vertical restraints, competition officials examine the manner in which prices are set along the distribution chain of products and services. The applicable legislation and case law on resale price maintenance establish the extent to which manufacturers can set and enforce the retail prices of their goods and provisions on price discrimination regulate the manner in which suppliers can offer their goods at different prices to competing distributors and retailers (47). As discussed in Section 7, infra, discriminatory pricing has a particular context when applied to multinational enterprises and their pricing practices with respect to subsidiaries, affiliated enterprises and independent firms.

137.   Provisions in competition laws which prohibit predatory pricing are of most direct relevance to the control of unfair pricing practices. This appears most directly in the Robinson-Patman Act in the United States, which prohibits price discrimination designed to eliminate competitors and competition in a market. Section D-4(a) of the UN Code on Restrictive Business Practices provides that enterprises should refrain from "Predatory behaviour towards competitors, such as using below-cost pricing to eliminate competitors..." when such acts or behaviour constitute "an abuse or

acquisition and abuse of a dominant position of market power". In some other OECD countries, laws against price discrimination may in some certain circumstances, be applied to predatory pricing.

138.   Under Article 86 of the Treaty of Rome, it is an abuse of a dominant position by:

   a) Directly or indirectly imposing unfair purchase or selling prices or other unfair trading conditions;

   c) Applying dissimilar conditions to equivalent transactions with other trading parties, thereby placing them at a competitive disadvantage.

With a view to achieving market integration and non-discriminatory selling prices within the EC, Article 86(c) has been applied to pricing practices of firms exporting into the Common Market. In a series of cases, the Commission has followed a policy of challenging practices by firms exporting to the EC of charging different prices to distributors according to the Member states in which the latter are located (48). Under EC law, both predatory and discriminatory pricing may be found to be illegal. "Predatory" pricing is defined as pricing goods at excessively low levels to put a competitor out of a market and "discriminatory" pricing as selective price reductions made to the customers of a competitor (49). In either instance, a challenged firm can assert that its pricing strategy was adopted to meet competition as a defence to allegations of unfair pricing.

139.   In the context of this study, it can be seen that a principal interest in the application of competition law to predatory or discriminatory pricing lies in the resemblance between such actions and actions brought under the antidumping provisions of the GATT or under national unfair trade legislation. In both situations, difficult questions emerge as to the methods by which to measure whether prices are below cost or "dumped". In Chapter 2, both the similarities and differences in the approaches taken under competition and trade law toward these types of pricing practices are examined.

   d) Restrictions relating to industrial property rights and to the transfer of technology

140.   The transfer of technology plays an important role in world trade. Not only do such transfers account for a considerable percentage of trade, but they also hasten the technological development of countries and the process of structural adjustment. Further, these transfers provide a means for firms to enter and trade in foreign markets despite trade barriers that may limit their ability to sell manufactured goods. The transfer and licensing of technology is facilitated by the existence of industrial property rights -- patents, trademarks, know-how, trade secrets -- which protect the interests of the transferor and ensure a return on the technology supplied. Since these grants create exclusive rights which may confer market power on the inventor or licensee, in some countries competition policy has been applied to such transfers to ensure that these rights are not used to unduly restrain competition. Of particular concern to this study are terms and conditions in the transfer of industrial property rights that unreasonably allocate markets, control re-exports or foreclose competition; i.e. practices which can restrict trade flows. Another important issue involves the use of certain business structures, e.g. joint ventures, to effectuate transborder technology

flows. To a large extent, these subjects have already been considered by the Committee (1972 report on Restrictive Business Practices Relating to Patents and Licenses; 1978 report on Restrictive Business Practices Relating to Trademarks) or are presently being addressed at Working Party level (joint ventures in natural resource exploration, development and/or production, and in research and development). Accordingly, this section briefly highlights some of the issues raised by the application of competition policy to trade in technology and reviews findings previously made by the Committee.

141. In 1972, the Committee issued a report on Restrictive Business Practices Relating to Patents and Licences, which was followed by a Council Recommendation in the following year. The Report generally concluded that there is no conflict between patent law and competition policy so long as "the fundamental objectives of the two systems are properly expressed" (50). Although a patent does grant a limited exclusivity to its inventor, the Committee concluded that this grant is fully in harmony with competition policy, since it promotes research and the practical application of inventions in the general interest, as long as the exclusive rights under a patent are exploited to work the invention and not to unduly limit competition (51). In most OECD countries, abuses of patent rights are usually dealt with under the patent laws, although competition policy may be applicable as well. In a few countries, particularly the United States, the report noted that competition laws are often applied to abuses arising in the licensing of patent rights, particularly the inclusion in licensing agreements of terms and conditions that are beyond the scope of the rights granted under the patent and that unduly restrict competition.

142. The Report also examined the effects of patents and licensing on international trade (52). Although no quantitative analysis of this question had been done, the Report indicated that "restrictive practices in the matter of patents and licences constitute a barrier to international trade." (53). This assumption was supported by facts brought to light in court cases, particularly in the United States. In these cases, practices which may be used for legitimate purposes, such as cross licensing agreements between firms or the establishment of patent pools whereby industry members agree to share patent rights, had been misused in agreements between competitors and produced such cartel-like effects as allocation and division of worldwide markets, output limitations and entry forclosure.

143. Several provisions that commonly appear in agreements to sell or license technology can have special impact on competition and trade. Under a vertical territorial restriction, the transferor restricts the geographic territory in which the transferee can use the technology or market the products made or services performed by the technology. A simple vertical territorial restriction and a technology licence, which basically represent a distribution arrangement with respect to a defined geographic area, is not inherently suspect; for reasons already noted above, such arrangements may be procompetitive and enhance efficiency. On the other hand, territorial restrictions in horizontal agreements between competitors to divide markets are very suspect under the competition laws of many countries. In the United States, domestic and international territorial limitations of a vertical nature in patent licenses are generally evaluated under a rule of reason and it is ordinarily considered illegal in the United States to use territorial restraints in licensing agreements between competitors as a device to divide world markets among them.

144. In the EEC, the policy toward territorial restrictions in technology transfers is broadly the same as for distribution agreements. However, there is a tendency to be more lenient with respect to such restrictions in technology transfers, in recognition of the fact that territorial protection may be more necessary for the introduction of new technology than for the distribution of goods which have already been successfully produced (54). In several cases, the Commission has opposed contract provisions which prohibit the licensor from exporting to another Member state (55), since such export bans constitute direct barriers to the free movement of goods in the Common Market (56). Bans on exports from the Common Market may be subject to challenge if they have effects within the market. In addition, the Commission has examined on a case-by-case basis certain types of patent pools, which are considered restraints of competition in regard to technological innovation.

145. Other provisions in licensing agreements can impact on competition and trade flows. For example, grantback clauses that require the licensee to provide the licensor with any new technological developments that are achieved through the use of the licence without recompense may in some circumstances be unreasonable. Such provisions can restrain competition, especially where the grantback is on an exclusive basis. In these and other practices, the balance must be drawn between the rights of the industrial property holder, the need to ensure that technological innovations are developed to promote the general interest, and the extent to which restrictive clauses in licensing agreements restrain competition.

146. Trademarks are another valuable industrial property right. They provide assurances to buyers as to the quality of goods and product origin by identifying the manufacturer or trader and distinguishing them from others. Trademarks can assist established firms to penetrate new export markets, and recently have come to have value in and of themselves separate from the product and thus increasingly are exploited through licensing and franchising. While concern may arise where trademark rights are used to allocate or divide world markets, a more important problem for trade and competition may be such unfair practices by competitors as using marks that are confusingly similar or the illegal practice of selling goods under counterfeit trademarks. These problems arise particularly with respect to luxury goods.

147. In its report on trade marks in 1978, the Committee concluded that the exclusive protection granted under trademark law would not be complete unless protection was extended to imported products, that is unless the trademark owner was allowed to prevent the parallel importation of products from a foreign country bearing an identical trademark or one which was confusingly similar. However, trademarks should not be abused for anticompetitive purposes. Thus, under competition law the trademark owner may only exclude imports when necessary to protect the distinctive sign which identifies his product from other products bearing infringing marks. In the area of distribution and franchising in national markets, exclusive trademark licensing agreements or exclusive distribution agreements for trademarked products are in principle permitted in most Member countries. Action may, however, be taken against such agreements by the competition authorities in certain well-defined cases (57).

148. Technology transfers can be achieved through the sale, assignment or licensing of technology. In addition, firms are increasingly forming joint

ventures to share technology and to jointly engage in such activities as research and development, manufacturing, resource exploration and sales and distribution. Although there is no commonly-agreed upon definition of joint ventures, they are a business structure that is something less than a merger and something more than a contractual agreement, and often result in creation of a third corporate entity by the two partners.

149. International joint ventures are particularly noteworthy, since they can make it easier for firms to enter foreign markets by forming a joint venture with a company in that market. Joint ventures have been especially common in the high technology field and have been seen as a way to obtain a foothold in tightly-controlled overseas markets. They may also be used to overcome import restrictions in particular countries. To explore the many issues raised by the use of joint ventures and their impact on trade, the Committee in 1982 issued a mandate to its Working Party on Mergers and Concentration to prepare a report on joint ventures by the end of 1985.

e) Countertrade

150. Countertrade generally refers to an international commercial transaction in which the seller must accept, in partial or total settlement of his deliveries, the simultaneous or deferred supply of products (or more rarely services) from the purchasing country (58). Countertrade began in the early 1970's in the context of East-West trade and has been used since the beginning of the 1980s by a number of developing countries which faced external imbalances (59). Certain OECD Member countries have become involved in countertrade by providing assistance to their domestic firms conducting private transactions with foreign governments demanding countertrade as a condition of import. In certain instances countertrade has also been practised at a governmental level, e.g. through arrangements limited to the sale of aircraft or military equipment.

151. A precise assessment of the importance of countertrade is not possible due to the fact that trade statistics do not distinguish between trade flows arising out of countertrade contracts and those that do not have such conditions attached. Estimates can only be made on the basis of countertrade arrangements that have been publicly announced. Secondly, definitions of countertrade vary considerably or the practice is often not defined at all. Three types of operation might reasonably be considered as countertrade: i) barter, counterpurchases and their variants, which add up to the total of so-called commercial compensation; ii) buy-back agreements and arrangements for the reciprocal exchange of goods under industrial cooperation agreements; and iii) switch operations and those linked to sales of military equipment. Based on this definition, countertrade has been estimated to account for not more than 5 per cent of OECD trade with the non-oil-producing developing countries, 10 per cent of the trade between developing countries and 30 per cent of developing countries' trade with the East. Countertrade thus seems likely to represent a maximum of 4.5 per cent of world trade.

152. Countertrade is expected to continue, if not increase, in the next few years as governments directly or indirectly encourage the practice as a means of promoting exports of goods which are either in excess supply or have limited market appeal. Another motive for countertrade commonly advanced is the growing burden of debt servicing and exhaustion of currency reserves for countries in chronic balance of payments deficit, thus leading the governments

of such countries to prefer transactions which are self-financing (61). Developing nations, in particular, are turning to countertrade in order to overcome their increasing difficulties to finance purchases abroad. A third reason for preferring countertrade is to circumvent anti-dumping and countervailing laws and regulations. Given the lack of transparency in such deals, the practice may conceal export subsidies, sales at dumping prices and more favourable financial terms than those allowed under multilateral rules.

153. Among its effects, countertrade has led to the growth of trading companies that offer services to small-sized exporters which lack the trade expertise and skills required to handle goods received in countertrade transactions (62). Commercial banks are also becoming involved in countertrade, acting as middlemen in identifying buyers for their customers' countertraded goods (63).

154. Due to the growth of countertrade, the OECD study examined countertrade transactions and analysed their trade policy implications. It was concluded that countertrade transactions generally are not conducive to the long-term expansion of trade and threaten an open, non-discriminatory multilateral trading system by emphasising reciprocity rather than price and quality as the criteria for the exchange of goods and services. Countertrade distorts trade flows by foreclosing market sectors to free competition, especially in the case of long-term arrangements requiring the exchange of fixed quantities of goods without reference to prices (64). Countertrade may also cause trade distortions which could aggravate the structural adjustments stemming from trade flows. These distortions may not only affect the market of the country to which the countertraded products are originally imported as payment for exports but also other markets not involved in the countertrade agreement. This situation will arise particularly when a multinational firm or a trading company is a party to the countertrade transaction in that it can divert the countertraded product for final sale into whichever of its markets is most profitable. Trade distortions may also result from geographic restrictions imposed on the disposal of the countertraded product. Finally, the increase in countertrade could lead to more direct government intervention in trade negotiations, with countries imposing countertrade requirements in order to promote domestic firms.

155. OECD Member countries have not adopted trade or competition laws which specifically cover countertrade transactions. Most Member countries indicate that countertrade transactions between enterprises would be subject to competition law, since there is no basis for distinguishing countertrade from other trade practices.

156. To date, there have been no cases brought by competition authorities directly involving the issue of countertrade nor otherwise analysing the application of competition laws to this practice. Nonetheless, by its nature, countertrade can resemble and produce effects similar to such vertical restraints as exclusive or reciprocal dealing. However, the extent to which competition laws on these practices might be applied to countertrade will depend on the degree of anticompetitive effects resulting from a specific arrangement. This, in turn, will largely depend on an analysis of the market power of the relevant parties and the amount of market foreclosure that occurs.

157. Although countertrade can resemble reciprocal dealing, which arises when a firm uses its purchasing power as an inducement to persuade a supplier

to buy its products, this practice has not often been challenged by competition officials. Countertrade may also foreclose small firms from international trade since they may be less able to sell or distribute the exchanged goods than their larger competitors. Of course, countertrade does foster commercial transactions where criteria of price, quality and service are replaced or supplemented by other factors. While this can produce allocative inefficiencies, it should be recognised that countertrade arrangements may enable trade to occur in circumstances where it would not otherwise be possible.

158. Countertrade also may be subject to review under unfair trade laws in Member countries. In the United States, trade laws do not distinguish between imports resulting from countertrade and imports from other trade agreements. Petitions for relief from countertraded imports may be brought under the general import relief statutes (antidumping, countervailing duty and escape clause) (65). If the countertrade contract involves trade with a "Communist country," Section 406 of the Trade Act of 1974 (19 U.S.C. §2436), which provides relief agains "market disruption" caused by imports from such countries, may apply.

159. Two of the seven investigations that the International Trade Commission (ITC) has conducted under Section 406 have involved countertrade agreements. Both involved imports of anhydrous ammonia from the U.S.S.R. These imports were the result of a long-term countertrade agreement between a U.S. firm, Occidental Petroleum Corporation, and the Soviet Union.

160. In the first investigation, No. TA-406-5 (October 1979), the ITC found that imports had caused market disruption, but the President declined to take action. In the second investigation, No. TA-406-6 (April 1980), the ITC found that no market disruption had taken place.

161. The antidumping law was utilized in a 1981 case concerning goods imported to the United States under a countertrade agreement, Truck Trailer Axles and Brake Assemblies from Hungary, ITC Inv. No. 731-TA-38. In that case, the ITC made a preliminary determination that there was material injury to the domestic industry by reason of imports of truck trailer axles from Hungary, but the investigation was suspended after an administrative settlement was reached.

f) Conclusions

162. There are a number of other practices that are common features in commercial transactions on the domestic and international level. From the standpoint of competition policy, one principal concern is that the terms and conditions in the vertical distribution of goods and services or in the transfer of technology, while often reasonable pro-competitive means to facilitate entry into new markets, are not abused to allocate and divide world markets. Analysis of these practices, and of business arrangements such as joint ventures, rests on a determination as to whether they excessively restrict competition. With regard to joint ventures, this issue is already being addressed in the work programme of the Committee. The Committee is also planning to review experience under the 1973 Council Recommendation on Restrictive Business Practices relating to the use of Patents and Licences.

163.   Although recognising the various reasons why countertrade agreements are used, in light of their potentially harmful effects on trade and competition, their uncertain status under competition laws, and their growing role in world trade, such agreements should be kept under review and, in particular, consideration should be given to steps that can be taken to increase the transparency of these agreements.

6. MULTINATIONAL ENTERPRISES AND INTRA-FIRM AGREEMENTS AFFECTING TRADE: MARKET AND PRODUCT ALLOCATION, TRANSFER PRICING, AND CROSS-SUBSIDISATION

a) Introductory remarks

164.   Over the past 20 years multinational enterprises ("MNEs"), ranging from small firms with one foreign subsidiary to large conglomerates with major enterprises in many countries, have been a growing phenomenon in the world economy.   Created through internal expansion, green-field foreign investment or international merger, MNEs have been a major vehicle for investment in both developed and developing countries, contributing significantly to the accelerated internationalization of business activities, and thus have become an important factor in the present structure of international trade.

165.   Intra-group trade between parent companies and affiliates accounts for a substantial share of total international trade.   While no exact and comparable data are available for the whole OECD area, a recent United Nations publication gives some indications of the proportion of particular countries' intra-group trade (66).   For the United States in 1977, 39 per cent of total imports and 36 per cent of total exports can be classified as intra-group trade.   These figures cover transactions between US parents and their foreign affiliates as well as those between US affiliates of foreign-owned MNEs and their parent companies abroad (67).   The proportion of intra-group exports in the total exports of the United Kingdom increased from 29 per cent in 1976 to 31 per cent in 1980 (68).   According to a study by Dunning and Pearce, a sample of 329 of the world's largest industrial enterprises for 1977 showed that one-third of all parent company exports consisted of intra-group sales, with the share varying from 45 per cent for US firms to 30 per cent for those based in Western Europe and 17 per cent for Japanese firms (69).   An UNCTAD estimate suggests that roughly 30 per cent of all world trade could be classified as trade between related parties (70).

166.   In 1977, the Committee of Experts concluded a major study on the Restrictive Business Practices of Multinational Enterprises (71) which led to the adoption of a Council Recommendation in 1978 (72).   The report highlights potential beneficial as well as negative effects of MNEs on competition in national and international markets and the main findings and conclusions of this report are still valid today.   The Report as well as subsequent investigations by individual Member countries do not suggest that MNEs either engage more frequently in anticompetitive behaviour than purely national enterprises or in types of restrictive business practices which are unique in terms of competition policy or substantive antitrust rules of OECD Member countries.   Nevertheless, according to the material collected for that report, the economic significance and the geographical reach of these practices tended to be greater than that of similar practices engaged in by national enterprises (73).

167.   In pursuing global strategies such as profit and growth maximization, MNEs may engage in intra-group arrangements with their subsidiaries or affiliates involving intra-group allocations of markets and production, transfer pricing and cross-subsidisation. Such practices may conflict with the policies of host countries and affect trade flows between Member countries. The Committee's 1977 Report did not put forward recommendations concerning such intra-group practices. Given the increasing importance of intra-group trade, the Committee feels that this matter warrants consideration in the context of the present study and accordingly the following sections focus on those intra-group practices where competition and trade aspects are closely interrelated. Sections B and C deal with the major issues arising as regards intra-group allocations of markets and production and with transfer-pricing and cross subsidisation. Inevitably, much of the analysis in these sections is tentative as inter alia, no reliable data exist as to the prevalence of such practices. That the latter do exist is borne out by information on cases brought by competition authorities.

168.   In Section d) below, the present policies of competition authorities toward these practices are set out. It will be seen that there is no general agreement on attitudes towards such practices. Although in most OECD Member countries competition laws are applied to intra-group practices only to the extent that such practices amount to an abuse of a dominant position adversely affecting competition outside the affiliated enterprises, these practices raise broader issues at the frontier between competition and trade policies. It is not the intention of the following sections to reach conclusions on policy or law enforcement approaches but rather to flag the main issues that have been brought to the Committee's attention and to indicate areas for further consideration on these issues.

b) Intra-group allocation of markets and production

169.   Multinational corporations often operate in national markets through subsidiaries or affiliates which are legally distinct entities, some only partially owned. In furthering their commercial interests, MNEs may make internal arrangements with their subsidiaries or affiliates restricting the range of products to be produced or the markets to be served by the component subsidiaries or affiliates in different countries. The strategies for accomplishing intra-enterprise market or production allocation are varied, ranging from such direct means as export or production restrictions imposed by parent firms on foreign subsidiaries and restrictions on patent and trademark licensing to more indirect strategies such as restrictive terms and conditions of delivery, restrictive procurement policies, including obligations to buy essential raw materials or semi-manufactures, and compensatory payments.

170.   It must be recognised that reasonable co-ordination of activities and allocation of tasks among firms belonging to the same group is a source of efficiency and from the point of view of the global strategies of an MNE may be necessary in order to maximise the performance of the group as a whole, to enhance the individual capacities of component entities and to reduce internal conflicts of interests. From this perspective, competition or at least uncoordinated competition does not exist between related entities within the same group. It nevertheless remains true that, in view of the high degree of internationalisation of business activities and the importance of MNEs in world trade, decisions to allocate production or markets between affiliates may raise concern in the home and host countries of such entities, in

particular in situations where MNEs hold a sufficient share in relevant markets to significantly influence trade flows.

171.   Several countries expressed concern with intra-group market allocations and procurement practices of multinational enterprises. For example, a recent study by Statistics Canada found that in almost all sectors of the Canadian economy the reliance of foreign-controlled firms on imports was much greater than that of their domestic counterparts. Export restrictions imposed by parent companies on their subsidiaries may conflict with export promotion policies of the host countries. One recent study concluded that freedom of component entities of MNEs to act as local profit centers, consistent with the need for specialization and sound commercial practice, could yield significant benefits for international welfare (74).

172.   In the course of the study of the CIME on trade-related investment measures such as performance requirements, some countries indicated that they found it necessary to impose export or local content requirements on foreign controlled enterprises to counteract intra-group restrictions. Such performance requirements, if used in a systematic way, may in themselves distort trade and competition in national and international markets. It is precisely the interaction between government intervention in international trade and practices by enterprises which raises issues of concern in the context of the present report. Also those measures act in certain circumstances as a disincentive to investment. The CIME has completed a report on this subject, while the Trade Committee is studying their implications for international trade (75).

c) Transfer pricing and cross-subsidisation

173.   Transfer pricing refers to the assignment of prices to goods or services transferred between members of a group. In an MNE many transactions normally take place between related entities, e.g. sales of goods, the provision of services, the licensing of patents and know-how, the granting of loans, etc. The prices charged for such transfers do not necessarily represent a result of the free play of market forces, but may, for a number of reasons and because the MNE is in a position to adopt whatever principle is convenient to it as a group, diverge considerably from the prices which would have been agreed upon between unrelated parties engaged in the same or similar transactions under the same or similar conditions in the open market (hereafter referred to as "arm's length prices") (76).

174.   "Cross-subsidisation" is a term sometimes used to describe transfers of resources from the sales of a line of a firm's products or services to support that firm's activities in another line or geographical area of its operations. There are a variety of techniques other than manipulated transfer pricing which can be used for this purpose within a group, including surrender of remuneration on invested capital and cover of operating losses. To some degree such activities are normal and inherent in the operations of companies whose various activities experience different levels and cycles of profitability. To the extent, however, that transfer pricing and cross-subsidisation techniques are abused, e.g. for manipulated pricing of exported and imported goods or services they can have a significant effect on international trade flows. Although such practices may be engaged in by domestic enterprises as well, in particular large diversified firms, a number of Member countries believe that the case of multinational enterprises is more

significant for two reasons: the negative effects of abuses may be greater given the magnitude of intra-group trade conducted by MNEs; and the operation of MNEs in separate national markets allows a greater flexibility in manipulated pricing through these mechanisms. On the other hand, transfer pricing policies by MNEs are subject to control by several national tax, customs or exchange control authorities and such controls may significantly limit the scope for abuse.

175. Where components of a multinational enterprise located in different countries sell to one another, the prices charged may have an effect on trade flows between those countries. Charging relatively higher prices will have benefits for the exporting country in terms of national income and balance of payments by adversely effect the importing country, while relatively lower prices have the opposite effect. Similarly, the prices charged for the imports of a component entity may weaken that entity's competitive position and its ability to export.

176. With the exception of a 1978 report by UNCTAD (77), studies on transfer pricing have, for the most part, focused on its use as a tax-evasion technique. Nevertheless, the 1977 Report on MNEs mentions a number of instances where the use of transfer prices constituted an important factor in abusive pricing strategies investigated by competition authorities in Member countries (87) and recent investigations in some Member countries concerning in particular the oil and pharmaceutical industries show that this is an area of continuing concern.

177. In assessing the pricing strategies of multinational enterprises it has, of course, to be recognised that there are cost differences between Member countries which tend to produce cost differentials. In addition, several factors outside the control of the MNE such as differences in tax rates, patterns of consumer behaviour, distribution systems, variations in exchange rates and state imposed price controls may have a disparate effect on prices. It is therefore important to distinguish abusive pricing practices from price differences which are induced by such factors. A recent decision of the French competition authorities provides an illustrative example of a situation where an abuse was found (79). According to that decision, the enterprise concerned was a multinational group manufacturing pharmaceuticals, which held a dominant position in the relevant product market. Its transfer prices widely exceeded comparable prices of outside enterprises without any economic justification for such differentials being apparent. In order to restrict market access by competitors, the enterprise engaged in selective low pricing stragegies for certain products which were compensated, at least in part, by artificially high prices for largely identical products sold by another subsidiary of the same group to a different category of customers. The decision of the European Court of Justice in United Brands gives an interesting example of abusive discriminatory pricing strategies where dissimilar conditions were applied to equivalent transactions with trading partners in several Member countries thus distorting trade and competition in the Common Market (80). Issues relating to transfer pricing were also relevant in the decision concerning the pricing practices of Hofmann La Roche in the Community and several Member countries (81).

178. As to domestic competition, the manipulation of transfer prices as a means of abusing a dominant position of market power can adversely effect competition by artificially raising or lowering prices, and in the latter

instance, possibly eliminating existing, efficient suppliers from the market and impeding new entry. The 1977 MNE Report (82) reflects concern relating to international predatory pricing which involves the supply of goods and services to a particular country at prices below cost for a certain period in order to drive competitors out of business. The relationship between problems of predatory behaviour and the application of competition and trade laws is discussed in Section 5(c) above and in Chapter II of this report. Views of OECD Member countries diverge as to the importance of these practices from the standpoint of competition law and trade policy. The large proportion of international trade attributable to intra-firm transactions has given rise to concern that these transactions hold potential for facilitating anticompetitive activity. On the other hand, transfer prices and cross-subsidisation are complicated tools and may be difficult to abuse within a complex business environment. These mechanisms, if used for anticompetitive purposes against third parties, can have detrimental effects on international trade and therefore may require continuing attention by governments, including competition authorities.

d) Assessment of intra-group practices under national competition laws and relevant international instruments

179.   As the Committee stated in its 1977 Report on MNEs, competition laws in most OECD Member countries provide that intra-group practices are not considered in and of themselves as harmful unless they amount to an abuse of a dominant position adversely affecting competition outside the affiliated enterprises. According to the theory of enterprise unity, corporations under common control, such as a corporation and its unincorporated divisions, may be considered a single economic entity from the perspective of competition law enforcement; accordingly coordinated conduct among component entities of the same group is the product of common control and should not be viewed as falling within the category of cartels or collusive activity prohibited under competition laws (83). It has been generally recognised that requiring individual entities within a single economic enterprise to compete and treating intra-enterprise directives or instructions which amount to an allocation of functions within that enterprise as restrictive business practices could discourage internal growth and decrease efficiency, and also create enforcement difficulties for competition authorities (84).

180.   The European Court of Justice in the Sterling Drug/Centrafarm case stated the rule under Common Market Law as follows:

"Article 85 is not concerned with agreements or concerted practices between undertakings belonging to the same concern and having the status of parent company and subsidiary, if the undertakings form an economic unit within which the subsidiary has no real freedom to determine its course of action on the market, and if the agreements or practices are concerned merely with the internal allocation of tasks as between the undertakings (85)."

It should be noted, however, that this decision concerned only the relations between a parent company and an affiliate and did not cover intra-group practices involving affiliates operating within the same product line.

181.   The Commission has followed this ruling but has suggested that in some circumstances minority ownership may be sufficient to negate this general

rule (86) and has also reserved the possibility of challenging intra-enterprise agreements under Article 85 when special circumstances indicate that the entities within the enterprise should be considered to have acted independently (87). Another approach has been taken by competition officials and courts in France, where intra-enterprise arrangements have been held unlawful if the entities concerned concealed the fact that they belonged to the same group and held themselves out as independent competitors. In Sweden, certain intra-group practices, for instance resale price maintenance and collusive tendering involving entities of the same group, may be considered as a violation of Section 2 of the Competition Act.

182.   In the United States, the courts have reached different conclusions as to whether, or the circumstancess under which, the "contract, combination or conspiracy" requirement of section 1 of the Sherman Act is met by intra-firm agreements. There have been few cases, however, in which such agreements have been found to constitute an unreasonable restraint of competition (88). A parent corporation and its controlled subsidiaries or affiliates may normally be operated as a single economic entity under which the head of the corporate group exercises management influence over its subsidiaries and affiliates to set prices, designate sources of supply, identify markets to be served and make other managerial allocations of functions among the group, without raising antitrust concern.

183.   The United States antitrust authorities have generally accepted the view stated in the 1955 Report of the Attorney General's National Committee to Study the Antitrust Laws, that a parent corporation may operate the subsidiaries that it fully controls as a single economic entity (89). The control test has generally been formulated in terms of whether the parent controls the majority of the voting stock of the subsidiary or the firm maintains effective working control (90). This issue is addressed in detail in Case A of the Antitrust Guide for International Operations (91). The key statement in the Report is as follows:

> "The use of subsidiaries is generally induced by normal, prudent business considerations. No social objective would be obtained were subsidiaries enjoined from agreeing not to compete with each other or with their parent. To demand internal competition within and between the members of a single business unit is to invite chaos without promotion of the public welfare. The substance of the Supreme Court decisions is that concerted action between a parent and subsidiary or between subsidiaries which has for its purpose or effect coercion or unreasonable restraint on the trade of strangers to those acting in concert is prohibited by Section 1. Nothing in these opinions should be interpreted as justifying the conclusion that concerted action solely between a parent and subsidiary or subsidiaries, the purpose and effect of which is not coercive restraint of trade of strangers to the corporate family, violates Section 1. Where such concerted action restrains no trade and is designed to restrain no trade other than that of the parent and its subsidiaries, Section 1 is not violated."

184.   As a general rule, therefore, the US antitrust authorities do not expect to challenge purely internal allocations of responsibilities within a corporate group which is under truly common ownership or control. Recently the Justice Department filed an amicus curiae brief supporting a writ of certiorari to the Supreme Court to address the question of whether joint

activities of corporations under common control should be deemed conduct of a single economic enterprise, rather than conspiracy in restraint of trade within the meaning of section 1 of the Sherman Act (92). The Supreme Court granted the writ of certiorari and the Justice Department filed an amicus brief in August 1983 adressing the substantive issues in greater detail.

185.   As it appears from the preceding paragraphs, in most OECD countries a challenge to internal allocation and pricing practices within a multinational as well as domestic groups is more likely to be based on an abuse of a dominant position if the firms involved hold sufficient market power to warrant such action.   There is case law in several Member countries where competition authorities and courts have considered intra-group relations and the market power of the group as a whole when applying competition law to abuses of dominant positions or predatory behaviour of group entities towards competitors (93).   For instance in the Continental Can case, the European Court of Justice in determining whether the enterprise concerned had a dominant position within the Common Market, took into account the market share of the subsidiary as well as the economic and financial power of the Group considered as an economic entity (94).   The same principle was applied in the Zoja/CS Case where the Court referred to the complete and effective control of the parent company over its subsidiaries (95).

186.   Application of national legislation to intra-enterprise practices by MNEs, however, presents several difficulties.   The burden of proof problems specific to transfer pricing, that is, determining "arm's length prices" and cross-subsidization have already been noted.   The problems of collecting documentation and other evidence at an international level requires little elaboration, being well-documented in case law as well as past and current studies by the OECD (96).   Although the 1979 OECD Council Recommendation (97) has encouraged co-operation in this area, problems of obtaining information persist.   The Committee has examined these problems in a recently published report and is presently reviewing the 1979 Recommendation with a view to strengthening its procedures to encourage cooperation in this area. Application of national legislation is further complicated by the issues associated with the exercise of jurisdiction over foreign firms or persons. For instance, relief requiring behavioural or structural change of the foreign enterprise may give rise to enforcement difficulties and disputes as to national sovereignty.

187.   At the international level, the competition chapter of the OECD Guidelines for Multinational Enterprises does address intra-group pricing in connection with the abuse of a dominant position calling upon enterprises to refrain from "discriminatory (i.e. unreasonably differentiated) pricing and using such pricing between affiliated enterprises as a means of transactions affecting competition outside these enterprises".   The UN RBP Code includes a similar provision.   Intra-group practices not affecting competition outside the affiliated enterprises are not addressed by the competition chapter of the Guidelines and are generally excluded from the coverage of the RBP Code. There are two further references to transfer pricing in the OECD Guidelines: one in the chapter on taxation (98), the other in the chapter on disclosure of information (99).   In addition, the relationship between intra-group practices and trade issues is reflected in paragraph 5 of the General Policies chapter of the Guidelines, according to which enterprises should "allow their component entities freedom to develop their activities and to exploit their

competitive advantage in domestic and foreign markets, consistent with the need for specialization and sound business practices."

e) Conclusions

188.   Practices like intra-group allocations, transfer pricing, and cross-subsidisation and their effects on trade and competition are of interest to policy makers, given the large proportion of international trade attributable to intra-group transactions. Competition laws in most OECD Member countries provide that intra-group practices are not considered harmful in and of themselves unless they amount to an abuse of a dominant position adversely affecting competition outside the affiliated enterprises. In dealing with such practices, cooperation between governments in the exchange of information according to the Committee's recent report on competition law enforcement is an essential element. In addition, Member countries should continue to use the consultation process provided in the 1979 Recommendation where problems of obtaining information arise. Similarly, use should be made of the provisions of the OECD Guidelines relevant to intra-group practices.

C. GOVERNMENT INVOLVEMENT IN AND REGULATION OF COMMERCIAL ACTIVITIES

1. BACKGROUND

189.   In view of the considerable extent of government involvement in commercial activity, such activity can be expected to have an important influence on the state of competition in international markets. This part of the chapter deals with three aspects of government activity which can affect competition and trade: public procurement policies, public enterprises and government regulated industries.

190.   Each of these categories raises important and complex issues for trade and competition policy. Government procurement is a significant component of national economies, and if used for protectionist purposes, e.g. to cushion domestic suppliers, can give rise to trade barriers or distort competition (if for example purchases are made above market prices in order to subsidise domestic firms). Public enterprises, whether fully or partly government-owned, can serve as a vehicle for governments to restructure their economies, channel investments and allocate domestic resources in pursuit of national programmes of economic and social goals. Concern arises, however, as to whether government support provides public enterprises with unfair competitive advantages in international trade. Finally, some sectors of domestic economies, e.g. utilities, energy and transportation, are commonly regulated by governments in the belief that competition in these areas does not produce a desirable outcome. However, where a regulated sector in one country engages in trade with a deregulated or non-regulated sector in another, considerable problems can arise with respect to the application of competition laws to such transactions, as has recently been the case in the shipping and air transport sectors.

191.   Available data on the public sector is not extensive, and is subject to definitional problems that make intercountry comparisons difficult. Nonetheless, it clearly appears that government involvement in commercial

activities is a significant component of domestic economies and a growing trend that is likely to increase. For example, a study done in 1979 concluded that the public sector represented 15.8 percent of the non-agricultural economy in the Common Market (100). The size of the public sector in the Community varies considerably by industry: from 6 to 7 percent in manufacturing (being especially large in chemicals), 30 percent in financial services and 70 percent in energy, transportation and telecommunications.

2. GOVERNMENT PROCUREMENT AND STATE TRADING

192.   An important feature of government activity has been a marked general increase in the amount of government expenditures for goods and services in all countries. At present, national government expenditures of OECD member countries account for approximately one quarter to one-half of their gross domestic product. In certain sectors, industries sell substantially more than half of their production to the State.

193.   As these figures suggests, governments have an influence on the competitive behaviour of the supplier markets. This influence could favour competition; e.g. a ministerial department or an agency could for example use its buying power to counter-balance the market power of its suppliers. Conversely, this influence can discourage competition; for example, a government may adopt specifications which only a very small number of suppliers are able to fulfil or use tendering procedures which exclude certain potential suppliers, for example small enterprises, or foreign enterprises when tendering takes place on a national basis. Government procurement policies may be responsible for higher costs if products are purchased at higher than domestic market prices in acquisitions from the private sector. This differential between procurement and market price represents a subsidy which can be used to expand sales to other purchasers (e.g., military procurement of aircraft may subsidize sales of civilian aircraft), or to sustain inefficient domestic producers and suppliers.

194.   In addition, Governments and their agencies have considerable power to encourage or restrict international trade by their procurement decisions. Not only are they large buyers of goods for national defence, health and other programmes but, in addition, they need not choose to buy from the cheapest source -- or make such a choice their regular policy -- and thus can favour domestic suppliers. Further, in their procurement policies, governments can set extensive technical standards, bidding requirements, financing conditions which, although directly precluding foreign sources, may nevertheless place foreign suppliers at an unfair disadvantage and thus operate as "hidden barriers" to trade.

195.   In light of the importance of government procurement in trade, this practice was added to the GATT discipline during the Tokyo Round of negotiations. The agreement reached on that occasion provides that products originating in the territory of the other parties to the Agreement and the suppliers of those products shall be accorded treatment no less favourable than that accorded to domestic products and suppliers. However, there are important limitations to the scope of application of this Agreement:

    -- It covers only goods and incidental services;

-- It applies only to procurement contracts of a value of SDRs 150,000 or more;

-- It recognizes the special nature of some aid programmes, which sometimes require that aid-financed procurements must originate in the grantor country;

-- It does not cover the procurement of arms, ammunitions, war materials or other procurements indispensable for national security or defence purposes or measures necessary to protect public order and safety;

-- It provides exemptions of a sectoral nature since it applies only to the specifically listed government entities and normally excludes power generation, transportation and telecommunications which constitute the traditional sectors of public authority activity.

The GATT Procurement Agreement covers only a relatively small proportion of public procurement by signatory nations. Nevertheless, the Agreement does create a set of rules designed to ensure that suppliers from each signatory country have an opportunity to bid for certain foreign government contracts.

196. Although significant interest has been expressed in a GATT context in the issue of state trading, this area has not been made the subject of a special accord. Rather, reliance has been placed on the provisions of Article XVII, which generally stipulates that state trading activities should conform on the standards for trade set by the GATT. Signatory countries report periodically on the activities of their state trading enterprises as provided by subsection 4 (§1) of this Article. In brief, the reports from non-Communist countries have encompassed state trading of agricultural products, but they have also included such trade in alcoholic beverages, coal and coal products, petroleum and petroleum products, pharmaceuticals, salt, steel and shipbuilding, as well as a broad category of products termed "inflammables". To cite an example of trading activities by government agencies, coal imports by the Central Electricity Generating Board in the United Kingdom are regulated in order to protect the national coal industry from low-price imports. Foreign producers have the disadvantage of negotiating with a single buyer, whereas the diversification of buyers would make it possible to obtain the supply of energy at the lowest possible prices. In some respects, state trading offers as many, if not more, opportunities for the provision of direct and indirect, open and hidden subsidies to particular industries as government procurement activities. Further, State-owned or controlled enterprises may set a higher priority on sales than profits, and this may result in operating losses which are covered by public revenues.

3. PUBLIC ENTERPRISES

197. This section does not deal exhaustively with all questions concerning public enterprises, but rather focuses on the consequences of their participation in international commercial activity in sectors in which private firms are also represented. The main issue for this study is thus public enterprises in the so-called "competitive sector" (automobiles, hydrocarbons, nuclear energy, chemicals etc.) in view of the strong international

competition to which they are exposed on both national and international markets (101). The report does not therefore touch on State-controlled monopolies (tobacco, alcohol etc.) or public services (transport, water, gas, electricity etc.) which generally operate largely or exclusively on the domestic market.

198.   The activities of public enterprises in the "competitive sector" can also have an important impact on international trade. As with private firms, public enterprises are often involved in the full range of export and import trading.   In addition, many public enterprises have established foreign entities or engaged in joint ventures with foreign private or public firms and thus have a multinational structure.   According to data published by the United Nations Centre on Transnational Corporations: "In the developed market economies, more than 40 State-owned enterprises had sales of over $1 billion each in 1981. (...) About half of these were involved solely in domestic activities;   of the remainder, about half could be considered directly comparable to private sector transnational corporations by reason of the internationalization of their activities. For example, ENI has more than 100 foreign affiliates, about half of which are in developing countries; British Leyland has some 90 affiliates and Renault over 60, at least a quarter being in developing countries" (102).

199.   If private undertakings determine their industrial and commercial strategy with a view to profitability, public or government-controlled enterprises can be subject to different factors in the pursuit by the public authorities of objectives in the general interest.   For even if public undertakings are managed in accordance with the criteria of profit and rentability, they may nevertheless have to pursue other objectives of a societal nature. For this and other reasons they are sometimes governed by specific regulations although by and large they apply the principles of private law in their commercial relations (unlike state monopolies and public services which are generally governed by public law).   In cases where the state seeks to further its economic and social policies, through its management of public enterprises, this may impose specific burdens on these enterprises, and such costs are sometimes offset by aids or subsidies designed to protect their viability (103). But difficulties from the point of view of competition and trade may arise from inequalities in the treatment accorded to public and private enterprises.   The State as shareholder or backer, may give public enterprises certain financial advantages which can influence their competitive position.

200.   A number of government aids specifically accorded to public undertakings may be subject to control. For example, the EEC Directive of 25th June 1980 on the transparency of financial relations between Member States and public undertakings, adopted pursuant to Article 90(3) provides a non-restrictive list: "the setting off of operating losses; the provision of capital; non-refundable grants, or loans on privileged terms; the granting of financial advantages by forgoing profits or the recovery of sums due; the forgoing of a normal return on public funds used; compensation for financial burdens imposed by the public authorities" (104).

201.   To gauge the effect of these measures on competition and trade, there are a number of questions that arise:

-- Can the government, through its provision of financial resources, be likened to a shareholder acting to promote the continuity or expansion of a private firm?

-- Does the competitive advantage constitute discrimination, in as much as it is not available to a private competitor in comparable circumstances?

-- Does government assistance take the form of a subsidy akin to the cross-subsidies which may be accorded within a national or multinational group of private companies?

As may be the case for internal practices within a single group of private companies, the financial relations between the State and public enterprises are not always transparent and this constitutes an impediment to the evaluation of these practices from the standpoint of competition and trade.

202.   In addition to this objective of transparency, mention should be made of the steps taken by several countries towards greater economic efficiency in the activities of the public enterprises by subjecting them to a greater degree to competitive pressures. The efforts at deregulation in various Member countries are one example of this approach. The aim is, inter alia, to encourage greater dynamism on the part of public undertakings by relieving them of excessive legal constraints, notably in the matter of State supervision. With the elimination of cumbersome administrative procedures, they may be better equipped to meet international competition since they can react more rapidly and independently in their decision-making. Furthermore, several countries are considering the possibility of privatising public enterprises in order to improve their efficiency. A major privatisation programme is presently under way in the United Kingdom.

4. REGULATED INDUSTRIES

203.   All categories of enterprises (public, private and mixed) are represented in the industrial sectors traditionally subject to specific regulation. In 1979 the Committee produced a report on competition policy in regulated sectors (105) which identified a number of industries which, due to the nature of their activities, can influence trade and are frequently subject to regulation: air and sea transport, energy and banking. The reasons most often given to justify the special treatment accorded to the regulated industries are the following (106): a "natural" monopoly situation in which there is room for only one viable firm in the market because of economies of scale or technical and physical factors; the need for the State to ensure the continuity of public services at a reasonable and non-discriminatory price to users; and the need to protect vital national interests such as energy supplies and national defence.

204.   It can nonetheless arise that the regulation remains although the motive for it has disappeared or lost much of its validity. For instance, in most countries, the telecommunications sector was, until recently, considered a "natural" monopoly because of the complexity of the techniques involved and the excessively high cost of the necessary equipment. Today, in a number of countries, a major part of the telecommunications sector, telephone services

and the telecommunications equipment industry, has been opened to competition and no longer receives special government protection.

205.   The regulation of industries that engage in international trade and/or their exemption from competition policy can have a significant impact on international trade in these sectors and conflicts can arise, as in recent years, due to differences in national approaches to regulation.   In countries where a "natural" monopoly exists, e.g. in telecommunications, the market power conferred by the government on the monopoly may create unfair advantages when it enters into trade agreements with suppliers of services operating on competitive markets.   Trade difficulties may also arise where international services are based on monopolistic structures, while domestic markets are organised on competitive principles.   Countries that have taken steps to deregulate certain sectors may experience problems in trading with countries where regulation remains the rule and in applying their competition law to such transactions.   Finally, in sectors such as air transportation and ocean shipping, where rates are set by intergovernmental agreements or by government-controlled private agreement, the resemblance of these practices to private cartels prompts concern on the part of competition authorities, particularly in those countries where the domestic sector of the industry is not regulated.   In fact, some of the most difficult international antitrust disputes have arisen over investigations in regulated sectors such as ocean shipping and air transportation.

206.   The following paragraphs, as illustrative examples, briefly mention three regulated sectors which appear to be of particular importance to international trade and competition.

207.   The shipping conference sector provides an excellent illustration of the complexity of the issue of regulated industries (107).   At present, there are over fifty major shipping conferences serving the world's main shipping trade routes.   The usual functions of conferences are the fixing of uniform tariffs, freight rates and practices relating to the receipt, carriage and delivery of cargo by all members of the Conference.   There is generally also an organisation to administer and enforce the agreement.   The main advantages claimed for the conference system are the provision of regular and frequent shipping services from a variety of ports and the provision of uniform, stable rates which do not discriminate between shippers in different locations. However, from the standpoint of competition policy, several aspects of shipping conference behaviour raise concern.First, there is joint fixing of uniform rates, tariffs and practices by members.   Second, there is discriminatory pricing between shippers for similar volumes and values of merchandise through provisions allowing "patronage" agreements.   Thirdly, there is discrimination in transporting merchandise of high value, so that a higher rate is applied to merchandise of high value compared with merchandise of lesser value which does not reflect transport cost differentials.

208.   As noted in a recent OECD report (108), shipping and in particular international liner shipping is totally or partially exempt from control under restrictive business practices legislation in most OECD Member countries, which generally approve the conference system as being desirable.   However, several countries have found it necessary to take action against certain conference practices (109).   Thus, the OECD Maritime Transport Committee is considering the development of guidelines concerning the application of competition policy to shipping practices which are designed to distinguish

desirable from undesirable conference practices as well as to minimise conflicts between countries when they do apply their laws to this international sector.

209.   International air transport is a sector in which the essential framework of operations is provided by bilateral agreements between states covering routes, capacity, frequency and tariffs.   Generally speaking, IATA, the trade association to which more than 100 scheduled international and domestic airlines belong, co-ordinates fares, rates, charges and levels of Agents renumeration.   Several tariff conferences have been established within IATA according to geographical area in order to determine cargo rates and passenger fares.   Participating members may also develop and adopt agreements on these matters.   But typically fares may only be charged with the approval of the contracting parties to the bilateral agreements and an airline will only be permitted to conduct its business in accordance with the permits granted by its domestic aeronautical authorities.   Air transport enjoys partial exemption from competition laws in most countries, some of whom regulate the fare co-ordination process itself as well as the fare agreements arising therefrom.   It should be noted, however, that in many countries airlines may and do file fares for approval by aeronautical authorities without prior coordination within IATA.

210.   As with other regulated sectors, some countries are making efforts to increase competition in domestic air transport markets.   But an extension of this philosophy of deregulation must take account of the existing international regulatory framework.   Otherwise there is potential for problems when their airlines compete with regulated or state-owned national carriers from other countries in the market for international services.   It may be more difficult to apply competition policy with respect to conduct in international air traffic where practices involve action of both private and public enterprises, owing to the important national and security interests seen in maintaining domestic airlines.   Divergent approaches to the utility of competition in this sector may also impede efforts at stimulating competition through deregulatory reform.   To date, the OECD has not carried out any in-depth study on air transportation, nor has the Committee assessed the role of competition policy in this vital sector.

211.   The telecommunications services and equipment industry is another area in which the public authorities play a role.   A recent OECD study noted that in virtually every country the provision of telecommunications services was carried out through a monopoly enterprise, frequently a public monopoly.   The equipment manufacturing industry is highly concentrated and, internationally, has always been an oligopoly.   The report recommends the introduction of more competitive procurement practices on the basis of competitive bidding. However, the report recognises the difficulties in some countries of extending competitive bidding to the full range of telecommunications equipment for technical, economic and national security reasons.   For instance, in some countries equipment procurement had been used to assist in financing firms considered important for national security reasons.   The report also suggests that consumers should be given greater choice in their purchase of terminal equipment by increasing the ease with which new terminal equipment can be certified for connection with the network.   The lack of competitive structures in most sectors of telecommunications has important implications for international trade.   International circuits linking countries with differing market structures and regulatory approaches can encourage the emergence of

restrictive business practices. Therefore, when a circuit links two countries, one of which has a number of competing providers of international services, while in the other services are provided on a monopoly basis, there is a danger that the monopoly provider will abuse its position to distort or unfairly exploit competitive conditions in the other country.

5. APPLICATION OF COMPETITION POLICY TO REGULATED INDUSTRIES AND PUBLIC ENTERPRISES

212. As discussed in Chapter III, the application of competition law to government commercial activities is generally subject to limitation under the doctrines of "sovereign immunity", "Act of State", and "Foreign compulsion". This section identifies exemptions from the law which may be given to regulated sectors and to publicly owned enterprises.

213. As regards regulated sectors, the report on competition policy in regulated sectors (see note 105) shows that the legal approaches are not the same in all countries. In some countries, it is considered that competition does not produce the desired effect in particular sectors and that in these sectors it is legitimate to substitute regulation for market forces. Government authorities may thus determine price and profit levels and other business terms and industry output targets and at the same time exempt the sector concerned wholly or partly from competition rules (for example, from merger control or from provisions governing restrictive agreements). In other countries, however, or in the same countries but for other industries, there is an observable tendency for the government to take more account of competition policy objectives or to give priority to such objectives. Thus, regulations and exemptions are kept to a minimum and issued only in exceptional circumstances since they are considered to result in increased costs and inefficiency.

214. In a many competition laws, some sectors enjoy different treatment from others. This is generally the case for those sectors discussed in the preceding section. The Committee's earlier report on regulated sectors noted the following distinction:

> "There are those countries where there are no or few express provisions exempting particular industries totally or partially from the competition laws but where a general provision exists which exempts actions resulting from the existence of another law or regulation or which enables such actions to be exempted by the competition authorities, if approved under another regulatory scheme. The second method of exemption is exemplified by countries which have laid down specific provisions in the text of the main competition legislation or in subsequent amendments providing that certain entire sectors or certain practices or agreements in certain sectors are partially or totally exempt from the operative provisions of the competition legislation but where, in the absence of such provisions, the competition legislation is considered to apply".

The choice of one or the other method or a mixture of the two does not prejudge the effectiveness of either system since each generally allows some margin of assessment on a case-by-case basis. Rather, the effectiveness of control depends on the willingness to enforce competition law in a given sector, especially where the competition authorities do not have the power to investigate on their own initiative but have to have cases referred to them by other administsrative bodies.

215.   When exemptions exist but the competition authorities retain some power to intervene, they generally attempt to ensure that the exemption granted is strictly limited.   Thus, abusive practices of shipping conferences have been challenged in Germany, Japan and the United States.   Similarly, in the air transport sector, the courts or administrative authorities in Denmark, Germany and the United States have examined exemptions resulting from airlines' membership in IATA.

216.   As regards publicly owned enterprises, a detailed review of national laws indicates that most countries in principle apply their competition laws to public enterprises but with different degrees of exemption.   In Japan, in the application of the Anti-Monopoly Act, there is in principle no difference in the treatment of private and publicly owned enterprises operating in the competitive sector.   However, some of the publicly owned enterprises are permitted by law to hold a monopoly position, including export and import activities.   For example, the Japan Cigarette and Salt Public Corporation has a monopoly right in the import of cigarettes and accordingly, only the importers commissioned by the Corporation can import cigarettes.   (Sections 2, 3 and 28 of the Tobacco Monopoly Act).   In Switzerland, Section 23(2) of the Cartels Act provides that "nothing herein contained shall affect ... such stipulations of the public law as may constitute exceptions to this Act". However, the Cartel Commission has interpreted this section in a restrictive manner (110), observing that it applies only when, in the general interest public law created a marketing system and special prices by granting an enterprise on a competitive position in the market.   When public law does not regulate competition or the competitive position of enterprises operating within a given market, the economic behaviour of all participants in that market, whether private public or mixed ventures, is governed by the provisions of the Cartel Act.

217.   In Finland, State-owned companies engaged in multinational trade are, with very few exceptions, in the same position as privately owned enterprises as regards competition laws.   In Denmark, public or regulated undertakings are exempted from the application of the Monopolies Act where their prices or business activities are determined or approved by public authorities.   In New Zealand, the only possibility for exemption results from express authorisation provided by another Act.   In Australia, the Trade Practices Act applies equally to private enterprises and to the Australian Commonwealth Government insofar as it carries on a business.   Specified public authorities may be exempted but this power has not been used to date.

218.   In France, Article 50 of the Price Ordinance No 45-1483 fully applies to both private or public business activities.   However, Article 51 exempts from the application of this ordinance "the activities of an enterprise or group of enterprises holding a dominant position when they arise out of the application of a legislative provision or regulation".   However, there is no a priori exemption: the Minister for the Economy and Finance has taken several decisions concerning practices by public or semi-public enterprises (e.g. involving the nationalised Gun Powder and Explosives Company, phytosanitary products and Havas D.O.M.).

219.   In Greece, the provisions of the Act of 26th September 1977 apply to both publicly-owned enterprises and regulated enterprises.   However, under Section 5, these enterprises can be exempted upon a decision of the Ministers for National Economy and for Trade after the advice of the Committee for Protection of Competition in cases considered to be of vital importance for the national economy.   In Spain, the Act against restraints of competition of 20 July 1963 applies to both publicly-owned and private enterprises.   However, Section 4 provides that "the prohibitions contained in Section 1 shall not apply to situations in which competition is restricted and which are expressly brought in being through the exercise of administrative powers in pursuance of any legal enactment".   As Section 1 only applies to concerted practices, the exception provided by Section 4 does not concern abusive practices.   In Belgium, Section 27 of the act of 27th May 1960 on the protection against the abuse of economic power provides that public enterprises do not fall within the scope of the   law.   In Norway, State-owned Monopolies are exempt from the obligation   to   be   registered   (the   Price   Act   of   1953   Section 34 sub-paragraph 2).   State-owned monopolies are also exempt from application of Section 42 of the Price Act which, under certain conditions, authorises the price authorities to amend or annul any regulation which has been made by a restrictive association

220.   In Ireland, certain service activities, notably land, air and sea transport, are excluded from the competition law.   The German Act against restraints of competition provides for exemption for certain sectors in which there is a high proportion of public undertakings (Sections 99 to 103 of the Act).   However, this does   not appear to be applicable in the international trade field.   In the United Kingdom, public or regulated enterprises which have international activities may be exempted from the provisions of competition law when a particular regulation is applied to them or when the competition laws themselves provide for exceptions in certain sectors of industry or commerce.

221.   In Canada, although exemption is not absolute, the regulated activities of a firm would not normally be subject, in practice, to application of competition law.   As concerns public enterprises, in a case in 1982, Regina v. the Uranium Canada and Eldorado Nuclear companies, the Supreme Court of Ontario found that that Act could not be applied to these companies since they were agents of the Crown.   This decision resulted in an appeal to the Supreme Court of Canada.

222.   In the United States, public enterprises involved in international trade are not treated any differently from other enterprises under antitrust legislation.   For example, a public railway was found to have formed a cartel with several private railway companies, with the object of harming a common competitor (111).   In the event of failure to comply with the obligations provided for in certain special regulations conferring a relative antitrust immunity, they become subject to antitrust provisions.   In 1983, several regulated road transport companies specialising in the transport of goods between the United States and Canada were charged with antitrust violations for having acted in excess of the immunity conferred on them by special regulations (112).

223.   In the European Economic Community, the public or private ownership of a firm is not taken into account for the application of the competition rules of the EEC Treaty.   In fact, article 222 provides that "this Treaty shall in

no way prejudice the rules in Member States governing the system of property ownership". However, considering the special character of the financial relations between governments and public undertakings, therefore, the Commission feels it must have access to the information necessary to apply Community competition rules equitably whether enterprises are under public or private ownership. The "transparency" Directive already mentioned (paragraph 14) should enable the Commission to assess whether the public undertakings in question benefit from transfers of public funds which might be termed aid. At the first stage, the "transparency" directive is being applied to the automobile, synthetic fibre, textile machinery, manufactured tobacco and shipbuilding sectors.

6. CONCLUSIONS

224. The commercial activity of governments, be it through procurement policies, public enterprises or regulation of industries, is of considerable importance in the domestic economies of OECD Member countries. As a result, such activity can exert a significant impact on competition in domestic markets and on international trade. Of particular concern is the extent to which the government's role, through, for example, specific procurement regulations or product standards, or through subsidies or financial support to enterprises at better than market terms, affects competition in domestic and foreign markets. Further, it may be more difficult for competition officials to apply their laws against the commercial activities of foreign governments that restrict competition in their markets than would be the case with private competition restraints. Greater transparency as to the Government's role in commercial activity is a necessary basis for assessment of effects of such action on trade and competition.

225. In the experience of several countries, efforts to apply competition laws to regulated sectors through deregulatory reforms have proved beneficial. Countries that have taken steps to deregulate certain sectors may however experience problems in trading with countries where regulation remains the rule and in applying their competition laws to such transactions. To improve this situation, cooperation between government authorities, including those responsible for competition policy, is necessary. The 1979 Council Recommendation on Exempted or Regulated Sectors is particularly relevant in this regard, since it calls upon Member countries to reconsider the continuing validity of present regulatory frameworks and whether the same objectives could be achieved by the operation of competition or through measures which restrict competition to a lesser degree. The Committee intends to examine in its future work programme the way this Recommendation has been applied.

CHAPTER II

COMPETITION-RELATED TRADE ISSUES

A. INTRODUCTION

226.   As it appears throughout this study, trade policy measures have a significant impact on competition in national and international markets. Competition policy which is designed to promote efficient functioning of markets has two substantial reasons for being concerned with a nation's trade policies. First, international trade serves to sharpen competition in the domestic market in terms of price, quality and incentives toward innovation and the development of new products and production processes. Second, barriers to trade which shelter particular domestic industries may have anti-competitive effects on national markets. The stated objective of such measures often is to provide domestic firms time to increase their ability to compete internationally. Nevertheless, most Member countries believe that in the long run, managed international trade and inward-oriented trade policies will frustrate the effective implementation of competition policy by favouring market structures that are unresponsive to competitive pressures. In sheltered economies, benefits accruing to specific national producers are generally accompanied by an overall reduction in efficiency and substantial welfare losses to be borne by consumers, taxpayers and/or other sectors of domestic production.

227.   The purpose of this chapter of the report is to examine a range of trade policy measures from the perspective of competition policy with a view to presenting a framework that competition and trade officials could use to assess the impact of such policies. The focus of this analysis is on non-tariff trade policy measures which give domestic producers an advantage when they compete with foreign firms. Non-tariff barriers have become increasingly important in determining trade flows as tariffs have generally been reduced to quite low levels, particularly among the OECD countries (113). Over the last ten years, protection of domestic industries has been carried out largely by the imposition of non-tariff barriers (114). Such measures are of particular relevance to competition policy for, unlike tariffs, which operate as an adjustment to prices, non-tariff barriers often act as absolute controls on trade flows and thus their impact on market structure can be both direct and substantial.

228.   Section B of this chapter deals with trade policy measures other than laws relating to unfair trade practices. Part 1, after noting the basic goals

of trade policy and competition policy, develops a general analytical framework which the Committee proposes for use by policy-makers to provide a more comprehensive basis for evaluating the effects of proposed trade measures. Part 2 provides, as background, a description of the main categories of non-tariff barriers and a brief description of the institutional setting in which trade policies are evolving. In Part 3, these categories of non-tariff trade barriers are analysed individually, applying the analytical framework developed in Part 1. Section C of the Chapter examines, from the perspective of competition policy, specific laws dealing with injurious or unfair trade practices. The conclusions of this chapter are set out in Section D.

B. TRADE POLICY MEASURES (OTHER THAN LAWS RELATING TO UNFAIR TRADE PRACTICES) AFFECTING COMPETITION

1. ANALYTICAL APPROACHES TO TRADE POLICY FROM A COMPETITION VIEWPOINT

a. The goals of trade policy and competition policy

229.   Throughout the post-war period the trade policies of the OECD countries have shared a common commitment, with varying degrees of qualification, to the achievement and maintenance of an open multilateral trading system subject to international rules. Such a trading regime brings opportunities for mutual gain as it encourages efficiency and adaptation to changed economic circumstances and hence to an increase in the quantity and variety of goods and services which are available in each participating country.

230.   In 1960, the OECD countries underlined their common commitment to the objectives of an open international trading system in OECD's Convention which, inter alia, provides that "the OECD shall promote policies designed ... to contribute to the expansion of world trade on a multilateral, non-discriminatory basis in accordance with international obligations" and states that in order to attain these aims, the Members agree "to pursue their efforts to reduce or abolish obstacles to the exchange of goods and services and current payments and maintain and extend the liberalisation of capital movements". In subsequent years, OECD Ministers have periodically reaffirmed this commitment, including, in particular, in the 1980 Trade Pledge, and more recently in the Communiqué of the 1983 Council Meeting at Ministerial Level, where

"Ministers agreed that, within the framework of their overall economic co-operation, strengthening the open and multilateral trading system is essential to support the recovery and the transition to sustained growth. They therefore agreed that the economic recovery, as it proceeds, provides favourable conditions which Member countries should use, individually and collectively, to reverse protectionist trends and to relax and dismantle progressively trade restrictions and trade distorting domestic measures, particularly those introduced over the recent period of poor · growth performance. They invited the Secretary-General to propose appropriate follow-up procedures. At the same time, they agreed that the work programmes now under way in the

GATT and OECD to improve the trading system and its functioning should be actively pursued" (115).

231.   Despite this general commitment to liberal trade policies, there have been numerous qualifications over the years, and during the past ten years in particular, there has been an increased resort to unilateral measures, bilateral arrangements and market-sharing so that the share of managed trade in the total trade of the market economies has increased. This trend is the result of a number of factors. Governments have sought to shelter weak industries and companies from the full impact of foreign competition and technological change. In a period of severe and prolonged recession with high unemployment and low profits, protectionist pressures that are of a social and/or political nature are magnified, particularly in sectors where there is a marked gap between capacity and demand or significant international differences in competitiveness in terms of cost or the level of technology, leading to large and rapid rises in import penetration. Protectionist measures have frequently been justified to protect domestic industries in order to carry out necessary adjustments and reduce the social costs of the latter. Unfortunately, the experience with such "temporary" trade measures has been that the pressure for adjustment is often not sufficient and that other countries take similar or retaliatory measures, and thus the measures tend to perpetuate themselves and to spread. In this regard, the OECD Ministers in May 1983, after noting a continuation and even extension of protectionist trade and domestic support measures observed that

"Such measures have contributed to slowing down the movement of resources into activities with greater growth and job-creating potential. A return to sustained growth requires more positive adjustment policies, more reliance on market forces and more productive investment" (116).

232.   Competition policy has as its central economic goal the preservation and promotion of the competitive process, a process which encourages efficiency in the production and allocation of goods and services, and over time, through its effects on innovation and adjustment to technological change, a dynamic process of sustained economic growth. In conditions of effective competition, rivals have equal opportunities to compete for business on the basis and quality of their outputs, and resource deployment follows market success in meeting consumers' demands at the lowest possible cost. In contrast, when suppliers face significant market imperfections, for example, as a result of monopoly or monopsony power, entry barriers or trade distortions affect allocative efficiency, the interests of consumers will suffer and the potential for sustained economic growth will be impaired.

233.   While economic efficiency as a result of competitive market structures can be seen as a central objective of competition policy, pursuit of this objective has also been qualified to differing degrees in the competition policies of the various OECD Member countries by other socio-economic objectives. In particular, competition policies often are aimed at such objectives as the dispersion of excessive concentration of economic power and the reduction of barriers to entry, which can be seen as contributing to the objective of promoting the competitive process over the longer run. In many Member countries, in addition to criteria of economic efficiency, other factors may be taken into account in the enforcement of competition policies,

in particular where a broad public interest test is applied to the assessment of restrictive business practices.

234. Trade and competition policies share a common economic objective of attempting to remove barriers to the competitive process and thus ensuring that markets are open to all producers. They thus appear as reinforcing each other. Governments have found it necessary, however, to take into account other economic or social factors which have led them to interfere with the competitive market mechanism and the pressures for such interventions are greatest in periods of prolonged recession. Nevertheless, the Committee reaffirms its view that competition policy, which has a long-term role in ensuring that market structures are competitive, is particularly important during a period of recession and thus its overall effectiveness should be maintained (117).

b. Implications of trade policy measures for competition policy

235. The previous chapter of this report examined the ways in which certain restrictive business practices can have significant effects on the competitive functioning of international markets and are thus of concern to trade policy. It is similarly the case that trade policy measures that result in barriers to international trade can have important detrimental effects on domestic market structures by diminishing competition. For example, a trade policy that permits domestic firms to co-ordinate their exports in a cartel-like manner may weaken competition to the extent that export co-ordination also facilitates co-ordination of domestic sales. On the other hand, trade policy that permits a free flow of imports is likely to cause domestic markets to behave more competitively. Thus, trade policy can either significantly promote or substantially impede the economic goals of competition policy. With national economies being increasingly linked and interdependent, trade liberalisation policies maintain a climate conducive to the effective functioning of competition in national and international markets.

236. Policy-makers should undertake a systematic and comprehensive evaluation of the likely effects of a restrictive trade measure, including, inter alia, the impact on the structure of domestic competition, before having recourse to such measures. To base a decision on a narrow consideration of the concerns of a specific industry or sector risks putting in place measures which, on balance, act detrimentally to the national economy, as well as to the common international objective of maintaining an open multilateral trading system.

237. Although in the real world policy-makers cannot fully apply theoretical standards of welfare analysis, estimation ex ante of relevant elements of the likely costs and benefits of trade measures and what would have happened in the absence of such measures will often shed light upon the appropriateness of a policy decision. In reaching a final decision on a trade policy measure, policy-makers will be able to weigh the various interests affected according to their governments' policy objectives, subject to the country's international obligations, particularly under the GATT, which circumscribe the available policy options. Analysis of the short and longer term effects of measures on the national economy and international welfare can thus provide policy-makers with a framework for developing an appropriate operational approach to evaluating trade policy measures, an approach which includes examination of the competition policy considerations concerning such measures.

238.   The Committee suggests that such a framework can most conveniently be provided in the form of a comprehensive check-list of the different categories of the likely gains and losses to an economy from proposed trade measures, thus serving as a means of comparing and contrasting the merits of alternative measures that are being considered.   The list should definitely include an evaluation of the impact of a measure on the structure of domestic and international markets.   Clearly, such a framework for assessing the costs and benefits of specific trade measures would have to be adapted to the specifics of each case, taking account of the characteristics of the markets involved. The practicability of undertaking quantitative estimation of the various relevant costs and benefits will differ from case to case and, in the end, policy-makers would still have to base their decisions on an approximation of the real costs and benefits of the measure.   But by seeking to identify, to the extent feasible, the short and longer term impact of a trade measure on the economy, they would be in a position to improve the basis for their decisions.   Through such an approach, some trade measures would no doubt appear self-defeating vis-à-vis the country's own interests and disruptive of international cooperation, despite their apparent attractiveness on the basis of a less comprehensive assessment.

239.   From the perspective of competition policy, the likely effects of trade measures on the structure of relevant markets and on the competitive process together with the longer-term effects of trade measures on structural adaptation in the sector concerned are of particular importance to developing trade policies which are beneficial to the long-term or dynamic competitive performance of national economies and thus to the national interest.   It should be stressed that, in addition to undertaking an analysis of the net effect on the national economy of alternative trade measures, governments must necessarily be guided by their international obligations (in particular, under the GATT) and should take into account the implications of their actions with respect to the common international objective of maintaining an open trading system subject to international rules.   The above proposed rationalisation of the decision-making process in formulating national trade policies would heighten awareness of the domestic costs of protection and would tend to narrow the range of issues to be resolved at the international level.

240.   An example of how an economic assessment of trade policy measures can be made operational can be seen in a 1980 Staff Report of the Bureau of Economics of the United States Federal Trade Commission (118).   After presenting different methodological approaches to estimating the major domestic economic effects of various import restraint policy measures, the report presents the results of five case studies of U.S. import restraints applied in the sectors of citizen band transceivers, colour televisions, sugar, non-rubber footwear, and textiles.   The case studies generally sought to estimate the gain to producers in the protected sector (the increase in the producers' surplus), the costs to consumers through higher product prices and foregone consumption (the reduction in consumers' surplus), the efficiency or deadweight losses due to diverting resources into the protected sector from high productivity uses, the increases in tariff revenues, and the job creation benefits (either in terms of the costs per job created or, more appropriately, the adjustment costs saved measured by the earnings losses that would have occurred absent the import restraint).   In four of the five cases, the import restraints were found to have significantly greater costs than benefits.   In two cases (C.B. transceivers and non-rubber footwear) the costs were estimated at 25 or more times the benefits.   In contrast, in the fifth case, the OMA on

colour televisions was found to have imposed no measurable costs nor to have generated any measurable benefits. This latter case illustrates the importance of considering the foreign reaction to a trade measure, for the OMA reportedly led to a ninefold increase in colour TV imports from a country not initially subject to the agreement (South Korea), a doubling of TV imports from Taiwan, another country not originally covered, dramatic increases in imports of incomplete receivers, and higher foreign direct investment by Japanese-owned companies in facilities in the United States. Exchange rate changes also diminished the estimated effectiveness of this measure. Several of these case studies also sought to estimate some of the second order effects of the import restraints, for example, the effects of restraints on apparel imports on domestic textile mill workers (whereas the primary effects would be on workers in the domestic apparel industry), but for the most part such estimates were quite difficult to make.

241. To be really comprehensive, the above examples of the assessment of costs and benefits of trade measures would have to be supplemented to include an evaluation of the likely impact of a measure on the structure of the relevant market and on the competitive process in that market, thus adding an important dynamic element to the analysis. The appropriate questions to ask in this connection are the following: How would the restraints on imports affect competitive pressures on domestic firms to modernise their facilities, to increase productivity, to close down inefficient units and to become more competitive internationally? Would they provide the necessary time and profit incentive for undertaking new investments both by existing firms and new entrants, including possibly foreign investors ? As presumably in all cases the immediate impact would be a reduction in competition in the relevant markets, the key question is how the situation is likely to evolve over the longer term, including the anticipated duration of the measure. In other words, what is the likelihood that reduced competition from foreign suppliers resulting from the restrictive trade measures would lead to a situation where the competitive process in the domestic market becomes weakened and conditions become more conducive to collusive behaviour with respect to prices, supplies and restrictions on prospective new entrants? Also, consideration should be given to the possible reactions to a measure by the governments whose economies are affected by the measure and the likely economic impact of such countermeasures. Finally, the effects on producers in other sectors of the economy due to the higher prices they would have to pay for the products of the protected industry and their likely actions, which could include efforts to find substitutes for those products, are important.

242. Drawing together the considerations set out in the preceding paragraphs, the following indicative check-list is proposed as a guide for policy-makers, it being understood that it would have to be adapted to the particular situation in question and that governmental policy considerations will determine the weight given to each item:

   a) What are the expected direct economic gains to the domestic sector, industry or firm in question (technically, the increase in producers' surplus) and also what jobs are expected to be created or protected by the measure?

   b) What are the expected direct gains to government revenues (e.g. from tariffs, import licences, tax receipts) and/or increased government costs (e.g. export promotion, government subsidies, lost tax revenues)?

c) What are the direct costs to consumers due to the resulting higher prices they must pay for the product in question and the reduction in the level of consumption of the product (technically, the reduction in consumers' surplus)?

d) What is the likely impact of the measure on the structure of the relevant markets and the competitive process within those markets?

e) In the medium and longer term perspective, will the measure, on balance, encourage or permit structural adaptation of domestic industry leading over time to increased productivity and international competitiveness or will it further weaken and delay pressures for such adaptation ? What will be the expected effect on investment, by domestic firms in the affected sector, by potential new entrants, by foreign investors?

f) What would be the expected economic effects on other sectors of the economy, in particular, on firms purchasing products from, and selling products to, the industry in question?

g. How are other governments and foreign firms likely to react to the measure and what would be the expected effect on the economy of such actions? Is the measure a response to unfair practices in other countries?

h. What are the likely effects of the measure on other countries ? How can prejudice to trading partners be minimized?

243.   The following sections of this chapter focus, for illustrative purposes, on how the above analytical framework can be applied to non-tariff trade barriers, of which there is a large variety. Some may be transparent, as in the case of formal import quotas, others disguised or even hidden, as in the case of certain forms of subsidisation or administrative trade barriers. For the purpose of the present analysis, these various measures are organised into broad categories of non-tariff barriers that appear to be of particular relevance to competition and competition policy. These categories, discussed individually below, are export promotion policies (including export subsidies), import substitution policies and export controls. In considering non-tariff trade measures under each of these headings, particular attention is given to their implications for domestic market structure and the competitive process in those markets. As it will appear in this analysis, some specific measures defy easy categorisation and policies from different categories may be employed as a package or may be substituted for one another to serve the same underlying purpose. Before embarking on this analysis, it seems useful to describe briefly the institutional setting in which these policies are evolving.

2. NON-TARIFF TRADE MEASURES: THE INSTITUTIONAL SETTING

244.   The GATT covers a wide range of government trade policies, including most of the measures discussed in this report. While previous rounds of

multilateral trade negotiations conducted within GATT led to significant tariff reductions, as a result of the Tokyo Round of multilateral trade negotiations, major non-tariff barriers to trade were subjected to GATT discipline with the aim of reducing or eliminating them. In April 1979, five agreements were concluded dealing with subsidies and countervailing measures, technical barriers to trade, customs valuation, government procurement and import licensing procedures; and Committees were set up to oversee operation of each agreement. The GATT Secretariat has established and is periodically updating an inventory of non-tariff measures affecting industrial products. The inventory lists hundreds of non-tariff measures grouped into five main categories: (i) government participation in trade and restrictive practices; (ii) customs and administrative entry procedures; (iii) technical barriers to trade; (iv) specific limitations such as quantitative restrictions, import licensing, export restraints, measures to regulate domestic prices, etc.; and (v) charges on imports (prior deposits, border tax adjustments, discriminatory credit restrictions, etc.). In the context of monitoring the implementation of the Code on subsidies and countervailing measures, the GATT issues annual reports including lists of measures that have been notified. The GATT is now in the process of developing an inventory of non-tariff trade measures affecting agricultural products.

245. Concerning safeguard restrictions, Article XIX of the GATT provides for emergency protection against sudden increases in the imports of a particular product. Under Article XIX, emergency action can be taken "if, as a result of unforeseen developments ... any product is being imported into the territory in such increased quantities and under such conditions as to cause or threaten serious injury to domestic producers of like or directly competitive products..." To be compatible with Article XIX, an application for emergency purposes of import restrictions must be non-discriminatory and the importer must consult the exporting countries, governments of these being in a position to demand compensation for the loss sustained by them or the residents of their territories as a result of the quantitative restraint. Negotiations to develop an agreed set of rules for the use of safeguard measures are continuing. In the meantime, the GATT Secretariat is periodically preparing, as an internal document, an updated list of measures which were taken and notified under Article XIX as well as other measures which appear to serve the same purpose, including voluntary export restraints and orderly marketing arrangements.

246. At the meeting of the Contracting Parties held at Ministerial level (24th to 29th November, 1982) GATT member governments noted that import restrictions have increased and a growing proportion of them have been applied outside GATT disciplines, thus undermining the multilateral trading system. This phenomenon, which is generally characterised as "new protectionism", reflects the relative stagnation of member countries' economies since the mid-1970s. It raises serious prospects that trade arrangements will increasingly be adopted on a bilateral or regional basis with abandonment of adherence to most-favoured nation treatment, which is one of the fundamental principles of GATT. In addition, as pointed out earlier, new protectionism is often characterised by a combination of government action and private restrictive business practices and thus raises concern from both the trade and competition policy perspectives. An important factor in these developments has been the increased resort to "voluntary" export restraints, which were discussed in the preceding chapter. While Article XIX of GATT lays down basic conditions circumscribing the recourse by importing countries to emergency

protection, it remains an unresolved issue within GATT as to the extent to which (if any) "voluntary" export restraints, because of their ostensibly voluntary character, are subject to this discipline. The problems arising from this situation for both trade and competition policy will be discussed below. Another interesting feature in the growing trend toward bilaterialism in international trade is the growth of countertrade and barter arrangements not only in the North-South and East-West contexts, but also within the OECD area (119).

3. ANALYSIS OF NON-TARIFF MEASURES OF PARTICULAR RELEVANCE TO COMPETITION

247. The framework for analysing trade measures proposed above, in particular, the indicative check-list of questions to be considered, is based on two principles. First, policy-makers should base their decisions on comprehensive analyses of the expected net benefits to the national economy of the measure under consideration. In the case of restrictive trade measures, there are always domestic losers as well as gainers. In many cases, the aggregate losses caused by a particular protectionist trade policy will exceed the gains. But the gains are typically shared by the producers and employees in a particular industry, while the losses are distributed among an enormous number of taxpayers, consumers, and firms in other industries. Thus, even when the aggregate losses from a protectionist trade policy exceed the aggregate gains, the losses experienced by any individual will be much smaller than the gains to individual members of a subset of the population favoured by those measures. This situation creates the risk of a bias in favour of protectionist trade policies because the losses caused by these policies are less visible than the gains and may be underestimated as a result. Accordingly, the Committee recognises that the more difficult problem facing policy-makers in this area is not identifying the likely net benefits but rather the political problem of effectively giving weight to the interests of the losers from such policies. Second, policy-makers should seek to identify the longer-term implications for their nation of proposed policy measures. In the case of trade policy measures, this means, in particular, that due consideration should be given to the longer-term structural implications for competition, innovation, adaptation to technological change and sustained economic growth. This is valid even in the case of seemingly short-term or "temporary" trade measures, for experience has shown that such measures often become longlasting precisely because their structural effects are such that they reduce the effectiveness of the dynamic competitive forces that are necessary to bring about a correction through structural adjustment to the problems that led to enactment of the measures. On the other hand, some would contend that it is in the longer term that protective measures can have a positive effect on the international competitiveness of the protected sectors.

248. In the light of the analytical framework developed above, the following paragraphs discuss three broad categories of non-tariff trade measures: export promotion policies (including subsidies), import substitution policies and export controls. The primary economic impact of these measures is considered first, followed by their implication for market structures and the process of competition, and their secondary economic impacts, including the potential cost of retaliatory measures by foreign countries. This analysis necessarily has to be of a general, qualitative nature, for in individual cases the effects of a measure will depend heavily on the particular situation, including the structure of the markets involved, the macro-economic

setting, etc., but it does serve to illuminate the nature of the economic effects that policy-makers should take into consideration.

a) Export promotion policies

249.   Exports can be promoted by a wide variety of specific measures that generally amount to the government bearing a portion of the private cost of production for export. Export subsidies are direct grants, tax credits or indirect payments to producers for each unit of a product they export. Internal production subsidies can have the same effect as export subsidies, especially to the extent that they are selectively focused on export sectors or are linked to local content or to export performance. The specific form of the subsidy involved in export promotion policies is irrelevant to the economic analysis of their impact. The impact depends on the size of the financial grant ultimately received by exporters from the government for each additional unit they export.

250.   An important element of the economic cost of an export subsidy is the cost to the government of the effective financial grant, a cost which falls diffusely on those whose taxes are used to provide the grant payments. Usually, the subsidy will result in exports being priced below their costs, and this difference will constitute the per unit primary economic cost to the economy implementing the measure. In addition, other efficient export industries may suffer as a result of the price of resources being bid up by the less efficient subsidised industry. This argument is less important in situations of significant unemployment. Indeed, the justification for a subsidy is usually based on the additional employment of otherwise under-utilised resources, in particular labour, together with the view that increased competitiveness through structural adjustment of industry will eventually enable it to compete internationally without the subsidy.

251.   Accordingly, the basic rationale for the government (and hence taxpayers) bearing a portion of the private cost of production by an industry for export (made usually in the context of structural unemployment or general recession) is that such a measure would result in the additional employment of otherwise under-utilised resources (labour, capital). Such resources earn more in the stimlulated sector than their opportunity cost, that is, what they could earn elsewhere in the economy; and the difference between earnings from the stimulated production and the return the resources could otherwise earn is the principal economic benefit to the country to be compared with the costs of the measure. In situations where there is effective competition in the markets, there should be no significant, persistent differences between earnings and opportunity costs. However, barriers to entry and resource immobility are common in the real world, and thus policy-makers are often faced with differences between earnings and opportunity costs and under-employment of resources. In many such cases, however, the barriers reflect deficiencies in the competitive process in the markets concerned (e.g. excessive concentration, barriers to entry) with regard to which a preferable policy response would be to seek to reduce those barriers through enhanced competition from foreign or domestic sources or to reduce impediments to the mobility of resources.

252.   Nevertheless, there can be situations of persistent structural rigidities and imperfections in markets which lead to differences between earnings and opportunity costs that reflect long-term underproduction and

structural unemployment and thereby significant economic and social costs to a nation. The economic gains from increased employment of otherwise under-utilised resources may significantly mitigate or even outweigh the primary economic costs of subsidies in such cases. In such cases, however, it would be preferable if incentive policies were applied to production generally and not just to production for export, as general production subsidies in most cases appear to be less harmful to the interests of trading partners than measures specifically aimed at export performance. General production incentives could be used, for instance, as a transitory measure to provide an industry with time to carry out the necessarily longer-term structural adjustments necessary to permit it to become internationally competitive and to mitigate the economic and social costs of that transition. But such a policy would make economic sense from a national point of view only in situations where there is a good prospect that this adjustment is feasible and will occur despite the reduction in competitive pressures. For this reason, subsidies under a time limit should be in proportion to the recipients own contribution, should have a clear objective, and their effects over time should be closely monitored. Such measures should be flanked by efforts by competition authorities to reduce to the extent feasible barriers to entry and other imperfections in the competitive process in the domestic markets concerned.

253. From the international perspective, it should be recognised that the economic costs of subsidised exports are in many respects borne by the more efficient producers of other countries. The future viability of the affected industry of these countries can be seriously undermined, leading to misallocation of resources and imbalances in the production and trade of goods. From the viewpoint of the self-interest of the country utilising such measures, it should be recognised that a likely result will be strong pressures for counter measures in the countries most adversely affected. While consumers of the subsidised exports in other countries will receive an economic gain which in aggregate terms may be significant, this gain will be distributed among an enormous number of consumers while the costs will be concentrated on a specific industry and political pressures from that industry for retaliation are often likely to prevail. Thus, it is not surprising that the Trade Committee has found that the use of export subsidies is increasingly being justified as a defensive action and that such measures have led to increased international frictions. The results can be an international race in which each government attempts to provide larger export subsidies to its national producers than those provided to their competitors. At each step of the race, the nation that is behind may be driven to increase its export subsidy, only to find that after retaliation it is once again behind. The nation that initiated the race with a subsidy intended to raise domestic production may find itself the loser of the race with diminished production instead. Or the initiating nation may ultimately prevail in the race but find that the expansion in domestic production is not worth the large amount of the subsidy necessary to win. The provisions of the GATT which are designed to avoid such a counter-productive race in subsidies are described below, including the measures agreed to at the Tokyo Round which clarify the acceptable procedures for applying countervailing duties to offset subsidies on imports.

254. In general, the costs of these policies will depend on the specific measures taken by foreign governments in response to export promotion. Consider first the simple case where only two countries are involved. A

countervailing duty exactly equal to an export subsidy eliminates the distortion caused by the subsidy. Domestic production of the exported goods returns to the pre-subsidy level because the subsidy and duty offset each other, restoring the private costs of export production to their original level. A subsidy and equal countervailing duty, therefore, have no impact on the national economy other than the social costs caused by the taxes levied to pay for the subsidy. There is a transfer from the subsidising country to the country collecting the duty, however, because the home country effectively pays the export subsidy to the foreign government. The home country is therefore in a worse situation with a subsidy and countervailing duty than with no subsidy at all. Typically, however, more than two countries are involved and the analysis of the likely net effect of the measure and resulting countermeasures is much more complex. Of particular concern are cases where subsidised exports displace exports from efficient producers in third markets, for in such cases, it is usually not possible for these efficient producers to secure the imposition of countervailing duties and their longer term viability may thus be affected.

b) Import substitution policies

255.   Import substitution policies protect home producers by putting foreign producers at a disadvantage in home markets. For the sake of analysis, these policies can be classified into two categories, depending on their direct economic effect: tariff-like policies (TLPs) that increase the price of imported goods and quantitative restrictions that directly limit import quantities. However, as will be discussed below, several protectionist measures defy this categorisation and have both price and quantitative effects.

i) Tariff-like policies

256.   TLPs are measures that, like tariffs, directly increase the price of imported goods. However, unlike tariffs, the price increase is not collected as tax revenue for the home government. Instead, they may permit the price increase to accrue to the importer or they may force up the price of imports by increasing the costs that the importer must bear.

257.   Examples of TLPs are minimum price restrictions that force foreign producers to sell their goods at a higher price than they would otherwise; improper use of anti-dumping actions as pressure for price increases; administrative entry procedures designed to impose costs on imports that must be recovered through higher prices; and, the improper use of product standards as trade barriers.

258.   The primary economic cost to a nation from imposing a tariff-like measure is the increased costs borne by consumers due to the resulting higher prices, including:

a) The higher costs of the imports of the product they continue to buy;

b) The differential between the price of the additional domestic production that imposition of the measure induces consumers to purchase and the price at which imports of the products would have been available in the absence of the measure, and;

c) The loss in consumer welfare associated with lower consumption (domestic production plus imports) of the product whose price is higher as a result of the tariff-like measure.

Domestic prices rise as a result of the TLP either because costs are driven up by production increases to accommodate diverted demand or because diminished import competition enables additional monopoly power to be exercised. A portion of the increased payments by consumers to domestic producers represents a transfer which nets out, from the overall national perspective, but the remainder represents a net "deadweight" or efficiency loss to the importing country, reflecting the domestic production of a product which could be obtained at a lower cost through importation.

259.   In essence, these primary economic costs arise because TLPS distort competition by disadvantaging imports so that higher-cost domestic goods inefficiently displace lower-cost foreign goods. In addition, efficient exporters may be injured because the prices of resources are bid up by the protected, inefficient sector. Against these costs are the gains to domestic resources, that is, to capital and labour in the protected industry and to suppliers to that industry. Similar to the case for export promotion policies, there may be situations where the expected gains from the stimulation of domestic production of under-produced goods or the stimulated utilisation of under-employed resources appear to outweigh the above costs, particularly where measures are used on a temporary basis with a view to easing the transitional costs of structural adjustment in the industry. In such cases careful attention should be paid to the factors which led to under-utilisation of resources and the need for structural adjustment. Imposing TLPs will reduce the competitive stimulus to adjust that is provided by imports, the extent of this reduction depending on the effective rate of tariff protection, and thus can be counterproductive from a longer-term perspective. Such measures can have significant detrimental effects on both competition and trade, in particular, in the case of an industry where the domestic market is relatively concentrated with high barriers to entry. The introduction of trade barriers would sharply reduce competition in that market. In such cases a more effective approach would be one directed at reducing the barriers to efficient utilisation of resources in that market and improving the domestic competitive process.

260.   As TLPs disadvantage imports from more efficient producers in other countries, there will be pressures on the governments of those countries to take defensive counter-measures, even though, in some cases, the price increases may accrue to those producers. The likelihood of retaliation will vary, depending not only on the level of protection provided by the TLP but also its particular form and the extent to which the measure falls under the international rules of GATT and/or national trade legislation. The possibility that the perceived gains from the measure could be quickly wiped out by counter-measures and that a competitive raising of trade barriers could develop should be evaluated.

ii) Quantitative restrictions on imports

261.   Quantitative restrictions place an upper limit on the quantity of foreign goods that can be imported. Quotas, VERs and OMAS clearly fall into this category. In addition, administrative entry procedures may impede the physical flow of imports and effectively cap the quantity of goods that can be

imported. Further, restrictive government procurement policies may limit purchases of foreign goods.

262. Some of the primary effects of quantitative restrictions are identical to those of TLPs. By decreasing the supply of imports, quantitative restrictions drive up their price in the home market and, in this regard, have all the negative primary economic effects of a TLP. And, at the same time, the same secondary impacts are relevant as in the case of TLPS. There is a basic difference, however, in that the margin between the resulting price of imports to consumers and the (lower) "world price" accrues to holders of the rights to import (unless it is taxed away by the government through fees for entitlements to import). As compared to tariffs, under quantitative restrictions no revenue accrues to the government taking the measure. The size of the margin gained by importers will depend, inter alia, on the demand for imports, price flexibility and the structure of the market affected.

263. Analysis of the competitive structure of the market is particularly important in the case of quantitative restrictions. When the participants in a domestic industry have market power, TLPs and quantitative restrictions can lead to quite different results. Quantitative restrictions can reduce the competitiveness of markets more than TLPs in cases where foreign producers exert an important competitive influence on the conduct of domestic producers. Consider first the case where there is a single domestic producer but that producer cannot charge a monopoly price because of foreign competition. That is, although the home producer controls domestic production, it cannot charge home consumers more than the prevailing price of competitive foreign goods. A TLP enables that domestic producer to raise its price but only by the amount by which the TLP raises the foreign price. If the domestic producer tried to raise its price even more, consumers would stop buying its goods and would instead buy more competitive foreign products at the post TLP price. A quantitative restriction would initially enable a single domestic producer to raise its price to the same level as it could under an otherwise equivalent TLP. But once imports reach the maximum permitted under the quantitative restriction, foreign competition no longer constrains the conduct of the domestic producer. More generally, if the domestic industry is competitive, a tariff and quota which result in the same volume of imports will have the same domestic price effect. If, however, the members of the domestic industry (excluding imports) have market power, then a quota will result in a higher domestic price than would a tariff which allows the same level of imports.

264. An additional possible impact of quantitative restrictions on consumers is that they affect the product quality chosen by importers. If the restriction applies to the number of physical units imported, and if importers' profits are approximately proportional to the value of sales, then importers have incentives to substitute higher quality units for what they would otherwise choose to sell. The rationale is that higher quality units would command higher prices, so that the value of sales and of profits would be greater, while the quantity imported would still meet the restriction. This effect is an added competitive distortion, inasmuch as more of the lower quality units would be sold absent the quantitative restriction. In such a case, the lower quality units offer consumers more utility for the price than do the higher quality units, and the substitution of the latter for the former results in further costs to consumers.

265.   In view of their absolute nature, their transparency and their treatment under the GATT, outright import quotas are very likely to lead to offsetting retaliatory action by affected countries.   Less transparent quantitative restrictions such as administrative entry procedures, being more difficult to evaluate, run somewhat lesser risks of leading to counter-measures.   Nevertheless, import quotas do constitute a significant share of the overall trade restrictions currently in place.   Unlike the quantitative restrictions targeted at particular foreign producers (usually the most efficient) discussed below, import quotas are generally non-discriminatory in application among importers and it is generally the least efficient importers which bear the greatest share of the resulting reduction in imports.

266.   Voluntary export restraints (VERs) and Orderly Marketing Agreements (OMAs) are forms of quantitative trade restrictions which, although often different from the perspective of the degree of government involvement in their arrangement and implementation and their status under competition laws as discussed in Chapter I, have identical economic effects and thus are treated together in the following paragraphs.   As with other quantitative restrictions, VERs and OMAs impact on consumption, prices, production, and employment in the importing country and upon profits, production and employment in the exporting country.   In addition, VERs and OMAs may affect the state of competition in both the export and import markets, facilitating interfirm cooperation in the former and reducing competitive pressures in the latter.   VERs and OMAs can also be expected to affect other exporters not covered by the arrangement and they may also impact on suppliers of raw materials to exporting countries.   Although they may create distortions identical to other quantitative restrictions, important differences can emerge with regard to the distributional consequences of VERs and OMAS, in part because of their typically bilateral nature.

267.   At the outset, it is important to realize the difficult measurement problems that arise in assessing the effects of VERs and OMAs.   Generally, the measure of a quantitative restriction is the amount by which it reduces imports of a particular good.   This can be difficult to measure with VERs and OMAs, because they rarely cover all foreign producers and exporters of a particular good.   As a result, the amount by which a country or producer entering into a VER or OMA decides to reduce exports to the home country may exceed the amount by which home imports of that good actually decline.   As the price of the good rises in response to the initial reduction in imports caused by the VER or OMA, producers not bound by the VER or OMA will increase their exports to the home country.   The increase in imports from these producers partially offsets the reduction in imports from producers who are bound by the arrangment.   For a realistic comparison with other quantitative restrictions, the measure of a VER or OMA is the amount by which it reduces the total quantity of imports from all producers and not simply the amount by which it reduces imports from producers covered by the arrangment.   Thus, the effects depend upon the cost differences among all the actual or potential exporters into the market.

268.   At a first step, VERs and OMAs, like other quantitative import restrictions, reduce trade levels.   This can be expected, because a VER or OMA will set limits on imports below the quantity that would be imported under unrestricted conditions.   The next effect is upon domestic prices, production and consumption.   When a trade restriction reduces the quantity of goods that

can be imported, domestic consumers are likely to pay a higher price for these goods. This increase in the price of foreign goods enables domestic producers to charge a higher price for their products and leads to an increase in domestic production. And because the price of imports and domestically produced goods is higher, overall domestic consumption declines. To some extent, increases in imports from countries not covered by a VER or OMA could offset some of these effects on domestic consumption and production. However, this is likely only to lead the importing country to seek to conclude VERs or OMAs with these other major exporting countries and foreign firms that produce the particular product, thereby expanding the amount of trade that is restricted (120).

269.   While import limitation measures can generally be expected to raise domestic prices, the nature of this effect can depend on the specific terms of a VER or OMA. First, the price effect would be expected to be larger, the greater the restraint on import volumes. Moreover, where a VER or OMA extends only to a particular product, exporters subject to the arrangment may exercise considerable leeway to shift to more expensive and more profitable models within the limits set, significantly raising prices in the domestic market (121).   In some instances, import limitation agreements may specifically set prices for imports, e.g. by setting a floor price for the products.

270.   Although a VER or OMA may tend to increase domestic production of a good and, indeed, this is the usual objective, its overall effect on employment and production may differ in the short and long term.   In the exporting country, the limit placed on production can exercise a harmful effect on workers either through job reductions or salary losses.   In the importing country, a VER or OMA could initially lead to an increase in employment in the protected industry. However, this increase in employment may not always correspond to increased production by domestic firms or a higher return to domestic shareholders. In some instances, a VER or OMA might encourage and foster moves by exporting firms to establish production units in their import markets. These moves can have favourable effects on taxes, employment, inward investment and balance-of-payments in the importing country.   But the qualitative effect of such moves on production and employment can depend on the type of products and extent of production transferred. For example, where only assembly operations are shifted to the importing market subject to a VER or OMA, the jobs created will be relatively unskilled and may not promote development of sophisticated domestic production which is internationally competitive.

271.   Different measures that reduce the quantity of goods imported by an identical amount will create identical distortions, i.e. they will cause identical increases in domestic production and reductions in imports and overall consumption. But the distributional consequences will vary according to the type of quantitative restriction that is used. Under tariffs, the home country retains the revenue generated by the import restriction through increases in domestic prices. This can also be the case where the importing country establishes quotas and either issues import licences to domestic importers or sells the licences to the highest bidder. Under a VER or OMA, however, the foreign producers retain any additional revenue due to the price increase resulting from the import restriction. Therefore from the standpoint of the exporting producers, a VER or OMA may have advantages as compared to other restrictive trade measures.

272.   The effect of VERs and OMAs may extend to other countries not party to the arrangment. Other countries into which the products are imported may request similar protection, particularly if the exporting country, after agreeing to a VER or OMA, increases shipments to these other markets. Other exporting countries not covered by the VER or OMA may benefit through increased sales to the importing country covered by the arrangment but may encounter increased competition from the exporting country which is partner to the arrangment in other markets. Also, an important "ripple effect" may be felt by suppliers of raw materials to the exporting country subject to a limitation arrangment. Countries that supply these materials for the product manufactured by the exporting country may encounter a contraction in production and employment as a result of limitation arrangments applied to customers for their resources.

273.   The use of VERs and OMAs will also be expected to impact on competition in the importing and exporting markets. Their effect can vary considerably depending on the terms of the agreement and the manner in which it is implemented. In the import market, a VER or OMA will reduce competitive pressures by limiting the presence of foreign producers. This reduction in what presumably had been strong competitive forces supplied by efficient foreign suppliers is likely to preserve some costly and inefficient domestic producers and can lessen incentives for technological development and innovation. As is noted in the discussion above on import quotas, a quantitative restriction on imports can sharply reduce competitiveness in concentrated and monopolistic markets to a greater extent than other trade restricting measures.

274.   The particular nature of VERs and OMAs presents certain risks to competition in addition to those stemming from quantitative restrictions in general. These arrangements are different from export cartels in that they are not formed to exploit market power but rather to avoid the imposition by the importing country of other trade restrictions. Nevertheless, since the total quota of exports under a VER or OMA is likely to be allocated among several producers, they can lead to and facilitate collusion on other matters among producers and thereby weaken competitive forces in both markets. In addition, an OMA or VER may prevent other firms in the exporting country from entering the market of the importing country, as this may be prohibited under the VER or OMA. Accordingly, competition authorities should consider carefully the competition policy implications of such arrangements and their implementation.

275.   A number of studies on the effects of OMAs, VERs or similar arrangements have been carried out in the United States concerning, in particular, the automobile and colour TV industries. While results of these studies cannot be generalised, the analysis carried out indicates that in the cases studied, VERs and OMAs often do not achieve their stated objectives, and even where they do, their economic costs may be high.

276.   To take one example, the 1979 Japanese automobile VER with the US for three years limiting shipments to 1.68 million cars annually appears to have been costly to the US consumer and of only rather limited value to the US automobile industry. In a brief before the International Trade Commission (ITC), the US Federal Trade Commission concluded that the proposed VER would be an inefficient way to increase employment, would increase the market power of domestic manufacturers in the small car market, would likely be

anti-competitive and could cost consumers between $3 to $5 billion annually (122). The VER went into effect in April 1981. The Japanese share of the market, which was then contracting, actually increased, and it has been estimated that the Japanese sold only 300,000 fewer cars than they would have in the absence of a VER. At the same time, to increase their revenues for the same number of imports, the Japanese producers shipped a higher percentage of luxury cars and expensive models. As a result, sales of more expensive models increased and those of small cars declined. The average list price of Japanese cars rose 8 per cent in the first two years of the agreement, as compared to the two previous years during which the inflation-adjusted price dropped 3 per cent (123). At the same time, the prices of American models rose sharply from 1979 to 1983. While median family income rose 21 per cent, prices of popular US model cars increased by 37 per cent to 59 per cent in the same period. In 1983, the purchase of a new car required an average 36.6 weeks of salary contrasted with 31.2 weeks in 1979 (124). Although some of the increases are undoubtedly the result of general inflationary pressures during this period, the VER does seem to have contributed to these higher car prices. The Japanese Government decided, as a temporary measure, to continue the VER in 1984.

277. Another study of the effects of OMAs involved those entered into by the US with countries producing colour televisions, as noted above in paragraph 15. In 1976, after selling 2.5 million sets in the US, Japan agreed to limit its imports to 1.56 million units annually for three years. Thereafter, imports surged from Taiwan and Korea, and they entered into an OMA in 1980. One study of these two agreements noted that foreign companies evaded them by producing partially completed televisions in the US, exporting them abroad for major components and additional assembly, and then reimporting them for final assembly. Reimported TVs were not covered by the OMA, and the 5 per cent tariff was levied only on the value added. Although US output of colour televisions rose to 10.7 million in 1980 from 7 million in 1977, nearly 3 million of those sets were largely foreign-made. The US work force producing colour TVs continued to decline - to 24,859 in 1980 from 29,104 in 1977 (125). The earlier cited study by the Bureau of Economics of the US Federal Trade Commission concludes similarly that the above factors together with the appreciation of the yen made this OMA virtually ineffectual. On the other hand, the costs to consumers and the inefficiency costs to the US economy were also found to be marginal (126).

278. A final example are the US OMAs on non-rubber footwear negotiated with South Korea and Taiwan in mid-1977. In the first year, the OMAs were calculated to have resulted in economic losses to the US economy over a four-year period of some $545 million, most of which was due to monopoly profits or scarcity rents created by the OMA and retained by South Korea and Taiwan. The major benefits were the avoidance of earnings losses by displaced workers. These employment gains were estimated at $8 million, implying net losses to the US economy of $537 million (127).

c) Export controls

279. Export controls can take the form of taxes on exports, industry-wide quantity restrictions, or quantity restrictions that apply separately to each major exporter(128). They sometimes are adopted in response to restrictions maintained in import markets. Where export controls are adopted only to implement a VER or OMA, they do not curtail output beyond the effect of that

arrangement, but they may suppress competition for shares of the exports permitted by the VER and thereby elevate the prices faced by the importing nation. Outside the context of VERs and OMAs, export controls tend to distort competition by both elevating price and curtailing production.

280.   Like an export tax, an export monopoly or an export cartel created to exert market power in international markets (129) raises the price received by the home country for the exported good by reducing the quantity of goods exported. Again, an export monopoly or cartel can only increase the price of a good if the exporting nation has the monopoly power in the relevant markets to restrict output. The major difference between an export tax and an export monopoly or cartel is that a monopoly or cartel enables the exporters to keep the revenue that would be collected by the government under an export tax. The national and international economic effects of an export tax and an export monopoly or cartel are basically the same. The net primary economic impact on a country which receives a higher price for its exports will be positive. However, the price increase will come at the expense of a reduction in the consumption of more competitively priced goods. While the costs to other countries will not usually be concentrated in a specific sector, governments may well decide to retaliate.

281.   The competition policy implications of such measures should be carefully weighed. Even if there is an apparent gain to the producing country, diminished world competition may lead to weakened home competition with social costs resulting in a net loss for the national economy. Higher prices abroad tend to pull domestic prices up with them, even if domestic producers coordinate only their foreign activities. Further, of particular concern to competition policy officials is that experience has shown it is difficult for domestic authorities to stop the domestic application of cartel mechanisms supposedly designed only for foreign use. Exchange of information, market sharing, compensation, and price coordination applied to foreign operations may spill over to domestic operations as well, diminishing domestic competition and harming domestic consumers, as well as the longer term ability of the industry in question to maintain its international competitiveness.

d) Interchangeability of trade barriers

282.   Various trade barriers can be used in conjunction with one another and as partial substitutes for one another. However, different trade policies that afford the same degree of protection to domestic producers can have quite different economic and competitive effects on the nation adopting the policy and on its trading partners.

283.   Among import substitution policies, tariffs are likely to result, in the absence of retaliation by other countries, in the greatest net economic benefit for the perpetrating nation. Under a tariff, the home government keeps the extra money paid by consumers for imports, while under most other import substitution policies this money is transferred to foreign producers or wastefully defrays artificial costs imposed on imports. This money is also captured by the home government under a quota system in which import licences are sold to foreign suppliers. However, as compared to quantitative restrictions of any kind, tariffs, unless set at a prohibitive level, insulate domestic producers less from potential foreign competition, and thus have a less detrimental effect upon domestic market structure, the effectiveness of

the competitive process and hence the long run capacity of the country for
sustained economic growth.

284. As tariff protection and import quotas have been subjected to GATT
rules and surveillance, it is noteworthy that there has been increased resort
to non-tariff import substitution policies, éspecially to voluntary export
restraints (VERs) and orderly marketing arrangements (OMAs), as discussed in
detail in Chapter I. The relative popularity of VERs and OMAs can be
explained by the fact that, compared to other techniques such as export
subsidisation or the import substitution measures described above, they offer
more flexible and, from the point of view of the countries concerned, less
objectionable means for achieving the same aim: that is, managing
international trade in particular products and within particular
regions (130). While export subsidies may provide diffuse benefits to foreign
consumers, they may injure foreign rivals and tend to lead to self-defeating
retaliation. Administrative entry procedures and artificial product standards
generate costs that absorb consumers' overpayments. On the other hand, VERs
and OMAs permit exporters to capture a significant portion of the price
increases borne by consumers. Thus, exporters can at least partially
compensate for the revenue lost from the quantity reduction. In comparison
with export cartels, which are difficult to sustain, because each member has
incentives to increase output and undercut the cartel price, the government in
the exporting country is likely to play a direct role in the case of OMAs
(more subtle but still usually significant, in the case of VERs), in
disciplining the arrangement through forbidding or discouraging price cuts and
production increases.

285. Hence, where international agreements discourage tariffs and
unilaterally impose quotas but permit or have an uncertain application to the
implementation of other restrictive policies, it is predictable that nations
seeking to protect their producers will turn to measures like VERs, OMAs, and
minimum price restrictions that benefit exporters and obtain (admittedly
grudgingly) the assent of exporting nations. Nevertheless, such restrictive
measures are not consistent with the principles of an open international
trading system embodied in GATT; and, as has been described at length above,
from an economic standpoint, they have similar primary and secondary economic
effects as the more traditional trade restrictions and non-tariff barriers.

C. SPECIFIC LAWS ADDRESSING INJURIOUS OR
UNFAIR TRADING PRACTICES

1. INTRODUCTION

286. Although competition law encompasses and prohibits a wide range of
anticompetitive commercial practices, in the past several decades, a separate
body of law has emerged dealing specifically with unfair practices in
international trade. While some countries had adopted unfair trade laws at
the turn of the century, the establishment of the GATT and subsequent
negotiations in the Kennedy and Tokyo Rounds led to international agreements
on such practices as dumping, countervailing duties and subsidies in the
1960's and 1970's, which have been incorporated in the national legislation of
many OECD countries. Despite apparent similarities in the goals of

competition and trade laws, there are significant differences in the way specific practices are addressed. These differences reflect some of the tensions described in the preceding section between the goals of competition policy and the effects of various trade-distorting measures. It is therefore important for the purpose of the present report to determine how competition policy and laws relating to unfair trade practices interrelate and, where conflicts exist, how these conflicts can be minimised.

287.   The following section begins with a brief summary of the coverage of unfair trade practices under the GATT agreements and the manner in which these provisions have been implemented under national legislations. This is followed by a description of enforcement actions and cases brought under laws relating to unfair trade practices. Finally, the section concludes by comparing and contrasting the general approaches of competition policy and laws relating to unfair trade practices. As it will appear from this discussion, there is a need for giving greater weight for competition policy considerations in the enforcement of these laws.

2. COVERAGE UNDER THE GATT OF UNFAIR TRADE PRACTICES

a) Subsidies and countervailing duties

288.   The main sections of the GATT relevant to these practices are Article VI (countervailing duties, antidumping), Article XVI (subsidies) and Article XXIII (dispute resolution), as well as implementing agreements reached during the Kennedy and Tokyo Rounds of negotiations.

289.   Subsidies are one of the most frequently used and controversial instruments of government policy (131). A principal concern under the GATT has been to identify subsidies granted by governments which, indirectly or directly, have the effect of distorting world trade and depriving other countries of legitimate trade opportunities. Article XVI of the GATT recognises that export subsidies may cause injury. Consequently, it provides:

i) That GATT member governments must avoid granting export subsidies on primary products which would result in them obtaining a more than equitable share of world exports in these products; and

ii) That, in the case of non-primary products, they shall not grant, either directly or indirectly, any form of subsidy which would lower export prices below prices in domestic markets.

Finally, Article XVI requires that a country notify any subsidy "which operates directly or indirectly to increase exports of any product from or to reduce imports of any product into its territory" (132).

290.   Whereas the term "subsidy" is not defined in the GATT, the Contracting Parties agreed in 1960 on a definition of export subsidies prohibited under Article XVI. This agreement provided an illustrative list of eight practices considered to be export subsidies.

291.   During the Tokyo Round, the issue of subsidies and countervailing duties was one of the main items on the agenda (133). The Tokyo Round made considerable progress on many of these issues. The Agreement on Subsidies and

Countervailing Duties ("Subsidies Code") expanded and modernized the list of prohibited export subsidies, endorsed a procedure for settling disputes which encompasses competition for third country markets, transferred minerals from the primary to the non-primary product category, and elicited a commitment to restrain the use of export subsidies on the remaining primary products and for production to the extent that they cause serious prejudice to the interests of other signatories. The criterion of "material injury" to domestic industry was recognised by all participants as a precondition to the assessment of countervailing duties under Article VI.

292.   Countervailing duties are levies on imported goods permitted under Article VI to offset any government subsidy on the "manufacture, production or export of any merchandise" (134)   These duties are only imposed against subsidised imports (as compared to general import duties) and, most importantly, the decision whether to countervail is made entirely by the importing country according to its own procedures (135).

293.   According to Article VI of the GATT, no countervailing duty shall be levied on any product in excess of an amount equal to the estimated bounty or subsidy determined to have been granted, directly or indirectly, upon the manufacture, production or export of any merchandise. In addition, a number of measures were agreed to at the Tokyo Round to clarify the countervail procedures. The right to impose a countervailing duty requires that the subsidy whose effects it should offset is such as to cause, or threaten, material injury to an established domestic industry, or is such as to retard materially the establishment of a domestic industry. Under the Tokyo Agreement, signatories are required to ensure that the imposition of countervailing duties is in accordance with the provisions of Article VI of GATT (i.e. includes a material injury test). The definition of material injury contained in this Article provides that the determination of injury should be based on an objective examination of both:

-- The volume of subsidized imports and their effect on prices in the domestic market for like products, and;

-- The consequent impact of these imports on domestic producers of such products.

According to the Agreement there has to be a causal link between the subsidized imports and the material injury to domestic industry. In addition, the Agreement provides:

i) Detailed provisions on procedures for countervailing investigations; ii) An obligation to consult with the exporting country before the opening of a countervail investigation; iii) that proceedings may be suspended or terminated if voluntary undertakings are accepted; and iv) Rules on provisional and retroactive application of countervailing duties (136).

b) Anti-dumping measures

294.   The term "dumping" refers to sales of goods in export markets at prices lower than the comparable sale price of like goods in the domestic market of the exporter. To implement Article VI of the GATT, which addresses this practice, the Kennedy Round negotiations led to an agreed Code on

Anti-Dumping. Agreement was reached with respect to the determination of injury and the establishment of a dispute settlement mechanism. The test of injury was revised to be consistent with the agreement reached on subsidies and countervailing duties, and specifies that both the volume of dumped exports and their effect on prices in domestic markets be considered in determining injury. An illustrative list of factors to consider in measuring the impact of dumping was made consistent with that for subsidies, as is the provision requiring that the injury alleged be the result of the dumping and not due to other economic factors (137). A footnote to the code provides that the injury to domestic industry be "material". In addition, the new Code strengthened the resolution procedures for Dumping disputes and provided for a conciliation role through a committee formed for that purpose.

295. Under Article VI and the implementing agreements, an anti-dumping case proceeds along the following lines. First, there is a determination by the importing country of whether dumping has taken place. This involves a comparison of the price in the foreign market with the comparable price charged for "like products" in the home market of the exporter. Where there are no comparable sales in the domestic market of the exporter, procedures exist for determination of a "constructed" price. The importing country then evaluates whether the dumped imports have caused material injury to domestic producers. The examination of the impact of the imports on the industry concerned includes an evaluation of all relevant economic factors and indices having a bearing on the state of the industry such as actual and potential decline in output, sales, market share, profits, productivity, return on investments or utilization of capacity, factors affecting domestic prices, actual and potential negative effects on cash flow, inventories, employment, wages, growth, ability to raise capital or investments. This list is not exhaustive, nor can one or several of these factors necessarily be decisive.

296. In addition, causality must be established, i.e. it must be shown that dumping and not other economic factors is the cause of substantial injury to domestic industry. During the investigation, provisions exist for requiring the exporter to post a duty or security bond in the amount of the anti-dumping duty provisionally estimated, pending final resolution of the case. Proceedings may be suspended or terminated upon receipt of undertakings by the exporter to raise its prices or cease exports. Ultimately, upon receipt of the facts and after all interested parties have had a full opportunity to defend their interests, the authorities of the importing country or customs territory exercise sole responsibility to determine whether anti-dumping duties should be levied and in what amount, although not to exceed the margin of dumping. Finally, the anti-dumping duty shall remain in force only so long as, and to the extent necessary, to counteract the dumping which is causing the injury to domestic industry.

297. The existence of the GATT Committees on Subsidies and Countervailing Duties and Anti-Dumping Practices serves as a restraint on the potential misuse of antidumping laws. Meetings of these Committees are held at frequent intervals and they provide an opportunity for representatives of signatory countries to express views on the operation of the accords and concerns about the provisions and applications of the laws of other signatories. Although delegates may not always be capable or willing to meet challenges posed to their country's laws in this context, the prospect that they may be called upon to do so operates as a restraining influence.

298.   As can be seen, there are a great many similarities in anti-dumping and countervailing procedures under the GATT, and the implementing agreements have been drafted and modified so as to assure a consistent approach.   Each of these measures seeks to provide a remedy against unfair, as opposed to fair, trade practices and concentrates on exports that are priced at a level which is deemed to be too low and which are prejudicial to domestic industry.   The procedures to investigate these practices are roughly the same, as are the tests to measure whether the requisite injury and causality are present.

299.   The main difference is that anti-dumping laws focus on the activities of the foreign exporters themselves whereas countervailing duties laws are concerned with the subsidizing behaviour of governments in the countries in which the foreign exporters reside.   Insofar as the latter involves policies and government action of another country, it is not surprising that anti-dumping actions have been much more frequent than countervail investigations.   It is also apparent that the same course of conduct can give rise to allegations of both dumping and subsidisation and thus there can be considerable overlap in the enforcement of laws relating to unfair trade practices.

3. NATIONAL LEGISLATION

300.   The development and enactment of laws relating to unfair trade practices in the OECD countries generally follows two patterns.   Some countries have not enacted their own legislation, but instead, as signatories to the GATT, rely directly on its provisions to regulate their international trade.   Other countries and the EEC have enacted specific laws or regulations that follow the GATT provisions.   The situation is somewhat different in the United States.   The U.S. enacted extensive trade laws prior to the GATT, some of which provided precedents for the GATT provisions.   These laws have subsequently been modified and amended to reflect GATT principles.   In addition, U.S. laws provide their trade authorities with broad authority to prohibit "unfair trade practices" in international commerce, extending to practices beyond those covered in the GATT.   Of course, it must be remembered that the competition laws in most Member countries permit competition authorities to regulate restrictive practices in international trade where the requisite jurisdiction exists.   And, as discussed infra, the line between a restrictive business practice and an unfair trade practice can be a fine one.

301.   In the European Community, the Treaty and Regulations provide a common framework for the ten member countries to regulate unfair trade practices. These are consistent with the GATT Codes with respect to dumping and subsidies, and, as EEC rules, are part of the law of each member state.   In the matter of dumping, private parties have the right to file complaints with the Commission or with Member states for transmittal to the Commission. Supensions of investigations after obtaining voluntary price undertakings have been frequent and provision is made for adjusting countervail and dumping duties to reflect public interest considerations.

302.   In a significant decision, the Court of Justice of the European Community recently held that private parties cannot directly enforce in national courts the obligations of the EC under the GATT.   However, the Court did confirm that as of July 1, 1968, the date when the common customs union went into effect, issues of GATT obligations and treaties were within the

jurisdiction of the Court, including cases involving determinations by national courts as to the compatibility of national laws with EC obligation (138). This jurisdiction is necessary to ensure a uniform interpretation within the Community of its obligations regarding third parties. In another recent case, the court held that private parties seeking protection under Community laws against dumping of foreign products on EEC markets, and where the Commission has announced, after investigation, that an anti-subsidy proceeding would not be opened, could appeal to the Court, if they believe that the Commission has not observed the procedural guarantees arising under Rule No. 3017/79, has manifestly erred in its consideration of the facts, has ignored signs pointing to the existence of an export subsidy, or has abused its power by basing its conclusions on improper grounds (139). The case involved an appeal brought by the vegetable oil industry concerning the failure of the Commission to initiate unfair trade proceedings following their petitions alleging subsidies of foreign soyabean oil cakes imported into the Community and seeking countervailing duties.

303.   In Australia, the Customs Tariff (Anti-Dumping) Act of 1975 regulates dumping and subsidised imports into Australia. Australia acceded to the GATT Antidumping Code in 1975.   Subsequent amendments to the Act reflect the revised GATT Anti-Dumping Practice Code and Subsidies and Countervailing Duties Code, to which Australia acceded in 1982 and 1981, respectively.   In New Zealand, regulations on dumping and countervailing duties are embodied in the Customs Act of 1966. Private parties have a role in initiating judicial or administrative proceedings in the enforcement of these laws only to the extent that the New Zealand industry can monitor competitive prices and lodge complaints.

304.   In Finland, the GATT agreements on dumping and export subsidies were incorporated into national law in 1980. Norway relies directly on the GATT and does not have separate laws. This area is adminstered by the Department of Trade. Similarly, in Sweden, there are no separate statutes, but, rather, direct reliance on the GATT Codes. Under the Swedish Customs Act, however, the government may decide that an anti-dumping fee or a countervailing duty should be added to any product in order to compensate for foreign dumping or subsidisation practices that harm Swedish industry. The authority responsible for unfair trade investigations is the Swedish Board of Commerce.

305.   In Spain, the GATT Agreements on Anti-Dumping duties and Countervailing Duties were adopted through Royal Decrees in 1982. Responsibility for enforcing the unfair trade laws lies with the Directorate General for Policy on Tariffs and Imports of the State Secretariat for Commerce. In Switzerland, the Customs Act provides for the imposition of antidumping or countervailing duties in order to compensate for foreign dumping or subsidisation practices. As to the criteria for application of this Act, the Swiss government relies directly on the relevant GATT Codes. In Japan, Article 9 of the Customs Tariff law addresses dumping practices and article 8 deals with countervailing duties. These statutes are based upon the terms of the GATT agreements. The laws provide that the government can terminate investigations upon an undertaking by a foreign exporter to revise its prices or cease its exports to Japan, in the case of dumping, or when a foreign government abolishes or reduces a subsidy or an exporter revises its prices, in the case of countervailing duties. In general, members of domestic industries can request investigations under the laws relating to unfair trade practices by submitting proof of the unfair practice and of the damage caused to the domestic industry.

306. Canada has several trade statutes to deal with unfair international trade practices. The Anti-Dumping Act deals with that practice, while Section 7 of the Customs Tariff Act, together with the countervailing duty regulations, address subsidisation. New legislation is under consideration which would combine the Anti-Dumping Act and countervail provisions and increase the transparency of investigatory procedures. Anti-dumping practices or countervail investigations can be and usually are initiated in response to complaints submitted by or on behalf of Canadian producers. Provided the complaint is properly documented and includes prima facie evidence of a material injury caused by dumping or subsidisation, the authorities proceed with an investigation.

307. Following a preliminary determination injurious dumping, provisional duties are customarily imposed and dumping cases are referred to the Antidumping Tribunal. The same procedures hold for countervail investigations, except that temporary relief can only be imposed pursuant to an order in Council. It is also through Orders in Council that these types of cases are referred to the Anti-Dumping Tribunal for a final determination on injury. The Anti-Dumping Act does not currently provide for the acceptance of price undertakings. A proposal to provide for this alternative is currently under consideration. On the other hand, voluntary undertakings are possible under countervail investigations. Finally, consideration is also being given to adopt procedures to permit the Anti-Dumping Tribunal to hear arguments and receive evidence with regard to public interest considerations during dumping and countervail inquiries.

308. In the United States, trade laws deal with dumping, subsidisation, unfair methods of competition, and violations of trade agreements or unfair or unreasonable practices by foreign governments. Each law generally regulates a distinct type of unfair trade practice, although there may be overlap in certain situations. The anti-dumping provisions of Title VII of the Tariff Act of 1930, 19 U.S.C. sections 1673 et seq., provide for an administrative procedure to investigate and offset dumping practices of foreign firms. This statute provides for the imposition of an anti-dumping duty equal to the "dumping margin" when the Department of Commerce determines that products are being sold or are likely to be sold in the United States at "less than fair value" and the U.S. International Trade Commission (ITC) also determines that an industry in the United States is materially injured, threatened with material injury, or its establishment materially retarded, by reason of imports of those products. Sales at "less than fair value" exist whenever the price of goods exported to the United States is less than the price at which such or similar goods are sold in the market of the exporting country for home consumption. If too few sales have been made in the home market to provide an adequate basis for calculation of a fair value, or, under certain circumstances, if the sales in the home market are determined to have been below cost, then the law provides alternate methods of calculating fair value.

309. An anti-dumping investigation is usually initiated by a producer, wholesaler, union, or trade association filing a petition with the Department of Commerce and the ITC. The Department of Commerce may also initiate an anti-dumping investigation on its own initiative if available information indicates that dumping may be occurring.

310. Section 734(b) of the Tariff Act of 1930 provides for the suspension of anti-dumping investigations if exporters who account for substantially all of

the imports of a particular product agree to cease exports completely or to revise their prices to eliminate completely the dumping margin. This provision has been used four times since 1979 to obtain undertakings by foreign exporters as to the price level of their products. The statute also permits suspension of anti-dumping investigations if exporters accounting for substantially all of the imports agree to eliminate the injurious effect of the dumping and to prevent price undercutting and suppression, and there are no dumping margins greater than 15 per cent of the weighted average dumping margin estimated during the investigation. However, this provision has never been used. The anti-dumping law does not permit the suspension of investigations on the basis of quantitative restraint undertakings by exporters, other than the complete cessation of exports.

311. Neither the Antitrust Division of the Department of Justice nor the Federal Trade Commission (the two competition authorities in the United States) have a formal statutory role in the enforcement of the dumping laws. However, the Tariff Act of 1930 directs that the International Trade Commission "shall in appropriate matters act in conjunction and cooperation with the Federal Trade Commission ... and [the FTC] shall cooperate fully with the [ITC] for the purposes of aiding and assisting in its work." 19 U.S.C. section 1334. Furthermore, both the Federal Trade Commission and the Antitrust Division may submit comments to the Department of Commerce and the International Trade Commission on particular aspects of an investigation.

312. The United States countervailing duty law, section 303 of the Tariff Act of 1930, 19 U.S.C. section 1303, provides that whenever a "bounty or grant" is paid or bestowed in a foreign country "upon the manufacture or production in such country", a duty equal to the amount of the bounty or grant will be levied upon imports of such articles into the United States. Where the subject imports are from "countries under the Agreement" (which generally includes countries to which the United States applies the GATT Subsidies Code) or are free of normal customs duties, the countervailing duty provisions of Title VII of the Tariff Act of 1930, 19 U.S.C. sections 1671 et seq. provide for the imposition of countervailing duties equal to the net subsidy, but only if the ITC makes a determination of material injury similar to that in dumping investigations,.

313. A countervailing duty investigation is generally initiated by the filing of a petition by a producer, wholesaler, union, or trade association. The Department of Commerce may itself initiate an investigation where available information indicates that a formal investigation is warranted. The countervailing duty law provides for the suspension of investigations if the government of the country in which the subsidy practice is occurring agrees, or if exporters who account for substantially all of the imports agree, to eliminate or offset completely the subsidy with respect to exports to the United States, to cease exports of those products to the United States completely or to eliminate the injurious effect of the subsidies by elimination of 85 per cent of the subsidy amount and prevention of price undercutting. The statute also provides that a countervailing duty investigation may be suspended where the foreign government agrees to restrict the volume of imports to eliminate the injury to the U.S. industry. The statute does not permit undertakings by private firms concerning the future volume of exports to the United States. As with the anti-dumping proceedings, neither the Justice Department nor the Federal Trade Commission have a formal statutory role in countervailing duty investigations. However, those agencies

may participate in those proceedings by submitting comments to the Commerce Department and the International Trade Commission.

314.   One of the novel aspects of U.S. law is section 337 of the Tariff Act of 1930, 19 U.S.C. section 1337, which declares unlawful unfair acts and unfair methods of competition in import trade, the effect or tendency of which is to destroy or substantially injure a domestic industry, efficiently and economically operated, or to prevent the establishment of such industry, or to restrain or monopolise trade and commerce in the United States. A striking feature of this statute is that its language resembles that of the U.S. competition laws, albeit in an international trade context. Although Section 337 might theoretically be invoked against restrictive business practices, it has rarely, if ever, been used in that context. Most of the cases brought under this statute have involved patent infringement. The ITC may not investigate dumping or subsidisation practices under this statute.

4. TRENDS IN ENFORCEMENT OF LAWS RELATING TO UNFAIR TRADE PRACTICES

315.   There has been a sharp increase in the number of investigations brought under laws relating to unfair trade practices in the past several years (140). Among the OECD Countries, however, this increase is to be found largely in Australia, the United States, Canada, and the EC, while other countries report no or very few actions. As it appears from the preceding section, in the former group of countries there exist detailed legal provisions, procedures and a corresponding administrative or quasi-judicial structure for the enforcement of unfair trade laws, whereas most of the countries in the latter group directly rely on the GATT Code. Most of the cases involved anti-dumping actions, as the U.S. is the only country to extensively apply countervail laws. Although the increase in the number of investigations undoubtedly reflects the difficult economic conditions of the recent period, this data must necessarily be qualified by the realization that the adoption of laws relating to unfair trade practices is a recent development in most OECD countries and thus historical comparisons are not possible.

316.   Australia, Canada, the United States and the EC have been by far the most frequent users of anti-dumping measures. In Canada, between 1971 and 1982, 176 investigations were initiated, only two of which involved countervail. Approximately one-quarter of these cases were dismissed for lack of evidence. Of the remainder, the Tribunal found material injury in about two-thirds of the investigations and some 10 cases are pending. The few countervail cases brought have resulted in two voluntary pricing arrangements concerning twine and cheese.

317.   In 1982, the EEC initiated 55 anti-dumping actions, a large percentage of which involved imports from centrally-planned economies. In 1981-82, the EC initiated 39 investigations, 17 of which were resolved through voluntary price undertakings.

318.   In the United States since January 1, 1980, the ITC has initiated approximately 135 dumping investigations. As of June 1, 1983, there were 87 anti-dumping orders in effect. The majority of U.S. cases involved OECD countries or their firms. Further, under longstanding administrative practice, U.S. anti-dumping cases are conducted on a country-wide basis, i.e.

all exporters or manufacturers from the country are covered by the investigation, unless expressly excluded. Since January 1, 1980, the ITC has initiated approximately 200 countervailing duty investigations. As of June 1, 1983, there were 50 countervailing duty orders in effect. There have been approximately 19 countervailing duty investigations suspended since 1979. Most of the suspensions involved agreements by the foreign government to refrain from subsidising exports to the U.S. or to impose an export tax offsetting completely the subsidy. There have been, however, one or two instances where exporters agreed to forego the subsidy. No countervailing duty investigation has been suspended on the basis of an agreement by the foreign government to restrict the volume of exports.

319. There has been an increasing trend in the number of anti-dumping complaints in Australia. During 1980-81, thirty-one formal dumping inquiries were notified and ten inquiries resulted in determinations by the Government that dumping duties should be imposed. The products concerned included hydraulic car hoists, power hacksaws, fire hose, pigments and carbonless copying paper.

320. There has been little or no enforcement of unfair trade laws in other OECD countries. The first two cases under the laws in Japan were brought in 1982; one involved an antidumping investigation against cotton thread imported from Korea and the second concerned a countervail case against cotton thread from Pakistan. New Zealand, Spain and Switzerland reported that anti-dumping petitions have been infrequent. In the past decade, one investigation of an anti-dumping practice took place in Sweden concerning tires.

321. Apart from the limited number of countries in which extensive use of laws relating to unfair trade practices occurs, several other trends emerge from a review of the GATT inventory of anti-dumping actions. First, anti-dumping laws have been mainly invoked against imports from industrialised countries, with less than twenty percent of the cases in recent years involving developing countries. Of these, most actions occur between OECD countries. In Canada and the United States, the vast majority of cases listed in the GATT inventory involve complaints against imports from other OECD members. This is somewhat less so in the EC, whose laws do not apply to dumping between members. The majority of EEC actions involve Eastern European countries. Second, the initiation of anti-dumping actions tends to be countercylical, with an upsurge in complaints recorded during recessionary periods. These complaints may involve imports which have been entering the country for years at low prices, but during periods of high unemployment and excess productive capacity, more frequent resort is made to anti-dumping and countervail actions. It may also be the case that exporters engage in more aggressive pricing behaviour during slack periods.

5. RELATIONSHIP BETWEEN LAWS RELATING TO UNFAIR TRADE PRACTICES AND COMPETITION POLICY

322. As the preceding sections of this Chapter have shown, trade policy measures exercise a significant impact on competition and on markets. This is also the case with the enforcement of laws relating to unfair trade practices. While designed to adjust competitive disequilibria brought about by unfair and injurious import pricing practices, the enforcement of these

laws can, in certain circumstances, restrict competition in domestic markets by raising entry barriers to foreign competitors. In this respect, two fundamental concerns arise for competition policy. The first is whether private firms abuse unfair trade laws by bringing actions to gain leverage over foreign competitors and either control or exclude their presence in domestic markets. Second, the question arises whether the effects on competition of proceedings under laws relating to unfair trade practices are adequately considered, in particular in the measurement of injury to domestic industry and in the level of relief granted. To explore these issues, this section compares the main approaches under competition policy and unfair trade laws and considers the possibilities for giving greater weight to competition policy considerations within the framework of these laws.

323. There are certain common elements in competition policy and laws relating to unfair trade practices. Both share the common objective of seeking to remove artificial distortions in markets. But differences emerge in the nature of the interests they seek to protect and in the ways in which standards are applied. The principal goal in competition policy is to preserve and maintain competitive domestic market structures and the efficient allocation of resources by prohibiting practices that restrain competition or impose barriers to new entrants. Emphasis is placed on market performance, costs and scale economies. The principal concern is to protect competition, and not competitors. Competition policy does not seek to protect inefficient competitors against lower prices that are achieved through efficiency, economies of scale, cheap labour or technological expertise, so long as the advantage is fairly attained. Nor, in most countries, does competition policy allow a departure from competitive principles for firms buffeted by recessionary conditions, shrinking markets or technological obsolence.

324. Laws relating to unfair trade practices, in contrast, aim to protect domestic industry from unfair import pressures causing injury to domestic competitors. Thus, the basic issue in the application of these trade laws is generally the legitimacy or illegitimacy of various competitive advantages which foreign producers enjoy over domestic firms and the resultant harm to domestic industry. Under these laws, the effect of the practices on competition in the market and the ultimate effect on consumers are not at issue, nor are they elements of the offence, except insofar as they relate to the causation of harm to the domestic industry. These differences in comparison with competition policy can be partly explained by the divergent concepts upon which rules of international trade are based and the different interests considered in formulating and applying trade policies.

a) Use of laws relating to unfair trade practices to restrain competition

325. In most countries, private firms can petition the authorities to initiate unfair trade proceedings and procedures exist to suspend investigations in response to undertakings by foreign firms to cease their exports or upwardly adjust prices. These procedures, if abused, can allow for collusive action on the part of domestic firms to restrain competition through the elimination of foreign competitors. Thus, an important concern is the possibility of domestic firms engaging in restrictive practices in their resort to laws relating to unfair trade practices.

326. At the outset, the threat of filing a complaint under such laws can be

used to exert pressure on foreign firms to modify their product prices or export strategies. This is particularly so since national laws generally require that foreign firms involved in unfair trade proceedings post a bond equal to the alleged amount of the dumping or subsidy during the proceedings. Once proceedings have been initiated, pressures can be brought to bear on foreign firms to accept voluntary undertakings to modify or cease their exports as a means to speedily resolve matters and avoid protracted and costly litigation. Domestic industries play a role in this process by informing governments whether a proposed undertaking provides a satisfactory basis for terminating an unfair trade proceeding, thereby allowing these firms to influence the competitive structure of their markets. In and of itself, the filing of a complaint under the laws relating to unfair trade practices by one or more domestic firms is not an anti-competitive practice. But where such complaints are baseless or the procedures are exploited to extract concessions from foreign firms through undertakings as a condition to remaining in the market, serious concerns arise as to whether domestic firms are abusing the unfair trade laws to restrict competition in their markets.

327.   This situation has received some attention in the United States for example. Under the Noerr-Pennington doctrine, provisions of the competition law prohibiting collusion or cartel-like behaviour do not apply to firms or industries when they petition the government for the passage of laws favourable to them, or for the application of existing laws (141). However, under the "sham exception" to this doctrine, baseless claims filed as part of a conspiracy to harass a competitor would not be immunised from prosecution under competition laws (142). Thus far, there has been only one case in which the applicability of the sham exception to an antidumping action was considered. Although, it did not decide the issue, the court did imply that a single harrassing antidumping petition was sufficient to state an antitrust claim (143).

b) Dumping and anti-competitive pricing

328.   The second broad issue is whether and to what extent competition policy criteria are considered in unfair trade proceedings. Although, to some extent a procedural question, involving the possibility for competition authorities to comment or participate in such proceedings, this issue also concerns the substantative approaches developed under law relating to unfair trade practices and competition law to assess injury and pricing practices.

329.   A major element under laws relating to unfair trade practices concerns the price of imported goods. Antidumping laws generally apply to sales in a market at prices lower than those charged in the home market of the exporting firm, provided that these practices result in material injury to domestic industry. It is not generally required that it be shown, under these laws, that the exporting firm intended to eliminate its competitors. Competition policy generally encourages price competition and intervenes only where pricing is predatory, i.e. set below cost with a view toward eliminating competitors, or set on a discriminatory basis, with a view toward restraining competition through the allocation or division of markets.

330.   It is in the measurement of the margin of dumping as opposed to anti-competitive pricing that competition and trade policy diverge. Dumping is generally defined only as the sale of products in foreign markets at less than the price at which they are sold in the home country. On the other hand,

a showing of predatory pricing under competition policy generally requires evidence of sales below production costs (144) or at excessively low levels with a design to put competitors out of business.

331.   In assessing the competitive impact of aggressive or low-cost pricing strategies, competition authorities usually seek to determine whether predation is likely to be successful.   Since competition policy encourages price competition, action against low prices will usually be taken only if it is likely that they will result in the irreversible exit of competitors from the market, thereby allowing the price cutter to acquire market power and subsequently raise prices (145).   Although a practice may cause a rival's exit, it may be predatory only if the practice would not be profitable without the additional monopoly power resulting from the exit.

332.   In this context, however, it may be difficult to measure the actual or potential market power of a foreign firm, because a foreign producer's share in domestic markets may not be a reliable indication of its chances for success in a predatory campaign.   While a small market share may indicate that successful predation will be difficult and a lengthy process, account must be taken of the firms productive capacity and resources in its home market.   The calculation of a foreign firm's production costs can also be more difficult, since account must be taken of government subsidies, tariffs, transportation costs and fluctuations in exchange rates.

333.   Analysis of international predation under competition policy must also consider the position of the exporting firm in its home market.   A foreign producer may have monopoly power in its home country, and therefore may set home prices substantially above marginal costs.   At the same time the producer may be willing to sell overseas at a price closer to (but above) its marginal cost of production.   While such sales may constitute dumping, they would not violate competition laws and in some instances may even be considered a procompetitive response of a producer seeking to enter new markets or expand its trade position.

   e) Injury

334.   Under the laws relating to unfair trade practices, following a showing of dumping or subsidisation, injury to domestic firms must then be established.   In applying the injury concept, these laws seek to protect domestic competitors against unfair competition from foreign firms.   In contrast, under competition laws, emphasis is placed on overall market performance and efficiency and not on the effect of a particular practice on an individual competitor.   Despite these differences in approach, the injury test, if vigorously applied, serves as a safeguard against the misuse of dumping or countervail laws as restraints to competition.   In particular, a finding of injury should be based on objective criteria after formal proceedings in which all interested parties are provided an opportunity to express their views.   Particular emphasis should be given to establishing a causal relationship between unfair pricing practices and injury suffered by domestic producers.   Competition authorities can play a useful role in this process to see that relevant market factors and the competitive behaviour of the industry concerned are taken into account when assessing injury under unfair trade laws.

335.   In some instances, where procedures permit, competition officials have

intervened in unfair trade proceedings to offer their views on the question of injury. In the United States, for example, the Department of Justice filed comments in 1981 with the International Trade Commission in the antidumping investigation of Truck Trailer Axles and Brake Assemblies, from Hungary, ITC Inv. No. 731=TA-38 (preliminary), arguing that the facts did not indicate there was a reasonable indication of material injury or the threat of material injury to the domestic industry. The Department filed its comments because it was concerned that the dumping laws not be used, without sufficient basis, to thwart attempts by foreign producers to enter the U.S. market. The Justice Department was also concerned that the imposition of antidumping duties would exclude an important competitor from the highly concentrated U.S. market. Later in that investigation, when the Hungarian producers were proposing to enter into a price undertaking with the Commerce Department, the Department of Justice filed comments with the Commerce Department indicating that it considered the price undertaking to be in the public interest because it would allow the Hungarian producer to continue as a competitor in the U.S. market.

336.   In some countries, consideration of the impact on competition of proceedings under laws relating to unfair trade practices is limited by the fact that respondents are generally not permitted to raise defences that would be available under competition laws. For example, defences which would normally be available in price discrimination cases, e.g. meeting competition or cost justification, are generally not accepted in anti-dumping proceedings (146). Similarly, the fact that lower import prices may reflect increased productivity due to technological advances is generally not taken into account in trade proceedings. In non-predatory pricing cases under competition laws, evidence that injury has been the result of the complainant's competitive inertia rather than of price differentials by the defendant is generally considered (147). Similar arguments raised by importers and the Department of Justice in anti-dumping proceedings have gone unheeded (148).

337.   In countervail proceedings, competition authorities have expressed concern as to the need to assess the impact of a subsidy on competition and to establish that the subsidy itself is the cause of injury. In the United states, in the countervailing duty investigation of Textiles and Textile Products of Cotton from Pakistan, ITC. Inv. No. 701-TA-62-63 (Final), the Department of Justice argued in written comments and oral arguments that since the imported products were underselling the domestic products by a margin significantly greater than the subsidy found by the Commerce Department, the subsidies on these imports could not have been a cause of any injury to the domestic industry. In another matter, the Federal Trade Commission filed a Prehearing Brief on April 7, 1983 with the Department of Commerce on the alleged subsidy of certain softwood lumber products from Canada. The Commission's analysis supported the Department of Commerce's preliminary determination that no countervailable subsidy resulted from the methods used by Canadian Federal and Provincial governments to set a price for standing timber that may be harvested and processed into lumber. As part of its presentation, the Commission argued that unjustified imposition of countervailing duties on Canadian lumber would raise costs to United States lumber consumers and adversely affect other segments of the economy, including the housing industry.

d) Remedies

338.   A final area in which it may be useful to consider the impact on competition of enforcement of laws relating to unfair trade practices is in the remedial relief granted in these cases.   In most countries, considerable discretion exists under these laws in determining whether or not to impose a dumping penalty or countervailing duty following upon a determination that a violation exists.   There is also discretion to fix the amount of the penalty or duty below the margin of dumping or subsidisation.   In this context, consideration of the competitive impact of penalties provided under laws relating to unfair trade practices would be useful in limiting the chilling effect that such remedies can have on competition in the markets concerned.

339.   As an illustrative example, in a brief filed in the complex countervailing duty investigation of carbon steel products from Belgium, U.S., Brazil, Germany, France, Italy, Luxembourg, the Netherlands and the United Kingdom, the US Federal Trade Commission assessed the effects of the planned imposition of countervailing duties on concentration in the domestic steel industry (149).   The brief first estimated the effect on industry concentration if duties led to the exclusion of imports and other foreign suppliers were not forthcoming.   To provide insight into the significance of these increases in concentration, the FTC analogised the situation to a merger between two firms and applied the merger guidelines it customarily uses in such cases.   On that basis, it concluded that elimination of the challenged imports could result in an increase in concentration sufficient to attract attention if such an increase were to result from a merger.

340.   In Canada, trade legislation makes explicit provision for the use of trade liberalising measures to combat restrictive business practices.   For example, certain classes of goods may be exempted from the Anti-Dumping Act. This authority was used to deny the pharmaceutical industry protection from dumping following a report by the Restrictive Trade Practices Commission that found the industry to be engaging in restrictive practices in the early 1970's.   Within the Community, although the relevant regulations do not refer to competition, in proceedings under laws relating to unfair trade practices concerning monopolistic or oligopolistic markets, competition aspects are taken into account.

D. CONCLUSIONS

341.   Trade policy measures can have a significant impact on the competitive processes in both national and international markets.   Where such measures restrict the pro-competitive effects of international trade in markets in terms of price, quality and incentives to innovate new products and production processes, they are of direct concern to competition policy authorities.   In some cases restrictive trade measures can be conducive to increased collusion between market participants.   In the long run, measures designed to shelter sectors from the incentives resulting from effective competition can reduce the ability of these sectors to innovate and grow in the domestic economy and to compete internationally, even though the stated purpose of the measures may be to give the sector time to adjust and become more competitive.

342.   The Committee therefore is of the view that policy-makers should, when considering a prospective trade measure, undertake as systematic and comprehensive an evaluation as possible of the likely effects of the measure, including, inter alia, the impact of the measure on the structure and functioning of the relevant markets and the long-term effects on the structural adaptation of the affected sector.   The checklist of the important effects of trade measures has been developed to provide a framework for such analysis (paragraph 242).   It is understood that it would have to be adapted to the particular situation in question and that governmental policy considerations will determine the weight given to each item.   Competition policy authorities could make an important contribution to such analyses, particularly with respect to the evaluation of the likely impact of the measure on the structure of the relevant markets and the competitive process within those markets.

343.   While a number of interesting national case studies of the economic effects of various trade measures have been identified, the Committee believes that considerable further analysis is needed to increase understanding of these often complex effects, particularly with respect to the newer forms of trade protection such as VERs and OMAs.   Within the OECD, it would be desirable to have further discussions, including inter alia exchanges of views and comparisons of national experiences with such measures from the perspective of both competition policy and trade policy authorities using the indicative checklist as a framework for the discussion.   The Committee has noted in this regard a need for exploring possible ways and means for increasing the transparency of these measures so that their effects can be better identified and monitored.

344.   With respect to laws addressing injurious or unfair trade practices, the Committee noted that these laws and competition policy share the common objective of seeking to remove artificial distortions in the marketplace. While competition policy is designed to preserve competitive domestic market structures and the efficient allocation of resources, laws dealing with unfair trade practices aim to protect domestic industry from unfair import pressures causing injury to domestic competitors.   Accordingly, in the enforcement of anti-dumping and countervail laws, different standards are applied to import pricing practices than if such practices were examined under competition statutes.   As a result, some actions brought under the unfair trade laws can reduce competition in domestic markets, particularly where high levels of concentration already exist, through the foreclosure of foreign firms.

345.   The Committee therefore considers that consensus should be sought on the extent to which policy-makers and enforcement authorities should give consideration to the impact on competition in domestic markets of actions taken under laws dealing with unfair trade practices.   First, care should be exercised to avoid a misuse of unfair trade proceedings by enterprises seeking to restrain foreign competition.   Second, further consideration should be given to the extent to which in administering laws dealing with unfair trade practices, it would be appropriate to take into account the structure and the functioning of markets and the competitive situation within these markets and the pro-competitive impact of foreign firms in domestic markets.   Injury and its causal relationship to unfair trade practices should continue to be assessed on the basis of objective criteria, in accordance with international rules, and following procedures where all interested parties are given an opportunity to express their views.

Chapter III

ISSUES RELATING TO THE FORMULATION AND IMPLEMENTATION OF
TRADE AND COMPETITION LAWS AND POLICIES

A. INTRODUCTION

346.   As discussed in the preceding two chapters of this report, the legal
and institutional framework for dealing with issues arising at the frontier
between competition and trade policies is not yet sufficiently developed to
permit a harmonised approach to these issues.   First, there remains
considerable uncertainty as to the applicability of existing national or
international legal instruments in a number of areas which are characterised
by a close linkage between government trade policies and private business
practices, e.g. export cartels, voluntary export restraints, government
sponsored cartels or monopolies.   Second, where existing instruments are
applicable, Member countries may experience enforcement difficulties given the
fact that the practices concerned are international in character and that they
may not fully be regulated by legal action taken at a purely national level.
Third, there are inherent tensions and inconsistencies in the implementation
of trade and competition policies within some Member countries which
underlines the need for cooperation between competition and trade authorities
to balance competing interests.   Finally, conflicting approaches of Member
countries in the application of their trade and competition laws to
international business transactions and disputes as to the jurisdictional
reach of such laws are a factor of disharmony in international trading
relations and may in themselves constitute barriers to trade.

347.   The basic question addressed in this chapter of the report is the
extent to which competition authorities can contribute to the development of a
harmonised framework for the formulation and implementation of trade and
competition law and policies. In this respect, two types of issues arise:

-- First, within their area of competence, competition authorities will
   have to consider whether the legal instruments available to them
   still meet the challenges of the present situation characterised by
   the interaction between government policies and private restrictive
   practices and the growing internationalisation of business
   activities. In particular, what are the means available to them to
   effectively apply their legislation on their national territory?
   What can be done to strengthen international cooperation to avoid

conflicts in competition law enforcement, using, where relevant, international instruments such as the 1979 Recommendation?

-- Second, given their expertise with the functioning of markets, competition authorities have an important contribution to make to the formulation and implementation of trade policies having an impact on competition. Are procedures available which provide for the participation of competition authorities in the decision-making process? What can be done to make such participation more effective?

This chapter of the report deals with both aspects. In section B, questions of law enforcement including jurisdictional issues are discussed while section C considers the involvement of and procedures for competition authorities to participate in the decision-making process on trade policy measures.

348. Section B starts with a discussion of the main reasons for jurisdictional conflicts arising between Member countries in the area of competition and competition-related trade measures. Drawing upon the findings in the previous chapters of the report, it then highlights procedural and substantive issues related to the application of competition law to foreign conduct affecting domestic markets on the one hand and to domestic conduct affecting foreign markets on the other. Problems relating to government sponsored or mandated restrictive practices are then discussed. Finally, the section reviews the main developments in national approaches and international cooperation that have been developed to resolve issues arising in the enforcement of competition and competition-related trade policies.

349. Section C first provides a survey of existing arrangements for participation of competition authorities in the formulation and implementation of trade policies. The next step is an evaluation of the different techniques which are being or could be used to make this involvement more effective and, in particular, the advantages to be gained from closer cooperation between trade and competition authorities. Section D presents the conclusions of this chapter of the report.

B. PROBLEMS OF LAW ENFORCEMENT INCLUDING JURISDICTIONAL ISSUES

1. MAIN FEATURES AND EFFECTS OF JURISDICTIONAL CONFLICTS ARISING IN THE AREA OF COMPETITION AND COMPETITION-RELATED TRADE MATTERS

350. Rules of jurisdiction determine the extent to which national competition laws will be applied to enterprises operating in domestic and foreign markets. Changed circumstances during the past several decades have heightened the significance of jurisdictional issues, particularly with respect to issues of the application of competition laws to foreign conduct, and have had an effect both on trade flows and on the relations between trading partners. The most significant change has been the rapid growth in world trade in the recent period and as a consequence, the increasingly international character of business conduct. The past two decades have also seen the adoption and enforcement of competition law in many OECD countries. Another important factor has been the increasing role of governments and

government-owned enterprises in trade. Conflicts of jurisdiction have arisen, often reflecting differences in the scope of competition laws and diverging trade policy approaches of Member countries. This is demonstrated by several major recent disputes, notably in the uranium, shipping and transportation sectors. Finally, there has been an increased resistance to enforcement efforts to collect information located abroad, which has resulted in the adoption and implementation of blocking laws in several countries.

351.   In general, there appears to be a correlation between jurisdictional approaches of Member countries and government decisions as to the national interest in applying competition policy to international trade (150). Jurisdictional differences can be magnified where one country's competition law is more extensive in scope and uses different criteria to analyse business practices than those of its trading partners. Despite a significant degree of harmonisation in competition law approaches among Member countries, which is reflected, inter alia, in the standards laid down in the competition chapter of the OECD Guidelines, differences remain. While in some countries the evaluation of restrictive business practices is primarily if not exclusively based on their effects on competition, in other countries such effects are part of a general economic analysis which allows for other factors to be considered. These two basic approaches concerning the application of competition policy reflect differing views of Member countries as to the consequences of various policies as well as differing economic interests, due to such factors as the size of national markets and the types of products involved.

352.   These factors, coupled with the importance attached to exports and trade as components of national economic growth, partly explain the policy adopted in Member countries of not applying their competition laws to conduct by their firms abroad, in the absence of effects on the domestic market. Nonetheless, it can be seen that this can result in conflicts between the export promotion policies of one country and the competition policy of its trading partners. Further, national approaches to jurisdiction may not always be suitable for resolving disputes that involve trading interests of countries. An important measure of the effectiveness of the present framework for international cooperation is its ability to ensure that all relevant interests are considered, and, where conflicts arise, that procedures exist to evaluate and weight the different interests.

353.   The scope of application of national competition laws can have an impact on corporate planning. Unless companies have a reasonable degree of certainty as to the laws that will apply to their conduct, they may be reluctant to enter new markets or engage in international transactions. Some firms contend that to the extent that their conduct abroad may be subject to competition policy in their home countries, they may be placed at a competitive disadvantage versus foreign enterprises. The enactment of competition laws in most OECD countries has served to minimise this problem. Nonetheless, firms based in countries that apply competition laws that are more extensive in scope and reach have sometimes claimed to be at a disadvantage against foreign rivals, e.g. in seeking partners for joint ventures or technology transfers, if they are subject to more stringent conditions with respect to ancillary restraints in such transactions (e.g. territorial restrictions). Thus, it has been argued that uncertainty as to the jurisdictional reach of national competition laws and the risk of being made subject to conflicting requirements can increase the costs of enterprises

engaged in international business transactions and constitute an impediment to trade.

354.   To assess the impact of the enforcement of competition policy on trade flows, it must be recognised that many other factors come into play when governments and enterprises make trade and investment decisions. Apart from economic interests, trade regulations and controls on export trade may be designed to pursue foreign policy objectives, and political and military concerns. Although the use of such regulations is more common in war time, in the form of trade boycotts, they have been increasingly used in times of peace to pursue one or more of the above objectives (151). For example, many countries place controls on the export of sensitive or strategic technologies and on the export of arms. Many require "end-use" certificates, which regulate the countries to which goods can be re-exported (152).

355.   While this chapter focuses on the issues that have arisen in the application of competition policy to international trade, the question of conflicting national requirements is a broad-based one that arises also in such areas as investment taxation, and securities and cuts across all forms of economic, political and social regulation. In this regard, the Committee on Investment and Multinational Enterprises (CIME) is examining the issue of conflicting requirements imposed by governments on enterprises and having effects on international business conduct, particularly those which may affect the climate for international investment. Based on the provisions relating to this issue contained in the Declaration and the Decisions on International Investment and Multinational Enterprises, this work programme aims at improving practical approaches to alleviate difficulties that may arise.

2. APPLICATION OF COMPETITION AND COMPETITION-RELATED TRADE LAWS TO FOREIGN CONDUCT AFFECTING DOMESTIC MARKETS AND FOREIGN COMMERCE

356.   There are essentially two types of jurisdiction that pertain to international conduct. Under the principle of territoriality, all OECD countries apply their laws to conduct that takes place within their national territory, regardless of the nationality of the persons or firm involved. In some Member countries, this principle is extended under the doctrine of effects to reach conduct abroad which has a direct and substantial effect on domestic markets or on the foreign commerce of the country claiming jurisdiction. In addition, the concept of "enterprise unity" has been used in some countries to establish in personam jurisdiction over foreign-based entities to the extent they may be held accountable for the acts of their affiliates present on the national territory.

357.   Jurisdiction may also be extended beyond domestic borders under the nationality principle. Even nations that apply the territoriality principle generally recognise that in certain circumstances, a nation may assert jurisdiction over its nationals, even when they are residing abroad. There is a parallel to "objective" territorial jurisdiction, which arises when there is a complex chain of behaviour which starts with acts abroad and ends with acts in the territory, and laws are applied to those who participate at an early point in the chain, so long as they can be linked directly to territorial results. Under the nationality principle of jurisdiction problems have arisen with respect to defining corporate nationality. The question of corporate nationality is an important aspect which is being examined by the Committee on

International Investment and Multinational Enterprises in its work on conflicting requirements.

a) Investigatory powers

358.   Procedural rules establish the framework for antitrust enforcement and litigation.   They address such questions as what types of information and evidence may be requested in an investigation, the mode used to consider competition cases - administrative, judicial, political, and, in some countries, which courts have jurisdiction to hear a case. These rules are typically codified in national laws that have application in other fields and are further developed though judicial and administrative decisions that interpret and elaborate the rules.

359.   To a large extent, procedural differences in the law, and in particular objections to extensive requests for information received from foreign authorities, have figured prominently in several of the major international antitrust disputes in recent years.   National fact-finding powers and the procedural rules for litigation vary widely, in part reflecting the differences between civil and common law countries.   Notable differences emerge in the parties that may be requested to provide information (e.g. third parties), in the amount and specificity of information they may request and in the use of voluntary versus compulsory measures to obtain evidence.   In cases with international elements, it may not be possible to establish whether sufficient links exist to assert jurisdiction without first collecting information from abroad.   Thus, companies may be requested to furnish information before it is clearly established that their conduct is subject to the foreign competition laws, although responding to such requests is not ordinarily an admission as to jurisdiction.

360.   In recent years, some Member countries (Australia, France, New Zealand and the United Kingdom) adopted legislative provisions or regulations to control or prevent the communication of information to foreign authorities, and similar legislation has been proposed in Canada.   The law in the United Kingdom further allows firms within the UK to recover from the party in whose favour the original judgement was given the non-compensatory element of any multiple damage judgement awarded against them by the court of a foreign country.   In 1983, the Australian Government introduced new legislation which would enable its Attorney General to make orders to, inter alia, recover-back all or a portion of foreign antitrust judgments, recover costs of Australian defendants in certain foreign antitrust proceedings, and the reciprocal enforcement by agreement with other countries of recover-back judgments.

361.   These prohibitory measures have been motivated by the need felt by these countries to protect sovereign national interests and reflect differences among Member countries, for example, in substantative or procedural competition laws, disagreements over the jurisdictional basis and the propriety or appropriateness of particular antitrust investigations, proceedings or sanctions in other countries.   Most of these statutes contain discretionary provisions which allow government authorities to restrict the transmission of information where significant national interests would be affected.   It is generally felt that these statutes have not posed insurmountable barriers to the collection of information located abroad, and they may have influenced the countries that do request information abroad to intensify their efforts to pursue evidence available in the national

territory. In addition, most competition authorities adhere to a policy of seeking to cooperate with information requests from their foreign counterparts, where these are compatible with sovereign national interests, and subject to general laws and safeguards concerning the confidentiality of documents and information.

362. The Committee extensively considered the issue of the collection of information abroad and made a number of specific suggestions in this regard in a Report issued in 1984 (153). In general, the Report indicated that "the seeking of information located abroad may also occur under legislation which confines subject matter jurisdiction to conduct taking place in the legislating country's territory. While the practice seems to be more frequent among those countries whose legislation incorporates some form of effects doctrine, most cases in which information located abroad is sought by those countries do not involve the application of the effects doctrine" (154).

363. The enforcement of laws addressing unfair or injurious trade practices (antidumping and countervailing) frequently will imply requests for information located abroad. Firms involved in such proceedings seem to have generally provided the information requested to avoid repercussions resulting from failure to comply. Central to this is the existence of international agreements within the GATT as to the scope of such unfair trade laws and the procedures for the collection of information.

b) Differences in procedural rules and remedies under competition law

364. In most OECD countries, the authority to enforce the competition laws is reserved exclusively to the government. However, in some countries there is an opportunity for private action. For example, in the EEC, the Treaty of Rome provides for private complaints to the Commission or to Member States for referral to the Commission concerning unfair trade practices (e.g. antidumping). Private complaints under the competition provisions (articles 85 and 86) can be brought to the Commission, to competent authorities in the Member States or in national courts. Further, in the United States, private parties enjoy the statutory right to bring suits under the antitrust laws, and at present, more than 90 per cent of antitrust cases in the U.S. are private litigation. Moreover, suits by private parties are covered by the same jurisdictional principles as those by the government, and thus can be brought with respect to conduct abroad if the requisite effects or links are proven.

365. Differences also emerge with respect to the nature and remedial aspects of national competition policies, which form an important part of the framework under which restrictive practices are assessed. In most OECD countries, competition proceedings are non-criminal in character, and remedial relief is prospective, designed toward regulating or prohibiting future conduct, while imposing fines for past violations. One exception lies in the area of merger control, in which many of the new laws enacted provide the right to dissolve a merger that has been found to be illegal or against the public interest as the case may be, although the emphasis remains on evaluation of a merger before it has been consummated. In the United States, certain aspects of the competition law are criminal in nature and the available remedies are more extensive. Under the Sherman Act, collusive or cartel-like behaviour can be punished by fines and/or imprisonment. In private litigation, a successful plaintiff can recover treble damages. It is especially this latter provision of the U.S. laws that has prompted

considerable concern on the part of foreign governments and enterprises operating abroad, particularly when it may not be clear whether their activities produce the requisite effects to be subject to the jurisdiction of U.S. antitrust laws.

c) Substantative aspects

366.   Most countries apply their competition laws so as to define the rules of conduct and practices that will be permitted in their domestic market. In so doing, the nationality of the firm or corporation is not a central consideration so long as its conduct occurs in the national market or in countries where the effects doctrine is applied, affects that market. By the process of entering a particular market, a company is expected, therefore, to follow the rules of competition that apply there as a result of its "presence" in that market. To some extent, officials may consider foreign imports and production in measuring the existence of market power with respect to a particular product or firm. Statutes relating to unfair trade practices, e.g. antidumping laws, also apply principally to the domestic market insofar as they establish whether imported goods are being fairly traded.

367.   Trade measures usually represent direct sovereign actions and thus action taken in accordance with such measures may in some circumstances be immune from laws which prohibit acts that restrict competition. For example, if a government requires its domestic producers to engage in an export cartel or VER, the resulting arrangement, according to the doctrine of foreign sovereign compulsion discussed below, is not subject to challenge under competition law by the government or private firms in the target market, depending on the nature and extent of the government involvement. On the other hand, if producers independently engage in a cartel, ordinarily this could be challenged under the RBP laws of the target market. Problems of competition law enforcement may also arise if concerted behaviour by producers has been tolerated or even actively encouraged by governments, in the absence of an element of compulsion. Thus government measures which require conduct having a restrictive effect on competition will usually not be subject to foreign or domestic competition law, while practices which produce the same result could be challenged if engaged in by firms acting independently. This highlights one of the concerns expressed in the report that direct government involvement in private restrictive business practices may frustrate the effective implementation of competition policy.

d) Parent-subsidiary relationships

368.   With respect to the dealings of parents and subsidiaries or other affiliated enterprises, issues arise as to the legal responsibility and liability of foreign entities for the conduct of their domestic affiliates and vice versa. Under the enterprise unity theory, resolution of such questions depends to a large context on the degree of control exercised by the parent over the subsidiary. While an enterprise is generally considered to be a legal citizen of the country in which it does business and subject to its laws, it may also be held to the laws of other countries in which its affiliates are located if those countries use the enterprise unity doctrine. Thus, in some cases, the enterprise unity doctrine has been used to hold companies responsible for conduct abroad or to obtain information located abroad.

369.   Some countries, such as the United States, and the European Commission, will hold a foreign-based parent responsible for activity within their markets, where the overseas company exercises a requisite degree of control over the local affiliate (155). For example, in the Dyestuffs case, the European Court found a foreign-based parent responsible for the acts of its subsidiary in the Common Market, since it exercised control and issued instructions to the subsidiary (156).

370.   Enterprise unity has also been applied by some countries to hold a domestic parent or subsidiary responsible for conduct of its affiliates located abroad. Most countries consider a subsidiary which is incorporated under the laws of the country where it operates to be a legal citizen of that country and therefore subject to its laws. However, where the domestic company exercises some control over the foreign affiliate and the conduct abroad results in effects on the domestic market, the parent can be held responsible under the competition laws of some countries. This is apparently the case in Germany, Sweden, Switzerland and the European Commission. In the United States, the courts have frequently held domestic parent companies of multinational enterprises' accountable for the restrictive behaviour of their foreign subsidiaries, provided of course that such restrictive behaviour constitutes a violation of U.S. competition law (157). For example, in the case of Continental Ore Co. v. Union Carbide and Carbon Co., the U.S. Supreme Court held Union Carbide and Carbon chargeable for an attempt to monopolise the vanadium market through certain activities of its Canadian subsidiary (158). On the other hand, countries which adhere to the territoriality principle of jurisdiction would object to any legal responsibility being attached to companies incorporated within their territorial jurisdiction on the basis of the enterprises unity theory, particularly where the company is acting in accordance with the laws and policies of the situs.

3. APPLICATION OF LAWS TO DOMESTIC CONDUCT AFFECTING FOREIGN MARKETS

371.   Despite the existence of jurisdiction over domestic enterprises, most countries, as a matter of policy, only prosecute conduct that produces harmful or anticompetitive effects in the domestic market. While this policy follows the view that competition law is concerned with the domestic market, it does not prevent domestic firms from engaging in collusive activity with respect to foreign trade. As a result, practices such as cartels, anticompetitive joint ventures and voluntary restraint agreements which might be prosecuted if pursued in domestic markets, will not be challenged when used to promote export trade, in the absence of anticompetitive effects on the domestic market. In effect, companies are given wide latitude when engaged in export trade and the responsibility for challenging such conduct is left to the importing country. In the United States, the Export Trading Company Act of 1982 was enacted to clarify this situation and reduce the risks of antitrust uncertainty to firms involved in exporting from the U.S. The Act allows U.S. companies to obtain advance certification of approval from the government that specified activities in export trade will not be subjected to treble damage liability, although persons who suffer injury as a result of violations of the statutory standards may still recover actual damages.

372.   On the other hand, conduct although exempted in the domestic forum, may be challenged under the laws of the importing country. This will depend

largely on the nature of the practice and the jurisdictional principles in effect in the importing market. For example, the actionable conduct of an export cartel, i.e. the collusive behaviour, often takes place where the companies are located, and not in the import market. If the importing country exercises effects jurisdiction, it can challenge this activity on the basis of the effects it produces in that market, even if the conduct occurs abroad. An importing country that applies territoriality, however, may not be able to challenge a cartel since there may be no actionable conduct in that forum.

4. PROBLEMS OF COMPETITION LAW ENFORCEMENT CONCERNING GOVERNMENT INVOLVEMENT IN COMMERCIAL ACTIVITIES

373. As discussed in Chapter I B of this report, governments can engage in commercial activities in a number of ways, including direct ownership of enterprises, regulation of industries, or through subsidies to private firms. As noted, with a few exceptions, government ownership of enterprises does not exempt public enterprises engaged in commercial activities from the requirements of national competition laws. A separate, but related question, is the extent to which government trade and commercial laws or policies serve to exempt restrictive business practices from competition law. Difficult questions of competition law enforcement may arise where competition authorities are required to evaluate practices by enterprises that produce anticompetitive effects in domestic markets, but which are encouraged or approved or even mandated by foreign governments pursuant to their trade policies.

374. The extent to which government involvement can exempt behaviour by foreign enterprises from domestic competition law is determined inter alia on the basis of the doctrines of sovereign immunity, Act of State and foreign compulsion. These doctrines are based both on judicial precedent and statutes. Further, these doctrines have been variously considered as principles of jurisdiction and substantive law, and even of procedure. Although they can apply to domestic firms as well, in the international sphere these doctrines can have an important limiting effect on the extent to which domestic competition laws are applied to conduct that occurs abroad, and in particular, business practices adopted in response to trade policies of other countries.

a) "Sovereign Immunity" and "Act of State" doctrines

375. The principle of sovereign immunity, i.e. that states are entitled to immunity from prosecution, has long been a basic doctrine of international law. Under the traditional view, the acts of a state received absolute immunity from suits under law, regardless of the circumstances. At present, with the increasingly active involvement of governments in commercial affairs, this doctrine has been replaced by the principle of "restricted" immunity. This principle is based on the view that States perform sovereign functions only when exercising legislative, judicial or administrative authority and not when they are engaged in essentially commercial activities (159). Therefore, when a State enters commercial areas and involves itself in business activities, under the doctrine of restricted immunity, it may be subject to legal action under the laws of another state including competition law.

376. The doctrine of restricted immunity is now followed by most OECD countries, although the interpretation of what constitutes "commercial activity" differs. By 1950, most civil law countries had adopted the principle of restrictive sovereign immunity (160). This change has now been followed by common law countries as well. In 1976, the U.S. enacted the Foreign Sovereign Immunities Act (FSIA) which codified existing national policy in this area (161). This statute recognises the general principle that foreign states are immune from jurisdiction in U.S. courts, but it sets forth several exceptions as well, including "commercial activity" of a foreign State. Under the statute, the test as to whether conduct is "commercial activity" is decided by the "nature" of the conduct, rather than its "purpose".

377. In the United Kingdom, the State Immunity Act, adopted in 1978 lists the specific commercial activities which are not covered by the principle of immunity. There are several decisions where British laws have been applied to commercial activities of foreign governments (162). In Canada, the Canadian State Immunity Act (CSIA) was enacted in 1981. The CSIA confers immunity on foreign governments vis-à-vis the Canadian courts. It also provides for important exceptions. In particular, section 5 of the statute provides that a State does not enjoy immunity relating to any commercial activity of the foreign State (Section 5).

378. Government action may also receive immunity under the "Act of State" doctrine. This doctrine is closely linked to sovereign immunity, as it compels courts to refrain from making politically sensitive judgments concerning actions by foreign governments. It reflects the view that certain disputes between sovereigns are better resolved through diplomatic and political channels, rather than through judicial procedures in the courts of the countries concerned. In Commonwealth countries, the Act of State Doctrine is part of the principle of sovereign immunity.

379. In the United States there are both important procedural and substantive differences between the two doctrines. Sovereign immunity is generally invoked at a preliminary stage to determine whether the courts possess jurisdiction to decide a matter. Where jurisdiction is found, the "Act of State" doctrine may nevertheless apply to preclude US courts from sitting in judgment on the public acts of a foreign sovereign executed on its own territory. Under this doctrine of abstention, challenges to such actions may be non-justiciable and should be addressed to the executive branch and pursued, if at all, through diplomatic channels. As several cases illustrate, the doctrines of "sovereign immunity" and "act of state" have a significant impact on law enforcement in the area of competition and trade, since they can serve to limit the application of competition laws to foreign activities that restrain competition in pursuit of trade policies. For example, in one case decided under the Act of State doctrine, a US court of appeals ruled that the doctrine applied to prevent the court from entering into a delicate area of foreign policy which the executive and legislative branches had chosen to approach with restraint, and therefore affirmed the dismissal of an antitrust suit brought against OPEC (163). Another recent decision held that New Zealand and Australian shipping companies could not invoke the Act of State doctrine to refuse to supply documents and information requested by the U.S. Justice Department, pursuant to an investigation into alleged anticompetitive practices by an ocean shipping conference (164). A third case in U.S. courts involved a monopolisation suit concerning military procurement policies of foreign governments. The court refused to dismiss the suit on the basis of

the act of state doctrine, because the basis of the suit was the practices of a competitor in the sale of jet aircraft and supplies abroad, and not the validity of the decisions of foreign governments in refusing to purchase from the complainant (165).

b) Foreign compulsion

380.   The Act of State and Sovereign Immunity doctrines provide that certain actions by governments or public bodies are not subject to challenge. Both doctrines have developed largely outside the antitrust area, although their application extends to antitrust suits. The foreign compulsion doctrine, on the other hand, has been developed in the antitrust area and provides that certain conduct by foreign firms acting pursuant to order by the State is not subject to antitrust liability. Under the foreign compulsion doctrine, which has largely been developed in the jurisprudence of the United States, conduct by a private firm which is compelled or required by a foreign government on its sovereign territory does not give rise to liability under the US antitrust law. However, the defense is not available if the conduct is based on mere encouragement or acquiescence by the foreign government. Whether the doctrine applies to conduct outside the territory of the state which seeks to compel the conduct is not clearly settled in US case law (166).

381.   This doctrine has important implications in the application of domestic competition laws to conduct that occurs abroad pursuant to the trade laws and policies of foreign nations. For example, to avoid potential liability of their auto manufacturers under U.S. competition laws following upon the VER entered into in 1981, Japan administered the VER and mandated the division of market shares among the firms so as to enable the firms to avail themselves of the sovereign compulsion defense. A broader question is the extent to which domestic laws which encourage the creation of export cartels can provide immunity for this conduct in foreign markets. Where these laws only provide assent or approval of such arrangements, but do not compel them, these cartels will remain subject to prosecution under some competition laws in foreign markets and will not usually be able to successfully raise the defense of sovereign compulsion.   In the US, for instance, courts have narrowly interpreted this doctrine and recognise the defense only where direct and specific compulsion can be shown (167).

5. NATIONAL AND INTERNATIONAL APPROACHES FOR DEALING WITH PROBLEMS OF LAW ENFORCEMENT AND JURISDICTIONAL CONFLICTS

a) National approaches to resolving disputes

i) Moderation and self-restraint

382.   As a standard to resolve disputes involving the application of competition laws, Member countries have increasingly used moderation and self-restraint, based on their understanding of public international law or their acceptance of the principles of comity. The term "Comity" has been used in many OECD documents and instruments as an expression of the willingness of countries to exercise restraint in international matters (168). In the view of most authorities, comity is a doctrine of restraint, i.e. based on a consideration of relevant interests, a sovereign may decide not to exercise its powers in relation to conduct or persons outside the forum. Unlike

international law, which is obligatory, the view is widely held that comity is a non-legal and discretionary standard. It presupposes that a sovereign considers it has a legitimate basis to exercise jurisdiction, and establishes the criteria that will be considered in determining whether to exercise that jurisdiction when other sovereign interests may be affected (169).

383. Although comity establishes a general principle to resolve disputes involving the application of competition laws, it does not provide specific criteria (170). To resolve jurisdictional questions, some courts in the United States have enumerated sets of criteria to be considered in weighing the relevant interests that should be considered in international competition matters (171). Legal scholars have proposed other sets of criteria to resolve jurisdictional disputes (172).

ii) Government intervention in private litigation under competition law

384. As we have seen, jurisdictional disputes often reflect underlying conflicts as to trade and economic policy. Even where moderation or self-restraint are exercised, the courts of one country may have a difficult task to ensure that all relevant interests are considered, particularly in private litigation (173). The question also arises whether it is appropriate for the courts of one country to engage in a balancing test involving the policies of other countries. This may reflect both institutional problems as well as differences as to the interpretation of comity. First, cases of international antitrust may involve both the private rights of firms and the policies of governments. Decisions involving a balancing of different interests can be exceedingly difficult when the interests of several countries are at stake (174). From an institutional standpoint, the courts of one nation may find it difficult to properly take account of or weigh the relevant interests of other countries. Moreover, resolution of jurisdictional questions at this relatively advanced stage, rather than when it is first determined to investigate a particular practice, elevates the risks and costs for all concerned, although it must be recognised that courts may not be in a position to rule on jurisdictional questions without an adequate factual basis. In addition, it is doubtful whether private parties are influenced by comity considerations in deciding whether and when to bring suits under competition laws.

385. Some steps have already been taken to increase the possibilities for presentation of foreign interests in litigation. The U.S. Supreme court has requested foreign governments to present their views as to their sovereign interests by way of amicus curiae briefs, and the Departments of Justice and State have, in particular cases, urged the courts to give due regard to the foreign government views expressed. A similar recommendation was made by this Committee in its Report on the Collection of Information Located Abroad. Further, in its bilateral agreement with Australia of 1982, the United States agreed to inform the courts handling private disputes, in respect to conduct which had been the subject of notifications and consultations between the two countries, as to the outcome of the discussions. In these cases, the government authorities will be able to inform the courts as to the Australian interests involved and the reasons why it declined to take action, to the extent those matters were addressed in consultations.

b) Progress towards cooperation

386.   To a significant extent, problems arising out of differences in competition policy have been mitigated by the development of national laws, bilateral agreements and international instruments.   As noted, most Member countries have enacted competition laws and recently, many countries have enacted merger control systems.   Further, the enforcement of competition policy by the European Commission under Articles 85 and 86 provides a more consistent framework for the members of the Community as well as its trading partners.   In the Stockholm Convention, which governs trade between the EFTA countries, Article 15, in particular, is concerned with restrictive business practices by private enterprises or public undertakings.   Through the Free Trade Agreements concluded between the EC and the EFTA countries, a free trade system comprising 18 countries has been established, and the Agreements also contain provisions on competition policy.   Other important developments have been the conclusion of bilateral agreements between countries, the elaboration of international instruments and the use of the notification and bilateral consultation mechanisms provided by the 1979 OECD Recommendation.

i) Bilateral agreements

387.   In its recent report on international cooperation in competition law enforcement, the Committee has recommended that Member countries which have not yet done so consider entering into bilateral agreements or understandings for mutual assistance in the collection of information abroad in antitrust proceedings.   The Committee intends to review at an appropriate time the experience with such agreements and will examine the possibility of developing common elements for bilateral conventions.

388.   To date, the United States has entered into such agreements with Canada, Germany and Australia and several other countries are considering such agreements.   The differences in the provisions of these agreements largely reflect different economic and enforcement policy approaches in Member countries and the history of relations between the parties to these agreements in regard to competition law enforcement.

389.   The recent U.S.-Australia agreement for instance explicitly recognises the need for cooperation between the two countries to avoid or minimize conflict, as well as in the enforcement of antitrust laws, where the proposed enforcement action of one country does not adversely affect the laws, policies or national interest of the other.   Some provisions of this agreement are worth mentioning here, because it reflects the close relationship between trade policies and competition law enforcement.   First, the agreement provides the Australian Government with the option of notifying the US Government of a policy it has adopted and which may have antitrust implications for the United States.   The nature of this provision is such that potential difficulties for Australian exporters can be identified and avoided before exporters have become committed to a course of conduct that might otherwise become the subject of antitrust concern or investigation under the US antitrust laws. The second kind of notification concerns decisions by the U.S. Department of Justice or the FTC to undertake an antitrust investigation.   Under this provision each is obliged to notify the Australia Government of any such decision that may have implications for Australian law, policies or national interests.   The Australian and U.S. Governments have accepted mutual

obligations to communicate their concerns arising out of notifications and each is entitled to request consultations.

ii) International instruments

390.   The work of the OECD Committee on RBPs, through its meetings and publications, has fostered a better understanding of the various competition laws and policies among OECD members and has provided guidance for countries considering new legislation.   The competition chapter of the 1976 OECD Guidelines on Multinational Enterprises and the 1980 U.N. Code on RBPs provide international statements on the principles of competition law.   Finally, the Tokyo Round of the GATT established a series of agreements with respect to certain non-tariff barriers and provides a mechanism to resolve trade disputes covered under these instruments.

391.   The OECD Guidelines make a specific reference to conflicting requirements that may be imposed on multinational enterprises as a result of different approaches by Member countries to law enforcement and concerning claims of jurisdiction.   Paragraph 11 of the Introduction to the Guidelines provides: "When multinational enterprises are made subject to conflicting requirements by Member countries, the governments concerned will co-operate in good faith with a view to resolving such problems either within the Committee on International Investment and Multinational Enterprises established by the OECD Council on 21st January, 1975 or through other mutually acceptable arrangements".   Also, the Revised Decision of the Council on Intergovernmental Consultation Procedures on the Guidelines for Multinational Enterprises states: "Member countries may request that consultations be held in the Committee on any problem arising from the fact that multinational enterprises are made subject to conflicting requirements.   Governments concerned will co-operate in good faith with a view to resolving such problems, either within the Committee or through other mutually acceptable arrangements." The above mentioned work programme underway in the Committee on International Investment and Multinational Enterprises is based on these provisions.

392.   To facilitate cooperation in the field of competition law enforcement, a number of procedures have been instituted in recent years.   The 1979 OECD Recommendation (which replaced earlier versions) provides inter alia for notifications, consultations and exchanges of information.   The Committee reviews experiences under this document on a semi-annual basis.   Examination of these experiences indicates that some 100 exchanges take place yearly and that the instrument has facilitated cooperation among officials in the investigation of business practices and enforcement of the law.   Further, the 1983 Report by the Committee on the Collection of Information Located Abroad noted the significant extent of cooperation that takes place in international investigations and made specific suggestions to improve the efficiency of exchanges between Member countries.   In addition, the Report noted that most of the Blocking Legislation enacted in the past decade provides discretionary authority to the responsible officials and that such discretion is often used to release requested information where significant national interests would not be jeopardized.   It also recognised that countries that do seek information abroad usually pursue voluntary means to obtain data, rather than compulsory measures.

393.   One of the principal virtues of the 1979 Recommendation and the bilateral agreements appears to be that through notification and consultation,

they allow countries to discuss problems in their incipiency before conflicts and costs escalate. In addition, the 1979 Recommendation refers to restrictive practices "in international trade" and "of whatever origin" and it may, therefore, provide guidance for developing ways and means to facilitate notifications and exchanges of views between Member countries on restrictive business practices which are influenced by government policies. The Committee is presently reviewing experience with the application of the 1979 Recommendation and exploring the possibility of further strengthening the procedures provided by the Recommendation.

C. THE INVOLVEMENT OF COMPETITION AUTHORITIES IN THE DECISION-MAKING PROCESS ON TRADE POLICY MEASURES

394. As it appeared in the previous parts of this report, restrictions on competition and trade frequently elude effective control when they arise at the frontier of competence of trade authorities and competition officials. In particular, Chapter II of the report sets forth a substantative checklist by which the effects of trade policies on competition and economic efficiency can be assessed. The following section examines how coordination of competition and trade policies is actually functioning at national and international levels and what steps could be taken to improve existing arrangements. For this purpose, a distinction is drawn between policy formulation and policy implementation, the latter including the assessment of the effectiveness of action taken. At each stage of this process, competition authorities have an important contribution to make given their expertise with the functioning of markets and the short and longer term effects of restrictive practices on market structures. In addition, certain non-governmental bodies such as consumer organisations and associations of wholesalers and retailers have an active interest in competition and trade policies affecting competition. The possibilities for these organisations to make their views known to trade policy decision-makers are discussed by the Consumer Policy Committee in a report to the Council (175).

1. PROCEDURES AT NATIONAL LEVEL

a) Participation of competition officials in the formulation of trade policies

395. Based upon the information provided by Member countries, there is no uniform framework for organising cooperation between competition and trade authorities on matters of common interest. Procedures vary from country to country and correspond to different organisational patterns of government and public administration. Two countries, namely Finland and the Netherlands, reported the complete absence of any arrangement to solicit the views of competition officials prior to the adoption of trade policy measures. In these countries, competition policy concerns seems to have little or no impact on the decision-making process in the trade area. For the remaining countries, the survey carried out by the Committee has revealed the following -- not mutually exclusive -- arrangements to ensure that consideration is given to competition policy concerns in the area of trade and trade-related measures:

-- Concentration of tasks relating to trade and competition policies in the same government department;

-- Participation of competition authorities in interdepartmental committees or task forces dealing with trade matters;

-- Informal ad hoc policy coordination and interdepartmental consultations involving competition authorities;

-- Statutory requirements to consult competition authorities prior to the adoption of certain trade or trade-related measures.

The following paragraphs provide illustrative examples of each of these arrangements.

396. In several Member countries, the formulation of competition and trade policies is concentrated in the same Government Department. For instance, in Germany, there is close co-operation within the Federal Ministry of Economics between the sections responsible for competition and trade questions. In France, competition and trade authorities are both placed under the authority of the Minister of Economic Affairs and Finance. A similar situation exists in Spain, where competition and trade policies fall within the competence of the same Ministry and State Secretariat. In Ireland, the Ministry of Trade, Commerce and Tourism is responsible for competition and trade questions. In Switzerland, the agency primarily responsible for trade policy as well as international competition matters is the Federal Office for Foreign Economic Affairs. This office has had a long experience of close co-operation with the Secretariat of the Cartels Commission. These two agencies both belong to the Federal Department of Public Economy and maintain regular contacts with one another. In the United Kingdom, the Secretary of State for Trade and Industry has responsibilities for both trade and competition. He is responsible, for example, for deciding whether to refer mergers (taking into account the advice of the Director General of Fair Trading -- DGFT) to the Monopolies and Mergers Commission and can veto references by the DGFT of either monopolies or anti-competitive practices. He has also to decide on action subsequent to investigations by the Monopolies and Mergers Commission.

397. In several countries where competition policy and competition law enforcement are either within the competence of an independent authority or shared between such an authority and other government departments, procedural arrangements have been established to ensure interagency coordination. In Germany, there are close contacts between the Federal Cartel Office and the Federal Ministry of Economics including, in particular, competition matters affecting international trade. They can, for instance, intervene against export cartels where anticompetitive effects violate the principles concerning trade in goods and commercial services accepted by the Federal Republic in international treaties. The same applies if the export cartel substantially impairs predominant foreign trade and payments interests of the Federal Republic. In Sweden, the Competition Ombudsman is normally asked to present written statements on legislative proposals, including those on trade matters, which may have effects on competition. Correspondingly, trade authorities are normally asked to comment on proposals concerning competition legislation. In Norway, the Price Directorate, which is in charge of competition policy, is a member of the Advisory Committee on trade policy questions of the Department of Trade. Further, the Price Directorate is often consulted on specific

issues within the competence of other departments, such as questions relating to the entry and establishment of foreign enterprises in Norway.

398.   In New Zealand, the Commerce Commission can, in connection with its investigations of monopolies, make recommendations to the Minister of Trade and Industry concerning import controls.   In France, under Section 1 of the Act of 19 July, 1979 the Competition Commission may be consulted by the Government on legislative proposals raising issues of competition and its opinions may be published by the Minister for Economic Affairs and Finance.

399.   In Japan, the Fair Trade Commission is the agency which enforces the Anti-monopoly Act and seeks to preserve and promote free and fair competition in import and export trade.   The competent trade authorities, when they intend to grant exemptions from this Act to import or export cartels, are mandated to negotiate with the FTC and, in some cases, to notify it.   This procedure is necessary in order to obtain an exemption from the application of the Monopoly Act.

400.   In the United Kingdom, the main executive arm of competition policy is the Office of Fair Trading (OFT) headed by the Director General of Fair Trading (DGFT).   In addition, the Monopolies and Merger Commission (MMC) has the task of investigating anti-competitive conduct, monopolies and mergers. The Restrictive Practices Court decides whether or not restrictive trading agreements are against the public interest.   The DGFT from time to time advises the Secretary of State for Trade and Industry on general policy matters related to competition, but apart from that there is no formal mechanism for these competition authorities to influence trade policy. However, there is contact between the officials dealing with competition matters and those dealing with trade matters on an ad hoc basis and interchange of staff between the Department of Trade and Industry and the Office of Fair Trading, and, to a lesser extent, the Monopolies and Mergers Commission.

401.   In Canada, several interdepartmental committees, such as the Committee on Low Cost Imports have been set up in which Consumer and Corporate Affairs, the Department in charge of competition policy, can participate, but the role of these committees in the formulation of trade policy has been declining. Under the Combines Investigation Act, the Director of Investigation and Research, who is responsible for competition law enforcement, may make representations or submit evidence to government agencies "in respect of the maintenance of competition".   This authority has been used on several occasions to make submissions in the context of inquiries into matters relating to Canada's import policies.

402.   In the United States, the Attorney General and officials of the Antitrust Division of the Department of Justice are regular participants in several established inter-agency committees dealing with trade policy matters, which are organised in pyramid formation.   At the top, at Cabinet level, is the Trade Policy Committee (IPC) and the Cabinet Council on Commerce and Trade.   Below this are the Trade Policy Review Group (TPRG) and the Trade Policy Staff Committee (TPSC).   Several meetings occur per week, on average, at subcommittee levels involving virtually all trade policy issues.   Within the limits of its resources, the Antitrust Division actively participates in these meetings, offering comments on economic and policy issues as well as legal views and antitrust advice.   The Federal Trade Commission participates

in these meetings on a case-by-case basis. Both FTC and the Department of Justice regularly take part in deliberations of the Interagency Committee on Foreign Investment in the United States (CFIUS) though neither is formally a member of that committee.

b) Participation of competition authorities in the implementation of trade policies and the enforcement of trade laws

403. As shown by the preceding review, most countries have more or less formal arrangements for the participation of competition authorities in trade policy matters. However, where such procedures exist, they are generally confined to the expression of opinions on draft legislation or regulation or policy formulation and, in many cases, consultation is on an ad hoc basis rather than systematic. In most countries, competition authorities are not involved in any meaningful manner in the implementation process of trade policies or trade-related measures. There are two notable exceptions: Canada and the United States, where competition authorities are authorised to participate or make representations in proceedings under unfair trade laws or where the authority in charge of these proceedings is requested to take into account the effects on competition of actions taken under trade laws.

404. In Canada, Section 19 of the Customs Tariff permits the government to reduce or remove any duty which is being used by producers to increase prices above those that should prevail in a competitive market. There is also provision for the exemption of certain classes of goods from the application of the Anti-dumping Act. This authority was used to deny the pharmaceutical industry protection from dumping following a report by the Restrictive Trade Practices Commission that found the industry to be engaging in restrictive business practices in the early 1970s. Proposals are under consideration which would give prominence to the public interest in decisions to levy anti-dumping duties.

405. In the United States, competition authorities are empowered to intervene in different types of trade proceedings before the Commerce Department and/or the International Trade Commission, e.g. injury determinations in anti-dumping and subsidy cases, "escape clause" cases and so-called unfair import competition cases. They have frequently availed themselves of this opportunity to present a competition view point in particular proceedings. For instance, the FTC participated in 1982 in a procedure before the Department of Commerce and the ITC concerned with anti-dumping and countervailing duties in respect of steel products imported from various European countries, Brazil and South Africa. The FTC pointed out to the ITC the consequences which the imposition of such countervailing duties would have on domestic competition. In a case where softwood lumber products were imported from Canada, the FTC, in a prehearing Brief submitted to the Department of Commerce in April, 1983, stated its opinion that the imposition of countervailing duties was not justified, that it would raise the prices paid by American consumers and would have adverse effects on other sectors of the economy, particularly the building industry.

2. THE INTERNATIONAL LEVEL

406. International organisations may intervene in various stages of trade policy decisions and in certain instances play a decisive role in the process

of policy formulation or implementation, or both. For the EC Member countries, trade policy falls to a large extent within the competence of the European Communities. The following paragraphs provide a brief summary of arrangements and possibilities for co-ordination of trade and competition policies within the EEC, EFTA, GATT and OECD.

407. The rules on competition contained in Arts. 85 to 94 of the Treaty of Rome establish a comprehensive system designed to ensure the effective functioning of a common market within the Community. Articles 85 and 86 in particular are both based on the criterion of effects of restrictive business practices on trade between Member states. Control over another important element, State aid and subsidies (Art. 92 of the Treaty) is an integral part of the Community's machinery for the prevention of barriers to trade and competition within the common market. The Commission, which is responsible for both external trade relations as well as competition policy, is able to assure cooperation between the two areas, where necessary.

408. In order to ensure that trade between the EFTA countries occurs under conditions of fair competition, Articles 13 through 17 of the Stockholm Convention contain a set or rules concerning competition. These rules aim at preventing distortions of competition in trade between the participating countries that arise through the use of protectionist measures or practices. The Articles address government aids, public undertakings (purchasing practices), establishment, and dumped or subsidized imports.

409. On a world wide scale, the first and most ambitious attempt to develop a multinational instrument for dealing with interrelated trade and competition issues was made in the context of the Havana Charter for an International Trade Organisation. In 1945, proposals were advanced to mutually establish and enforce standards for the conduct of commercial relations and the control of restrictive business practices was included as an integral part of the proposed scheme (Chapter V of the Havana Charter of 1948). When by 1951 the Havana Charter had failed to obtain the necessary number of ratifications, an attempt was made in ECOSOC to revive Chapter V as a separate instrument. In May 1953 an ad hoc Committee established by ECOSOC presented a report recommending an international agreement on restrictive business practices. As this report did not attract sufficient support, the project was definitively abandoned in 1955.

410. In essence, the text of Chapter V of the Havana Charter and the ad hoc Committee's proposals sought to establish procedures for consultations, complaints, co-operative enforcement action and a mechanism for studying and recommending improvements in the handling of restrictive business practices affecting international trade. Efforts to insert similar elements into the GATT were made between 1954 and 1960, but a working party appointed to examine these proposals failed to agree on a compromise. Finally, the Contracting Parties adopted in 1960 a resolution simply recommending that "at the request of any contracting party a contracting party should enter into consultations" on allegedly harmful restrictive practices and the party requested should accord sympathetic consideration with a view to reaching mutually satisfactory conclusions. Parties were supposed to report to the Secretariat the nature of any complaint and the fact that a mutually satisfactory conclusion had been or could not be reached. No such reports have been made to date.

411.   Trade policy issues can be discussed in a multidisciplinary manner involving various bodies such as the Trade Committee, the Economic Policy Committee, the CIME and the Consumer Policy Committee. The preparation of the present report has led to a constructive dialogue between the Committee of Experts on Restrictive Business Practices and the Trade Committee and close cooperation between both Committees will be pursued on issues of common interest. In the course of this report, numerous references have been made to the 1979 Council Recommendation concerning cooperation on restrictive business practices affecting international trade. This Recommendation provides an important framework in which contacts between competition and trade authorities can be organised to deal with issues where restrictive practices by enterprises and government trade policies are closely interrelated. As requested by the 1982 Ministerial Council, the Committee is reviewing this Recommendation and intends to report to the Council in 1985. In the course of this review, particular attention is being given to the possibilities for strengthening the existing procedures for notification, exchanges of information and consultations at bilateral level and within the Organisation. In addition, consideration will be given to clarifying the scope of the Recommendation and to elaborating complementary mechanisms for dealing with issues arising at the frontier between competition and trade policies, in particular those discussed in the present report.

D. CONCLUSIONS

412.   In light of the increasing internationalisation of business conduct, the rising importance of trade as a component of national economies and the development of competition law in most OECD Members, there is a strong interest in controlling restrictive practices on the part of either foreign or domestic firms which create anti-competitive effects on domestic markets. On the other hand, policies designed to promote export trade or to regulate imports, through the creation of such structures as export cartels, import cartels, trading companies or joint ventures, can be of limited effect depending on the jurisdictional reach of the competition laws existing in target markets. In this context, jurisdictional rules and international arrangements need to reflect the growth and development of the world trading system to ensure that all relevant interests are considered and disputes avoided as far as possible when questions of jurisdiction over international conduct arise and to provide businesses with reasonable certainty as to the laws applicable to their transactions. Although there seems to be growing observance of moderation and self-restraint, in the absence of multilaterally agreed upon criteria, unilateral approaches are not likely to be successful in resolving all conflicts which may arise. With due regard to the situs of conduct, jurisdictional rules should be based on reasonable standards that allow for the consistent and effective implementation of the laws and policies of the countries affected. In this connection, while significant differences remain among Member countries, the Committee recognises the desirability of achieving international agreed criteria for avoiding or resolving jurisdictional differences of this nature.

413.   There is a strong common interest among OECD Member countries in overcoming difficulties arising from competing claims of jurisdiction over international business activities and there have been encouraging signs in the

development of cooperation between governments, in particular in the competition area. On whatever basis jurisdiction is applied, competition authorities may need to obtain information located outside the national territory in order to adequately evaluate the nature of practices under review and the impact of such practices on competition in the domestic market. The notification and consultation procedures provided for under international instruments and bilateral agreements have provided a useful first step in creating channels to resolve conflicts between the competition policies and trading interests of countries.

414.   Given their expertise with the functioning of markets and the short and longer-term effects of restrictive business practices on market structures, competition officials can make an important contribution to the formulation and implementation of trade policies. In most countries, arrangements of a formal or more frequently informal nature exist to obtain the advice of competition authorities on trade policy measures likely to affect competition. Nevertheless, experience shows that procedures do not always suffice to bring to bear on trade policy any real influence based on the criteria of competition. This situation could be significantly improved if policy makers undertook, where appropriate with the assistance of competition authorities, an analysis of the likely effects of prospective trade measures, guided by a checklist of quantitative and qualitative criteria as described in Chapter II of this report.

415.   Given the diversity of government structures in Member countries, it is neither possible nor desirable to propose a single institutional framework in which coordination between trade and competition policies could be organised. Stress should be laid not on rigid procedural arrangements, but rather on creating the necessary conditions under which competition policy considerations can effectively be brought to the attention of policy-makers in the formulation and implementation of trade policies. For this purpose, competition authorities should be provided, subject to legal constraints, in a timely manner with relevant information on the nature and motivation of proposed trade policy decisions and be invited to express their views on all such decisions likely to have a significant impact on competition. Corresponding to different organisational patterns of government and public administration, there are various options for organising such participation, such as informal but regular contacts, establishment of standing interdepartmental committees or formal public hearings. On their part, competition authorities should be sensitive to the realities and developments in international trade including in particular trade rules and the growing internationalisation of markets. Thus, there is a need for a two-way co-operation between trade and competition authorities so as to better promote the efficient functioning of markets within an open international trading system.

416.   In the next phase of its work, the Committee will consider steps that could be taken at international level to improve longer term cooperation on issues arising at the frontier between competition and trade policies. In this context, it will study the means by which the mechanisms that have proved beneficial in promoting cooperation in the competition area could be strengthened and whether they could be applied to trade matters having a substantial effect on competition. The review of the 1979 Recommendation which is presently underway will be an important part of that exercise. Within the Organisation, the Committee will continue to cooperate closely with

the Trade Committee and other bodies dealing with trade or trade related matters within the area of their competence. It will provide, where appropriate, its advice to these bodies on issues likely to have a bearing on competition.

NOTES AND REFERENCES

CHAPTER I

EXPORT CARTELS AND SIMILAR ARRANGEMENTS

1.   Export Cartels, Report of the Committee of Experts on Restrictive Business Practices, OECD, Paris, 1974, p. 7.

2.   Rahl, "International Antitrust Policy", Northwestern Journal of Law and Business, 2:336 (1980), p. 354.

3.   Id.

4.   See, e.g., United States v. General Electric Co., 82 F. Supp. 743 (D.N.J. 1949); United States v. General Dyestuffs Corp., Cr. 111-135 (S.D.N.Y. filed 1941); United States v. General Analine and Film Corp., Cr. 111-136 (S.D.N.Y., filed 1941); United States v. Imperial Chemical Industries, Ltd., 100 F. Supp. 504 (S.D.N.Y. 1951); United States v. U.S. Alkali Export Ass'n., 86 F. Supp. 59 (S.D.N.Y. 1949); United States v. National Lead Co., 63 F. Supp. 513 (S.D.N.Y. 1945).

5.   Due to the Supreme Court's decision in the oil field pipes case in 1973 and before the 1980 Amendment to the Act, "pure" export cartels did not need to be notified to the Federal Cartel Office so that data for the period 1973 to 1980 are not reliable.

6.   F.T.C., Economic Report on Webb-Pomerene Associations: A Fifty Year Review (see also OECD report on Export Cartels (1974), para. 69).

7.   F.T.C., Webb-Pomerene Associations: Ten years later (1978), p.15.

8.   Hearings H.R. 2326 before the Subcomm. on Monopolies and Commercial Law, House of Rep. Comm. of the Judiciary, 97th Cong., 1st Sess. (1981) pp. 163-4.

9.   See OECD Report on Export Cartels, op. cit., Chapter II and Annexes for data up to 1972.

10.   Webb-Pomerene Associations: Ten Years Later, op.cit., p. 12.

11.   See OECD report on Export Cartels, Annex V, Tables 3 to 5 for summary of statutes, area of operation, function, etc., analysed in 1967 report.

12.   See, e.g., FTC Report on Webb-Pomerene Associations, A Fifty Year Review, op.cit., pp. 32-4.

13.   Export Cartels, pp. 47-48.

14.   Id., p. 51.

15.   See David A. Larson: "An Economic Analysis of the Webb-Pomerene Act", The Journal of Law and Economics (1970), p. 497.

16.   Webb-Pomerene Associations: Ten Years Later, op.cit., pp. 13-14.

17.   Id.

18.   Foreign Trade Antitrust Improvements Act of 1982, Section 2 (Title IV of Export Trading Company Act of 1982).

19.   United States v. Alkali Export Association, 86 F. Supp. 59 (S.D.N.Y. 1949); United States v. Minnesota Mining and Mfg. Co., 92 F. Supp 947 (D. Mass. 1950); United States v. Concentrated Phosphate Export Association, 393 US 199 (1968); United States v. Anthracite Export Association, 1970 Trade Cases para. 73,348 (M.D. Pa. 1970); In re General Milk Co., Inc., 44 F.T.C. 1355 (1947); In re Carbon Black Export Inc., 46 F.T.C. 1245 (1949); Florida Hardrock Phosphate Export Association, 40 F.T.C. 843 (1945); Export Screw Association of the U.S., 43 F.T.C. 980 (1947); Sulphur Export Corp., 43 F.T.C. 980 (1947); Phosphate Export Association, 42 F.T.C. 555 (1946).

20.   86 F. Supp. 59, (S.D.N.Y. 1949).

21.   92 F. Supp. 947 (D. Mass. 1950).

22.   See also the suggestions made in the report by the Committee of Experts on Restrictive Business Practices on Competition Law Enforcement: International Cooperation in the Collection of Information, OECD, Paris, 1984, pp. 75-76.

IMPORT CARTELS

23.   Monopsony power can of course be exercised without a cartel; dominant domestic firms, trading companies, public corporations and state buying agencies may all be able to influence the price and quantity of products they import.

24.   United States v. Sisal Sales Corp., 274 U.S. 268 (1926).

25.   Continental Ore Co. v. Marion Carbide Corp., 370 U.S. 690 (1962).

26.   Judgment of 26 March 1963 L.R. 4 R.P. .....

27.   Decision of the Japanese Fair Trade Commission, 31 March 1983.

28.   Re National Sulphuric Acid Association Ltd's Agreement (1963) L.R. 4 R.P. 169. In Australia the Trade Practices Commission authorised a joint buying agreement for sulphur from overseas by six major Australian fertiliser manufacturers.

29.   United States v. C. Itoh and Co. et. al., Civ. No. C-82-810 (W.D. Wash, 1982).

TRADING COMPANIES

30.   Cascade Steel Rolling Mills Inc., v. C. Itoh & Co., et al., 499 F. Supp. 829 (D. Ore. 1980). The defendant Japanese trading companies include Kanematsu-Gosho, Ltd., Nichimen & Co., Ltd., Nisshu-Iwai Co., Ltd., C. Itoh & Co., Ltd., Mitsubishi Corp., Mitsui & Co., Ltd., Sumitomo Shoji Kaisha, Ltd., and Marubeni Corp.

31.   This case has generated several decisions in the Court of Appeals for the Fifth Circuit, under the name Industrial Investment Development Corp. v. Mitsui & Co., Ltd., including decisions on the application of the act of state doctrine [594 F. 2d 48 (1979)], subject matter jurisdiction [671 F. 2d 876 (1982)], and standing [1983-1 trade cases, para. 65, 360 (1983)].

32.   Four of the defendants were Japanese trading companies. Those companies were C. Itoh & Co., Ltd., Mitsui & Co., Ltd., Shinko Sangyo Trading Co., Ltd., and Toshoku Ltd.

33.   United States v. C. Itoh & Co., Ltd., et al., Civil No. C-82-810 (W.D. Wash., 1982).

VOLUNTARY EXPORT RESTRAINTS

34.   In the United States, the Trade Act of 1974 authorises the President to use OMAs as a means of implementing relief in "escape clause" cases. In addition to or in lieu of effecting tariff increases or quotas on imports of the pertinent product, the Trade Act authorises the President to "negotiate, conclude, and carry out orderly marketing agreements with foreign countries limiting the export from foreign countries and the import into the United States of such article." 19 U.S.C. § 2253(a)(4).

        Thus, there is a direct statutory basis for the negotiation of OMAs. On the other hand, United States law does not specifically authorise voluntary export restraints for purposes of import relief. VERs sometimes do occur where import relief has not been granted under the Trade Act of 1974. A voluntary export restraint can be negotiated under the President's general authority on foreign affairs, but no antitrust immunity arises for the enterprises participating in such a restraint. See Hindley, "Voluntary Export Restraints and Article XIX of the GATT", Trade Policy Research Centre (1978), p. 22 (hereinafter, "Hindley").

35.   The GATT Secretariat maintains an inventory of safeguard restrictions, including VERs, and is presently engaged in a study of this question. It is not likely that this list is exhaustive. Consequently, the business and economic press remains a major source of information on VERs.

36. Hindley, op. cit., p. 2.

37. De Kieffer, "Antitrust and the Japanese Auto Quotas", VIII Brooklyn Journal of Int'l Law pp. 59-63.

38. Id., p. 63.

39. Id., pp. 64-75. Nonetheless, this did not fully preclude the possibility of private antitrust litigation against the Japanese companies, which is available under the US laws. In fact, one US dealer of Japanese autos sued the manufacturer as a result of losses arising out of the VER. The dealer alleged that the supplier had cut its shipments in half and that the cars received were loaded with optional equipment, reducing the dealer's profit margin.

OTHER BUSINESS PRACTICES AFFECTING INTERNATIONAL TRADE

40. See Duro-dyne/Europair OJ L29 (1975) p. 11.

41. See Grosfillex/Fillistorf JO N° 58 of 9/4/64 and Rieckermann/AEG-Elotherm JO N° L 276 of 14/11/68.

42. Grundig-Consten v. Commission, Joined cases Nos 56-64 and 58-64, 1966 (ECR), p. 429.

43. OJ L 57 of 25/3/67, p. 849.

44. OJ L 173 of 30/6/83 and OJ C 355 of 30/12/83 (communication).

45. See United States v. Arnold Schwinn & Co., 388 US 365 (1967).

46. See Continental TV. Inc v. GTE Sylvania, 433 US 36, 51-59 (1977).

47. These two practices have also been addressed at the multilateral level. The OECD MNE Guidelines provide generally that enterprises should refrain from "discriminatory (i.e. unreasonably differentiated) pricing and using such pricing transactions between affiliated enterprises as a means of affecting adversely competition outside these enterprises. Section D-4 of the 1980 UN RBP Code also refers to discriminatory pricing.

48. See, e.g., United Brands Co. v. Commission. In the United Brands case, the court held that a vertically-integrated US-based supplier abused its dominant position by charging different prices to different markets where the price differentials were without objective justification and had the effect of tending to maintain substantially different price levels in each of the Member states. In the same case, the Commission further alleged that excessive prices imposed by a firm in a dominant position violated Article 86 as well.

49. EEC Interim Measure 83/462, ECS/AKZO, 1983 OJ L252/13.

50. OECD report on Restrictive Business Practices Relating to Patents and Licences, 1972 p. 19.

51.   Id.

52.   Id., pp. 16-18

53.   Id., p. 16.

54.   See, e.g., Nungesser and Eisele v. Commission, Case 258/78.

55.   See, e.g., AOIP/Beyard, (1976-78 Transfer Binder) CCH Comm. Mkt. Rep.
       para. 9801, pp. 9793-6 to -7;

56.   AGA v. Steel Radiators, Seventh Report on Competition Policy, pp. 105-7
   •   (1978).

57.   See OECD report on Restrictive Business Practices Relating to
       Trademarks (1978) pp. 70-72. The Antitrust Division of the US
       Department of Justice filed an amicus brief in the appeal of Bell and
       Howell: Mamiya Co. v. Masel Supply Co., 548 F. Supp. 1063 (E.D.N.Y.
       1982). The brief advocated that the Second Circuit Court of Appeals
       should affirm the district court's decision that a US trademark holder
       was entitled to relief for trademark infringement when parallel imports
       bearing the same mark were sold in the US without permission of the
       trademark holder. The Justice Department argued that the Lanham Act
       properly grants the right to enjoin such importation, and that the
       district court's injunction does not conflict with federal antitrust
       policies since, inter alia, there was no evidence that the plaintiff
       enjoyed market power in any relevant market. Brief for the United
       States of America, Amicus Curiae, in Bell and Howell: Mamiya Co. v.
       Masel Supply Co. (2d Cir., No. 82-7857). The Court of Appeals reversed
       the district court's decision to grant preliminary relief on other
       grounds, without reaching the issue.

58.   See East-West Trade, Recent Developments in Countertrade, OECD, Paris
       (1981) ("East-West Trade") pp. 5, 9.

59.   See, e.g., "New Restrictions on World Trade", Business Week July 19,
       1982 ("Business Week") pp. 128-29; "The Explosion of International
       Barter", Fortune, February 7, 1983 ("Fortune"), p. 89. As to
       industrial nations, Canada, Switzerland, Sweden, Austria and other
       European countries have linked purchases of costly items such as
       aircraft or hospital equipment to the export of their products. A new
       variation in a few Western countries is tying approvals of investment
       proposals to export commitments. Business Week at 128, 132. Some
       countries such as Romania and Indonesia have government-mandated
       countertrade requirements for a large portion of government contracts
       awarded to foreign companies. See also East-West Trade, Annex I.

60.   See Business Week pp. 128-29, 132.

61.   See, e.g., Business Week at 128 and East-West Trade at 5-6. The East
       European countries view countertrade as a lasting and increasingly
       prevalent aspect of their trading relationship with the West. See
       East-West Trade, p. 57.

62. Business Week, pp. 129-130, Fortune, pp. 93-95.

63. Business Week, p. 131.

64. See East-West Trade, op.cit., pp. 7-8.

65. Section 201 of the Trade Act of 1974, 19 U.S.C. § 2251 et seq.

MULTINATIONAL ENTERPRISES AND INTRA-FIRM AGREEMENTS

66. Transnational Corporations in World Development Third Survey, UN Centre on Transnational Corporations, 1983, paragraphs 478 to 480.

67. Department of Commerce, Survey of Current Business.

68. See Overseas Transactions 1979 and 1980, Business Monitor (London, HM Stationary Office).

69. J.H. Dunning and R.D. Pearce, The World's Largest Enterprises (Gover 1981) p. 132.

70. Dominant Positions of Market Power of Transnational Corporations, Use of Transfer Pricing Mechanism, UNCTAD 1978.

71. Restrictive Business Practices of Multinational Enterprises, OECD, 1977 (hereafter cited as "MNE Report").

72. Council Recommendation concerning action against restrictive business practices affecting international trade including those involving multinational enterprises [C(78)133(Final)].

73. MNE Report, paragraph 191.

74. See Hedland, Johansson and Otterbeck, Autonomy of Subsidiaries in Multinational Companies, Research Paper, Institute of International Business, Stockholm School of Economics (to be published).

75. See International Investment and Multinational Enterprises, the 1984 Review of the 1976 Declaration and Decisions, OECD, 1984, Chapter IV, for an account of the CIME survey.

76. Transfer pricing and multinational enterprises, Report by the Committee on Fiscal Affairs, OECD 1979. Of course, transfer pricing policies are subject to the controls and constraints imposed by tax authorities in order to prevent tax evasion.

77. Dominant Positions of Market Power of Transnational Corporations, Use of Transfer Pricing Mechanisms, UNCTAD, 1978.

78. See MNE Report, paragraphs 71 to 78.

79. Decision of the Minister of Economic Affairs and Finance concerning Boehringer, Bulletin Officiel de la Concurrence et de la Consommation of 31 August 1983.

80. United Brands v. Commission, Case 27/761 Court of Justice Reports 1978-2.

81. MNE Report, paragraph 77.

82. Id., paragraph 65.

83. International Investment and Multinational Enterprises: Responsibility of Parent Companies for their Subsidiaries, OECD 1980, paragraphs 51 to 55.

84. MNE Report, paragraph 200.

85. Centrafarm v. Sterling Drug, Case No. 15/74, [1974] ECR 1147 See also Commission, Sixth Report on Competition Policy, paragraph 39 (1977); Commission Response to Parliamentary Question, May 13, 1977. But cf. Kodak-Pathe, 05 No. L 147 of 7th July 1970.

86. Response by the Commission to Written Question No. 67/80, 23OJ Eur Comm (No C 167) 28, 3 Comm. Mkt. Rep P 10,245 (1980).

87. See Commission of the European Communities, Sixth Report on Competition Policy, p.32 (1976).

88. In a few instances, courts have found illegal parent-subsidiary agreements that in fact substantially restrained competition outside the enterprise, e.g. that have been employed as part of an anticompetitive scheme to drive competitors from the marketplace or to monopolise a market. Such cases typically involve a parent and subsidiary which hold themselves out as competitors, or an ownership interest used to disguise a pre-existing conspiracy to restrain trade. See U.S. 134 (1968), Timken Roller Bearing Co. v. United States, 341 U.S. 593 (1951). The use of section 1 in such circumstances has been criticized. Section 2 of the Sherman Act, the primary U.S. statute that prohibits anticompetitive single-firm behaviour, would more appropriately apply to prescriptive conduct by a single corporate group that amounts to monopolization or attempted monopolization.

89. Report of the Attorney General's National Committee to Study the Antitrust Laws 34 (1955).

90. Effective working control has been found to exist even though there was only a five percent holding. United States v. Citizens & Southern National Bank, 422 U.S. 86 (1975).

91. Department of Justice, Antitrust Guide for International Operations 10-14 (1977).

92. Brief for the United States as Amicus Curiae Supporting Petitioners' Writ of Certiorari to the U.S. Supreme Court in Copperweld Corp. v. Independence Tube Co., No. 82-1260, 1983.

93. Responsibility of Parent Companies for their subsidiaries, op.cit., paragraphs 59 to 62.

94. Europemballage Corp. & Continental Can v. Commission, European Court of Justice Reports 1975, 215.

95. Cases No. 6 and 7/73, E.C. of Justice Reports, 1974-3.

96. Competition Law Enforcement: International Cooperation in the Collection of Information, OECD, 1984.

97. OECD Council Recommendation Concerning Co-operation Between Member Countries on Restrictive Business Practices Affecting International Trade/[C(79)154(Final)].

98. The relevant provision of the taxation chapter of the Guidelines reads as follows:

   "Enterprises should:

   1. ....

   2. refrain from making use of the particular facilities available to them such as transfer pricing which does not conform to the arm's length standard for modifying in ways contrary to national laws the tax base on which members of the group are assessed".

99. Under (VIII) of the disclosure chapter of the Guidelines, enterprises are called upon to disclose "policies followed in respect of intra-group pricing".

GOVERNMENT INVOLVEMENT IN AND REGULATION OF COMMERCIAL ACTIVITIES

100. European Centre of Public Enterprises. Cited in La Revue Economique No. 3 of May 1983 (Presses de la Fondation Nationale des Sciences Politiques, Paris): 15.8 per cent constitutes the average of the three percentages calculated in accordance with the following criteria: wage earners (11.9 per cent), value added (13.2 per cent), gross fixed asset formation (22.5 per cent).

101. According to the Commission Directive of 25th June 1980 on the transparency of financial relations between Member States and public undertakings, a "public undertaking" is taken as "any undertaking over which the public authorities may exercise directly or indirectly a dominant influence by virtue of their ownership of it, their financial participation therein, or the rules which govern it" (Official Journal of the European Communities, No L 195/35 of 29th July 1980).

102. United Nations Centre on Transnational Corporations: "Transnational Corporations in World Development", Third Survey, United Nations, New York, p. 51, 1983.

103. CIME: International Investment and Multinational Enterprises: Mid-term Report on the 1976 Declaration and Decisions (OECD, 1982), p. 69.

104. Article 3, Note 1, of the Directive quoted above. The validity of the latter has been confirmed by the Court of Justice following an appeal by three Member States (Judgments in Joined Cases Nos 188 to 198 80 (France, Italy, United Kingdom/Commission of 6th July 1982), cf. 12th report, paragraphs 222-224).

105. Competition Policy in Regulated Sectors, OECD, 1979.

106. Idem, p. 9

107. In the framework of the United Nations, a Code of Conduct for Liner Conferences regulates the activities of the Conferences.

108. Report by Maritime Transport Committee on Competition Policy in Shipping: situation in OECD Member countries, para. 132 (1983).

109. Op. cit., paragraphs 189, 191-2 and 210.

110. Ruling on the milk market (CC, publ. 4/1969 p. 34).

111. US v. Baltimore and Ohio R.R. et al., Cir. No. 81-936 (DDC, 1981).

112. US v. Niagara Frontier Tariff Bureau, Inc., Civ. 83-1681 (DDC, 1983).

CHAPTER II

113. By the beginning of the Tokyo Round of GATT negotiations in 1973 the average level of tariffs had fallen to about 6 per cent and that Round resulted in further cuts of about one-third.

114. See, e.g., S.A.B. Page, "The Revival of Protectionism and its Consequences for Europe", Journal of Common Market Studies, Vol. XX, No 1, September 1981, pp. 17-40.

115. OECD Press Release [Press/A(83)25] of 10th May 1983.

116. Id., paragraph 13.

117. See also the Role of Competition Policy in a Period of Economic Recession, with Special Reference to Crisis Cartels, OECD, Paris, 1981, paragraphs 47 to 50.

118. Morris E. Morkre and David G. Tarr, The Effects of Restrictions on United States Imports: Five Case Studies and Theory, Staff Report of the Bureau of Economics to the Federal Trade Commission, U.S. Government Printing Office, June 1980. For another interesting example, See Comment by the Federal Trade Commission's Bureau of Competition, Bureau of Consumer Protection and Bureau of Economics on Countervailing Duty Investigations Before the U.S. Department of Commerce on the Matter of Certain Steel Products from Belgium, Brazil, the Federal Republic of Germany, France, Italy, Luxembourg, the Netherlands, Romania, South Africa, Spain and the United Kingdom, May 1982.

119. The competition issues raised by counter-trade arrangements between enterprises are discussed in Chapter I(5)(e).

120. For example, the US OMA with Japan on colour television receivers in 1977 was followed two years later by an agreement with Korean and Taiwanese manufacturers following a surge in US imports from those countries.

121. Gomez-Ibanez, Leone and O'Connell, "Restraining Auto Imports: Does Anyone Win", Journal of Policy Analysis and Management, Vol. 2 No. 2, (1983), See text and studies cited at 199, Fn. 9, 10. (Hereafter "Gomez-Ibanez"). Bergsten, "On the Non-Equivalence of Import Quotas and VERs", in Toward a New World Trade Policy: The Maidenhead Papers, (Lexington, Ma: Lexington Books, 1975).

122. Antitrust and Trade Regulation Reporter, October 9, 1980, A-17.

123. Report in Wall Street Journal, May 2, 1983 ; Gomez-Ibanez, supra.

124. Report in Wall Street Journal, August 4, 1983, p. 7.

125. Study by Victor Canto and Arthur Laffer, reported in Business Week, January 31, 1983, pp. 9-10.

126. Morkre and Tarr, supra, page 193.

127. Id., Chapter 7.

128. This section does not consider the effects of trade embargos imposed for foreign policy and/or strategic considerations.

129. Such export cartels should be distinguished from cooperative arrangements having the objective of grouping smaller firms together to achieve economies of scale in competing in international markets without exerting market power.

130. See also, text at Chapter I, Section B(4).

131. Long, "The Tokyo Round of Multilateral Trade Negotiations, GATT Publication (Geneva 1979), p. 54 (hereafter "Long").

132. Id., p. 55.

133. Id., p. 53. See also Baldwin, "The Multilateral Trade Negotiations". American Enterprise Institute (Special Analysis) (1979) at 11. (hereafter "Baldwin").

134. Baldwin p. 12.

135. Id., p. 12.

136. Long, p. 131.

137. Baldwin, p. 13.

138. Jointed cases 267/81, 268/81 and 269/81; Judgment of 16 March 1983, European Court Reports, 1983-4, p.801.

139. The Federation of the Vegetable Oil Industry in the EEC (FEDIVOL), Case 141/82 -- Fedivol Judgment of 4 October 1983; reported in "European Law Letter", November 1983, pp. 12, 13. (Decision not yet published).

140. The data in this section is based both on individual country responses to the questionnaire and on cases listed in the GATT inventories. Under Article 14:4 of the GATT, signatories to the Anti-Dumping Practice Code are required to file semi-annual reports to the Committee on Anti-Dumping Practices regarding actions which have been taken. Similar reporting requirements exist with respect to countervail and subsidies. It should be noted that data among countries are not always comparable, since investigations involving more than one company may be reported as one or several investigations, according to national practice.

141. United Mine Workers v. Pennington, 381 U.S. 657 (1965); Eastern R.R. Presidents Conference v. Noerr Motor Freight, 365 U.S. 127 (1961).

142. California Motor Transp. Co. v. Trucking Unlimited, 404 U.S. 508 (1962).

143. Outboard Marine Corp. v. Petzel, 1979-2 Trade Cas. [CCH] § 62,792 at 78,603.

144. For example, the Japanese VER concerning passenger car exports to the United States was initiated only after a decision by the U.S. International Trade Commission that Japanese automobile imports were not a substantial cause of injury to U.S. producers.

145. In the U.S., predatory intent is inferred where prices are set below average variable costs. This is the so called "Areeda-Turner test".

146. In the United States, See, e.g., Primary Lead Metal from Australia and Canada, Inv. No. AA 1921-134/35, 39 Fed. Reg. 2,156 (1974).

147. See, e.g., Hanson v. Pittsburgh Plate Glass Industries, 482 F.2d. 220 (5th Cir. 1973), cert. denied, 414 U.S. 1136 (1974).

148. See generally, Report of the Ad Hoc [ABA] Sub-committee on Antitrust and Antidumping,
43 Antitrust L.J. 653 (1974), Footnote 15.

149. Prehearing Brief of the FTC, August 27, 1982.

CHAPTER III

150. See generally, Hawk, "International Antitrust Policy and the 1982 Acts: the Continuing Need for Reassessment", 51 Fordham Law Review (1982), pp. 201-254.

151. See Rosenthal and Knighton, National laws and International Commerce, London 1982, pp. 53-67.

152. Id.

153. Competition Law Enforcement: International Cooperation in the Collection of Information, OECD, Paris, 1984.

154. Id., p. 4.

155. Restrictive Business Practices of Multinational Enterprises, 1977 OECD Report, §§ 130-140.

156. Id., See also Europemballage, Continental Can Inc. v. Commission (1973), Judgment in Case 6/72 of 21st February 1973 [E.C.R. 215] United Brands Co. v. E.C. Commission (1978) Judgment in Case No. 27/78 of 14 February 1978 [E.C.R. 207].

157. OECD Report on Restrictive Business Practices of Multinational Enterprises (1977), §§ 137-40

158. 370 U.S. 690 (1962).

159. See generally text and notes at Coad, Brian, "Recent Development: the Canadian State Immunity Act", Law and Policy in International Business, Vol. 14, No.4 (1983), pp. 1197-1220.

160. Id., at 1199. See also Lauterpacht, "The Problem of Jurisdictional Immunities of Foreign States", 28 British Y.B. Int /. L. 220, 250-72 (1951).

161. 28 U.S.L. 41602, et. seq. The U.S. informally adopted restrictive immunity in the so-called Tate Letter. See Letter from Tate, Acting Legal Advisor, U.S. Department of State, to Perlman, Acting Attorney General (May 1952) 26 Dept. of State Bulletin 984 (1952).

162. Trendtex Trading Corporation v. Central Bank of Nigeria, (1977), I Q.B. 529; See now Congresso I Partido (1981), 3 W.L.R. 321.

163. International Ass'n. of Machinists v. OPEC, 649 F.2d 1354 (9th Cir. 1979) Cert. denied, 454 U.S. 1163 (1982).

164. Associated Container Transportation Ltd. v. U.S., Hamburg-Sudamerikanische Dampfschiffahrts-Gesellschaft, Eggert and Amsinck dB/a Columbus Line v. U.S., Farrell Lines, Inc. v. U.S., Nos. 82-6242, 82-6314, 82-6316, CA 2, (22 April, 1983).

165. Williams v. Curtis-Wright Corp., No. 82-5141, CA 3 (Nov. 29, 1982).

166. See Continental Ore Co. vs. Union Carbide and Carbon Corp., 370 U.S. 690 (1962); Interamerican Refining Corp. vs. Texas Maracaibo, 307 F. Supp. 1291 (D. Del. 1971); Linesman vs. World Hockey Assn., 439 F. Supp. 1315 (D. Conn. 1974); Department of Justice, Antitrust Guide for International Operations 50-52 (1977).

167. See, e.g., U.S. v. The Watchmakers of Switzerland Information Centre, Inc., CCH Trade Cas. (1963); Continental Ore Company v. Union Carbide and Carbon Corp., 370 U.S. 690 (1962).

168. See, e.g., OECD Report on the Collection of Information, op. cit., (1984); In the mid-1970's, the U.S. Justice Department announced in its "Guide to Antitrust Operations Abroad" that it would observe comity considerations in exercising its discretion to investigate and prosecute business practices. The Department indicated that it would consider conflicting national interests of foreign countries when deciding whether to pursue cases involving conduct that occurs abroad.

169. Maier, Harold G., "Extraterritorial Jurisdiction at a Crossroads", American Journal of International Law, Vol. 76 (April 1982), pp. 280-81.

170. See Shenefield, John, "U.S. Antitrust in the International Arena. The Problem and Some Solutions", 15 Swiss Review of International Antitrust Law (June 1982), p. 17.

171. In the first case to use a balancing test, Timberlane Lumber v. Bank of America, 549 F. 2d 597, 614 (9th Cir. 1976), the Court set out the following criteria:

1) The degree of conflict with foreign law of policy;

2) The nationality or allegiance of the parties and the location or principal places of business or corporate parties;

3) The extent to which enforcement by either state can be expected to achieve compliance;

4) The relative significance of effects in the U.S. as compared with those elsewhere;

5) The extent to which there is an explicit purpose to harm or effect American commerce;

6) The forseeability of such effect, and;

7) The relative importance to the violations charged of conduct within the U.S. as compared with conduct abroad.

In Mannington Mills, Inc. v. Congoleum Corp., 595 F.2d 1287 at 1297-98 (3d. Cir. 1976), another federal court added the following factors to be weighed:

1) The availability of a remedy abroad and the pendency of litigation there;

2) Whether an order for relief would be acceptable in the U.S. if made by the foreign nation under similar circumstances;

3) Whether a treaty with the affected nation has addressed the issue;

4) If relief is granted, whether a party will be placed in the position of being forced to perform an act illegal in either country or otherwise be under conflicting requirements by both countries, and;

5) The possible effect upon foreign relations between the two countries if the court exercises jurisdiction and grants relief.

172.   See, e.g., Restatement of Foreign Relations Law of the United States (Revised) Tent. Draft No. 2 (1981).

173.   See, e.g., Rosenthal and Knighton, pp. 26-28.

174.   For example, in the Mannington Mills case, the plaintiff sued for monopolisation, claiming inter alia that the defendant had blocked U.S. Competitors overseas by fraudulently obtaining patents in 26 foreign nations.

175.   Consumer Policy and International Trade, OECD, 1984 (forthcoming).

OECD SALES AGENTS
DÉPOSITAIRES DES PUBLICATIONS DE L'OCDE

ARGENTINA – ARGENTINE
Carlos Hirsch S.R.L., Florida 165, 4° Piso (Galería Guemes)
1333 BUENOS AIRES. Tel. 33.1787.2391 y 30.7122

AUSTRALIA – AUSTRALIE
Australia and New Zealand Book Company Pty, Ltd.,
10 Aquatic Drive, Frenchs Forest, N.S.W. 2086
P.O. Box 459, BROOKVALE, N.S.W. 2100. Tel. (02) 452.44.11

AUSTRIA – AUTRICHE
OECD Publications and Information Center
4 Simrockstrasse 5300 Bonn (Germany). Tel. (0228) 21.60.45
Local Agent/Agent local :
Gerold and Co., Graben 31, WIEN 1. Tel. 52.22.35

BELGIUM – BELGIQUE
Jean De Lannoy, Service Publications OCDE
avenue du Roi 202, B-1060 BRUXELLES. Tel. 02/538.51.69

BRAZIL – BRÉSIL
Mestre Jou S.A., Rua Guaipa 518,
Caixa Postal 24090. 05089 SAO PAULO 10. Tel. 261.1920
Rua Senador Dantas 19 s/205-6, RIO DE JANEIRO GB.
Tel. 232.07.32

CANADA
Renouf Publishing Company Limited,
61 Sparks Street (Mall), OTTAWA, Ont. K1P 5A6
Tel. (613)238.8985-6
Toll Free: 1-800.267.4164
2182 ouest, rue Ste-Catherine,
MONTRÉAL, Qué. H3H 1M7. Tel. (514)937.3519

DENMARK – DANEMARK
Munksgaard Export and Subscription Service
35. Nørre Søgade
DK 1370 KØBENHAVN K. Tel. +45.1.12.85.70

FINLAND – FINLANDE
Akateeminen Kirjakauppa
Keskuskatu 1, 00100 HELSINKI 10. Tel. 65.11.22

FRANCE
Bureau des Publications de l'OCDE,
2 rue André-Pascal, 75775 PARIS CEDEX 16. Tel. (1) 524.81.67
Principal correspondant :
13602 AIX-EN-PROVENCE : Librairie de l'Université.
Tel. 26.18.08

GERMANY – ALLEMAGNE
OECD Publications and Information Center
4 Simrockstrasse 5300 BONN Tel. (0228) 21.60.45

GREECE – GRÈCE
Librairie Kauffmann, 28 rue du Stade,
ATHÈNES 132. Tel. 322.21.60

HONG-KONG
Government Information Services,
Publications/Sales Section, Baskerville House,
2nd Floor, 22 Ice House Street

ICELAND – ISLANDE
Snaebjörn Jónsson and Co., h.f.,
Hafnarstraeti 4 and 9, P.O.B. 1131, REYKJAVIK.
Tel. 13133/14281/11936

INDIA – INDE
Oxford Book and Stationery Co. :
NEW DELHI-1, Scindia House. Tel. 45896
CALCUTTA 700016, 17 Park Street. Tel. 240832

INDONESIA – INDONÉSIE
PDIN-LIPI, P.O. Box 3065/JKT., JAKARTA, Tel. 583467

IRELAND – IRLANDE
TDC Publishers – Library Suppliers
12 North Frederick Street, DUBLIN 1 Tel. 744835-749677

ITALY – ITALIE
Libreria Commissionaria Sansoni :
Via Lamarmora 45, 50121 FIRENZE. Tel. 579751/584468
Via Bartolini 29, 20155 MILANO. Tel. 365083
Sub-depositari :
Ugo Tassi
Via A. Farnese 28, 00192 ROMA. Tel. 310590
Editrice e Libreria Herder,
Piazza Montecitorio 120, 00186 ROMA. Tel. 6794628
Costantino Ercolano, Via Generale Orsini 46, 80132 NAPOLI. Tel. 405210
Libreria Hoepli, Via Hoepli 5, 20121 MILANO. Tel. 865446
Libreria Scientifica, Dott. Lucio de Biasio "Aeiou"
Via Meravigli 16, 20123 MILANO Tel. 807679
Libreria Zanichelli
Piazza Galvani 1/A, 40124 Bologna Tel. 237389
Libreria Lattes, Via Garibaldi 3, 10122 TORINO. Tel. 519274
La diffusione delle edizioni OCSE è inoltre assicurata dalle migliori librerie nelle
città più importanti.

JAPAN – JAPON
OECD Publications and Information Center,
Landic Akasaka Bldg., 2-3-4 Akasaka,
Minato-ku, TOKYO 107 Tel. 586.2016

KOREA – CORÉE
Pan Korea Book Corporation,
P.O. Box n° 101 Kwangwhamun, SÉOUL. Tel. 72.7369

LEBANON – LIBAN
Documenta Scientifica/Redico,
Edison Building, Bliss Street, P.O. Box 5641, BEIRUT.
Tel. 354429 – 344425

MALAYSIA – MALAISIE
University of Malaya Co-operative Bookshop Ltd.
P.O. Box 1127, Jalan Pantai Baru
KUALA LUMPUR. Tel. 51425, 54058, 54361

THE NETHERLANDS – PAYS-BAS
Staatsuitgeverij, Verzendboekhandel,
Chr. Plantijnstraat 1 Postbus 20014
2500 EA S-GRAVENHAGE. Tel. nr. 070.789911
Voor bestellingen: Tel. 070.789208

NEW ZEALAND – NOUVELLE-ZÉLANDE
Publications Section,
Government Printing Office Bookshops:
AUCKLAND: Retail Bookshop: 25 Rutland Street,
Mail Orders: 85 Beach Road, Private Bag C.P.O.
HAMILTON: Retail: Ward Street,
Mail Orders, P.O. Box 857
WELLINGTON: Retail: Mulgrave Street (Head Office),
Cubacade World Trade Centre
Mail Orders: Private Bag
CHRISTCHURCH: Retail: 159 Hereford Street,
Mail Orders: Private Bag
DUNEDIN: Retail: Princes Street
Mail Order: P.O. Box 1104

NORWAY – NORVÈGE
J.G. TANUM A/S
P.O. Box 1177 Sentrum OSLO 1. Tel. (02) 80.12.60

PAKISTAN
Mirza Book Agency, 65 Shahrah Quaid-E-Azam, LAHORE 3.
Tel. 66839

PHILIPPINES
National Book Store, Inc.
Library Services Division, P.O. Box 1934, MANILA.
Tel. Nos. 49.43.06 to 09, 40.53.45, 49.45.12

PORTUGAL
Livraria Portugal, Rua do Carmo 70-74,
1117 LISBOA CODEX. Tel. 360582/3

SINGAPORE – SINGAPOUR
Information Publications Pte Ltd,
Pei-Fu Industrial Building,
24 New Industrial Road N° 02-06
SINGAPORE 1953. Tel. 2831786, 2831798

SPAIN – ESPAGNE
Mundi-Prensa Libros, S.A.
Castelló 37, Apartado 1223, MADRID-1. Tel. 275.46.55
Libreria Bosch, Ronda Universidad 11, BARCELONA 7.
Tel. 317.53.08, 317.53.58

SWEDEN – SUÈDE
AB CE Fritzes Kungl Hovbokhandel,
Box 16 356, S 103 27 STH, Regeringsgatan 12,
DS STOCKHOLM. Tel. 08/23.89.00
Subscription Agency/Abonnements:
Wennergren-Williams AB,
Box 13004, S104 25 STOCKHOLM.
Tel. 08/54.12.00

SWITZERLAND – SUISSE
OECD Publications and Information Center
4 Simrockstrasse 5300 BONN (Germany). Tel. (0228) 21.60.45
Local Agents/Agents locaux
Librairie Payot, 6 rue Grenus, 1211 GENÈVE 11. Tel. 022.31.89.50

TAIWAN – FORMOSE
Good Faith Worldwide Int'l Co., Ltd.
9th floor, No. 118, Sec. 2,
Chung Hsiao E. Road
TAIPEI. Tel. 391.7396/391.7397

THAILAND – THAILANDE
Suksit Siam Co., Ltd., 1715 Rama IV Rd,
Samyan, BANGKOK 5. Tel. 2511630

TURKEY – TURQUIE
Kultur Yayinlari Is-Türk Ltd. Sti.
Atatürk Bulvari No : 191/Kat. 21
Kavaklidere/ANKARA. Tel. 17 02 66
Dolmabahce Cad. No : 29
BESIKTAS/ISTANBUL. Tel. 60 71 88

UNITED KINGDOM – ROYAUME-UNI
H.M. Stationery Office,
P.O.B. 276, LONDON SW8 5DT.
(postal orders only)
Telephone orders: (01) 622.3316, or
49 High Holborn, LONDON WC1V 6 HB (personal callers)
Branches at: EDINBURGH, BIRMINGHAM, BRISTOL,
MANCHESTER, BELFAST.

UNITED STATES OF AMERICA – ÉTATS-UNIS
OECD Publications and Information Center. Suite 1207,
1750 Pennsylvania Ave., N.W. WASHINGTON, D.C.20006 – 4582
Tel. (202) 724.1857

VENEZUELA
Libreria del Este, Avda. F. Miranda 52, Edificio Galipan,
CARACAS 106. Tel. 32.23.01/33.26.04/31.58.38

YUGOSLAVIA – YOUGOSLAVIE
Jugoslovenska Knjiga, Knez Mihajlova 2, P.O.B. 36, BEOGRAD.
Tel. 621.992

Les commandes provenant de pays où l'OCDE n'a pas encore désigné de dépositaire peuvent être adressées à :
OCDE, Bureau des Publications, 2, rue André-Pascal, 75775 PARIS CEDEX 16.

Orders and inquiries from countries where sales agents have not yet been appointed may be sent to:
OECD, Publications Office, 2, rue André-Pascal, 75775 PARIS CEDEX 16.

67849-07-1984

OECD PUBLICATIONS, 2, rue André-Pascal, 75775 PARIS CEDEX 16 - No. 43063 1984
PRINTED IN FRANCE
(24 84 05 1) ISBN 92-64-12625-2